Praise for *Black Folk* T0013723

"[Randall Kenan] dreams a path forward using resources that lie deep in the past. This applies to the whole of *Black Folk Could Fly*, a collection of essays that, while less known than his celebrated fiction—many appeared as introductions or in small magazines— provide rare insight into Kenan's life and mind, while retaining the humor, humanity and elegant power for which he is loved. In a sense, the collected pieces function as memoir, or as a series of love letters to the forces that shaped the writer."
—Kinohi Nishikawa, *New York Times*

"Randall Kenan's erudition was matched only by his imagination, his love for his homeplace only by his vast appreciation of elsewhere, his profound engagement with Black culture only by his daring and thoughtful explorations of its broader meanings. Few writers are as secure in their various identities as he was and as generous in celebrating the worlds of others. This collection is a tribute to one of the great writers in the African American tradition and assures his place in the canon. It also reminds us how much we need to hear his voice today." —Henry Louis Gates Jr., author of *The Black Church*

"Almost everything in the inimitable sound of Randall Kenan's baritone voice is contained in this collection of beautiful thinking and feeling. The warm, mercurial intelligence of Kenan's smile, especially, is made word here, thank goodness."
—Terrance Hayes, author of *American Sonnets for My Past and Future Assassin*

"In these wonderfully far-ranging essays Randall Kenan writes with wit, warmth, and humility about Baldwin and Bergman and Blackness and the great Eartha Kitt. Best of all, he writes about himself: his fascinating childhood, his relationship with the South, his thoughts on *Star Trek* and race and writing and pop culture and barbecue. He understood we live in perilous times; he understood the necessity of joy." —Margot Livesey, author of *The Boy in the Field*

"Each essay in this collection is an education, an illumination, a bridge from the past to the present, to the future, as long as Randall Kenan's writing is read. The breadth of his knowledge of life, food, literature, American history, his own history, touches down here again and again in moments of mixed grace, candor, and wit. The result is a book you sit with instead of rush through, lingering like you might with a friend when you just don't want to say goodbye."
—Alexander Chee, author of *How to Write an Autobiographical Novel*

"Rich in texture and scope, this posthumous collection of selected writings is one to savor. Kenan never shies away from big questions, never once pulls a punch. His understandings are carefully considered, and his knack for capturing the people and places he knew and loved are in many ways unprecedented and unechoed. He was quite simply one of the greatest writers the state of North Carolina ever produced."   —David Joy, *Garden & Gun*

"Randall's character was composed of science fiction novels, church suppers, long days spent in the tobacco field, and nights spent at the movie theater, all of which he covers in these essays. . . . I couldn't help but feel that Randall was welcoming me home again."
—Wiley Cash, *Assembly*

"*Black Folk Could Fly*, a collection of Randall Kenan's work, contains some of my favorite food writing this year. The way he evokes tastes and textures speaks to my stomach, but it's how he ties food to people and places and moments—and uses it to ask real questions about the world around us—that really makes it stand out for me."

—Danielle Davenport, *Bon Appétit*

"Randall Kenan's posthumous collection of essays soars. . . . [H]is pieces on Southern foodways sparkle with personality and color. . . . [H]is acute attention to sense of place permeates his work, no matter the genre. One of the hallmarks of his writing is his ability to put his audience in vivid, sensory-filled spaces."

—Latria Graham, *Atlanta Journal-Constitution*

"Stirring, deeply thought-through essays and letters on topics ranging from sexuality and racism to foodways and the sense of place. . . . A superb introduction to a writer deserving much greater recognition."

—*Kirkus Reviews*, starred review

BLACK
FOLK
COULD
FLY

BLACK
FOLK
COULD
FLY

SELECTED WRITINGS

Randall Kenan

W. W. NORTON & COMPANY
Celebrating a Century of Independent Publishing

For information about special discounts for bulk purchases, please contact
W. W. Norton Special Sales at specialsales@wwnorton.com or 800-233-4830

Manufacturing by Lakeside Book Company
Book design by Chris Welch
Production manager: Lauren Abbate

Library of Congress Cataloging-in-Publication Data

Names: Kenan, Randall, author.
Title: Black folk could fly : selected writings / Randall Kenan.
Description: First edition. | New York : W. W. Norton & Company, Inc., [2022]
Identifiers: LCCN 2022019924 | ISBN 9780393882162 (cloth) | ISBN 9780393882179 (epub)
Subjects: LCSH: Kenan, Randall. | Authors, American—20th century—Biography. |
African American authors—20th century—Biography. | LCGFT: Essays.
Classification: LCC PS3561.E4228 Z46 2022 | DDC 813/.54 [B]—dc23/eng/20220609
LC record available at https://lccn.loc.gov/2022019924

ISBN 978-1-324-06459-6 pbk.

W. W. Norton & Company, Inc., 500 Fifth Avenue, New York, N.Y. 10110
www.wwnorton.com

W. W. Norton & Company Ltd., 15 Carlisle Street, London W1D 3BS

1 2 3 4 5 6 7 8 9 0

CONTENTS

INTRODUCTION

TAYARI JONES

Randall Kenan was an extraordinary writer and thinker, due in no small part to the fact that he was an exemplary human being. He listened as carefully as he spoke. He read even more than he wrote. He was somehow clear-eyed, yet optimistic, reverent of the past, but seldom nostalgic. He was a country boy and a man of the world. I was fortunate to know him as a mentor and friend, but if you are holding this book in your hands, then you are positioned to receive your blessing as well. These twenty-one works of nonfiction offer an experience that is like a walking expedition through a beautiful and intricate landscape, led by a tour guide who visits the popular attractions but also insists on stopping by the ancient cemeteries, telling the stories behind every stone. He will invite you to high tea, also insisting that you stop for a pulled-pork sandwich and, when you get to the pit, the man behind the grill will call him by name. *Follow me*, Kenan seems to say with every word, every image. *I will show you the way.*

For Kenan, all roads lead to—or from—Chinquapin, North Carolina. He was born in Brooklyn, New York, to unmarried parents, and at the age of six weeks old, he went to live with his father's people, who gave him a legacy rich beyond measure. If you are to understand anything about Kenan, you must know this. His origin story undergoes very slight variations in each telling; the difference is in the tone rather than the substance. He was "stolen away" from New York. Or, his grandfather "sent for" him. He identifies himself as "illegitimate," with irony, I believe. When he describes his grandfather as "kindhearted," this is deliberate understatement. What remains constant is the fierce love and connection he feels for the family who raised him. The love shared between Kenan and his kin is enhanced by the unbidden nature of the relationship. He revels in the bond the way you might revel in finding romantic love—rejoicing in the wonder and miracle of it all.

The stories of Kenan's childhood signal the complexity of the man, and indeed the writer, he would become. Fans of his fiction will see the obvious likeness between the imaginary town of Tims Creek and the very real setting of Chinquapin. But in his nonfiction, we can see the ways that his remarkable early life is yellow bricks on the avenue he would travel for the rest of his days. In Chinquapin, "unincorporated, and rural, largely tobacco fields and cornfields, and hog farms"—he learned that identity could be kaleidoscopic, colorful, and breathtaking, like the aurora borealis he saw over his cousin's house when he was eleven years old.

Imagine the boy-Randall and the seeming contradictions of his young life. He was born in the North but raised in the South. His parents were unable to care for him, but his other relatives loved him so much there was a little scuffle over who would be granted the pleasure of his custody. He was so country that one of his earliest memories was a fight with a rooster and his first glimpse into the workings of sexuality was witnessing a rendezvous between hogs. Yet in this same environment, he became an insatiable reader with a particular penchant for science fiction. Born in 1963, he lived a racially segregated life, but came to be an "affirmative action baby," matriculating at the University of North Carolina.

With this rich backstory, it may seem obvious that Kenan would become a great writer. However, his early ambition was to be a scientist. Luckily (for us), a biology teacher pulled him aside. "There's no shame in being a writer," he said, gently nudging Kenan toward his destiny.

As his muse, Kenan chose "Blackness," a terrain so vast, beautiful, and tangled that no writer—even one as brilliant as Kenan— could ever map it out. But the pleasure is in the journey. To get to the heart of Blackness as "an emotional condition," Kenan mines his own family history, the stories of the dead in a neglected Richmond cemetery, the primacy of basketball, gospel, blues, the Bible, and anything else that involves humanity.

———————

FOR A MAN of Kenan's generation, any quest to understand Blackness would obviously lead to James Baldwin. Despite the obvious parallels between the two men—both Black, both queer, both writers—the two stood on opposites sides of a generational and regional divide. Kenan had to learn to love the work of Baldwin, to see beyond the obvious to access their shared humanity. With Kenan, every route is circuitous and unanticipated. The highway to his fulsome appreciation of James Baldwin passes through the great Swedish filmmaker, Ingmar Bergman.

As comfortable in the cineplex as the library archives, Kenan held great appreciation for pop culture. He was especially fond of the chanteuse Eartha Kitt. While many people remember her for her trademark purr and audacious holiday ditty "Santa Baby," in her Kenan saw much more. He admired her diva persona—who doesn't?—but remembers the day she made Lady Bird Johnson cry by speaking about the evils of racism and imperialism. On one occasion, he had the opportunity to meet the star in her dressing room and walked away with a new understanding of Southern hospitality, and Southern identity more generally.

Who would be surprised that a writer of such vast curiosity and ambition that he attempted to define Blackness would attempt the same with *Southernness*? His investigation of Blackness sent him on an adventure that allowed him to meet with fascinating folks all over the country. His investigation of Southernness allowed him to eat his way across the region.

Kenan was a great student of Southern foodways. He studied in the library, reading the reflections of scholars and practitioners. But he also studied the old-fashioned way—with a napkin tucked into his collar and fork in hand. He had strong opinions about the best way to prepare barbeque—though he would eat it whether it was served with or without sauce and whether that sauce was tomato-, mustard-, or vinegar-based. To him, the scuppernong is a perfect grape and one of the great cultural treasures forever lost to humanity is his great-aunt's recipe for muscadine wine. From the flavor of that wine, "harsh, sweet, and bracing," he learned one of life's great lessons: "You don't drink life because it's good for you, you drink life because it's good."

As we end this book, reaching the conclusion of this guided excursion, we realize that we have been gifted a tour of the world, when we thought we were just visiting the South, mostly in this small town of Chinquapin. And perhaps we thought the voice of our guide was the words of a single man, but that one man contains multitudes, much in the way a single drop of pondwater viewed under a microscope is revealed to be a universe.

The title of this book, *Black Folk Could Fly*, is a reference to the African American folktale of the Africans who flew back to Iboland after the slave ships arrived on the shores of America. Kenan ends his letter to his godson with a suggestion that he take comfort in this mythology. However, I can't imagine that Kenan himself longed to fly away. Perhaps the boy-scientist in him would appreciate a celestial view of this planet or an overhead view of the aurora borealis that so captivated him as a child. But Randall Kenan, the man revealed on these pages, was most at home when he was at home. He returned to North Carolina before "reverse migration" was a chic term tossed about on the pages of the *New York Times*.

When I met him, the year was 2005. I was a debut novelist and he was the lone Black faculty member at the Sewanee Writers Conference, the premier gathering for writers in the South. He and I were seated in the guesthouse on campus, known as the Rebel's Rest.

"How do you stand it?" I asked him, crinkling my nose as though some Confederate dust might somehow soil my red-and-white dress.

"It's our home, too," he said.

Recently, I found a photo, likely taken that same day. I am leaning over the table, feeding Randall from a ceramic bowl. His eyes are shut and his lips smile even as they close over the spoon. Try as I might, I don't remember what was in that bowl, but I know that it was Southern and I know that it was good.

RANDALL KENAN DIED in 2020. He was laid to rest at the Kenan Family Cemetery in Chinquapin, North Carolina. May his words live on as he rests in peace among his kin.

BLACK
FOLK
COULD
FLY

A Change
Is Gonna Come

A LETTER TO MY GODSON

One is responsible to life: It is the small beacon in that ter-
rifying darkness from which we come and to which we shall
return. One must negotiate this passage as nobly as possible,
for the sake of those who are coming after us. But white Americans do not believe in death, and this is why the darkness of
my skin so intimidates them. And this is also why the presence
of the Negro in this country can bring about its destruction.
It is the responsibility of free men to trust and to celebrate
what is constant—birth, struggle, and death are constants, and
so is love, though we may not always think so—and to appre-
hend the nature of change, to be able to be willing to change. I
speak of change not on the surface but in the depths—change
in the sense of renewal.

—James Baldwin, *The Fire Next Time*

Dearest Jailen,

Nine months before you were born, your grandfather, Mr. John
Wallace Brown, died.

In every aspect but one, he was my father. I first met him when
I was five years old, visiting your grandmother's home in Harlem,
USA. He took a shine to me straightaway. Recordings exist of me

asking him silly questions. ("Can you eat a thousand biscuits?") He took the entire family to Chinatown, I remember, and he took me to his gym. Your grandfather had been a boxer, but by the time I met him, in his late thirties, he had become a trainer of other boxers. The gym was in uptown Manhattan in the 150s, a dankish, run-down place, smelling of sweat and blood and smelling salts, but it held my fascination for decades. (A few years before he died, I casually mentioned to your grandfather that I had read the great jazz trumpeter, Miles Davis, liked to box. Your grandfather said, Of course, he knew that. Davis used the same gym. You saw him, he told me.)

The year your mother was born, your grandfather and grandmother left New York for North Carolina, your maternal homeland. I was ten years old that year.

Many people had an enormous influence on my mischievous mind—undoubtedly the greatest of them being your great-grandmother, who took me in as an infant. But the impact your grandfather had on me was profound.

He had been a civil servant for the City of New York for over twenty years, but he dressed like a duke and carried himself like a crown prince (a large part of that coming from the physical grace he had learned as a boxer; part coming from a certain confidence and leonine heart). He was not himself college educated, but he was more curious about the world than most college professors I would come to know, and he was possessed of a wisdom forged in hand-to-hand combat with life. He bequeathed to me at an early age a love of jazz, especially Wes Montgomery, Billie Holiday, and Sarah Vaughan, ("the Divine One"). He respected Dinah Washington the way some people respect the Pope.

He was independent, but not haughty. He believed in decency and courtesy. If someone demonstrated a need, he would lend the proverbial hand, though he was always on the lookout for being taken advantage of. He blamed this innate suspicion and a dogged frugality on being raised during the Great Depression.

He was not a perfect man. He would be the first to admit to a Tasmanian-devil temper. But I never saw him harm anyone, though I well knew he was more than capable.

Chinquapin was and is a small, unincorporated village, and the only fire protection is volunteer. Soon after arriving as a full-time resident, your grandfather joined the Fire and Rescue Squad as a fireman. At the time, few of the Black men in the community felt welcome on the force, founded and run by the local white farmers and schoolteachers and plumbers and truck drivers who owned homes in the area. But your grandfather often said: If I expect them to come to my house if it's on fire, I should be willing to go to theirs. He studied at the local community college for his certification as an emergency medical technician. (I still remember the things he taught me about checking someone's vital signs; about how to deal with someone having an epileptic seizure; about how to stanch the flow of blood and figure out if a fracture is simple or compound.)

Most weekends, the Fire and Rescue Squad would hold Saturday benefit suppers selling fried chicken, pork barbecue (a local favorite and specialty), slaw, potato salad, hushpuppies. Friday afternoons men would begin slow-roasting the whole hog in a shed behind the firehouse. This process lasted all night. Often on those Friday nights, your grandfather would be on call there overnight and would help watch the hog. Many times I would stay with him, and we would roast a chicken along with the hog—wrapped in aluminum foil, drenched in a local sauce, spicy and good, placed among the coals. That chicken still ranks as some of the best food I have ever tasted.

On at least two occasions, in the very wee hours, your grandfather answered calls from accidents involving my classmates. One involving a fatal gunshot wound, one involving a ruinous car accident.

Being there, watching him deal with the death of young people, was an odd place for me; the sorts of events that brace the soul and make you ponder your own mortality and the randomness of life. These were people I knew. On those nights, after delivering the bodies to the hospital, your grandfather would be tired but restless, and he would wax philosophical, speaking of many things, trying in his way to make sense of the world for him and for me. He was a great talker.

Years later, as an adult, I would come to devote many years to traveling and to writing about African American lives, and to a quest toward understanding the meaning of "Blackness," a journey that continues for me. During these wanderings and wonderings I always return to your grandfather and to the many lessons he taught me, both directly and by example. Of the many things I learned from all the people I've written about all across North America, the consonant element about their identity, the thing that forged who they were, what gave them their vision of themselves and the world, was this sense of family, those early people who helped shape who they were—this was the bedrock of their identity. Of course this is true for everyone, of any color, but it is surprising how often we let that truth slip from our thinking. Like them, you will need to know a great deal about your past, where you come from, what your people were like—really like—what they thought of you, in order to better understand yourself. You need to know how your own blood lived and faced adversity and of what their character was composed. And though your own journey will no doubt be easier for you than it had been for your grandfather and for me, your path will not necessarily be an easy one. So much of that passage will ultimately depend upon you.

For many in the world, in their jaded eyes, alas, now and for many years to come, you will be a demon. For the next thirty years or so, you will be among the most despised group in your homeland: the young African American male. *The Black male.* This will not be a reality; you are much more than that. But, as an idea, this view of you will have great power. The world will, with a great deal of might and resource, try to define you. But you must know better. You must remember you are not a problem.

These days people can be so trite when discussing the idea of race and its attendant problems. Too many reach instantly for bromides and hackneyed phrases that merely restate positions, rehash old battles, resurrect silly stereotypes. These silly ways of thinking aren't going away anytime soon, but you need not subscribe to them or pay them much heed. The world is no longer—it never really was—about simply Black and white. Don't heed people who tell you differently. The old American order of white versus Black is fast changing, and you will have a real opportunity (one of the greatest opportunities in history) to break free of such limited thinking. Many people are threatened by this new and burgeoning reality.

But "pluralism" is the watchword of the future. "Multiculturalism" doesn't come close to encompassing the battles to be waged, the alliances that need to be made. Black folk are no longer the great minority in this nation, and our continued enduring and prevailing rest with an understanding of how we fit in the new demography. History, alas, does not privilege the people on the side of right; history never does. Might is not always right; but knowledge will always defeat blunt force in the end. Know the past, learn from the past, but don't be a slave to it: keep moving forward.

In a way—barring some racial cataclysm between now and then—your generation will be the freest people of color this nation has ever engendered: free of racial guilt, free of the burden of representation, free of expectations, high or low—you will not be expected to lift up the race, nor will you be shackled with the hope that your every step will drag along an entire population toward some Promised Land: You will have achieved that land, for better or for worse, borne up on the wings of those who came before. Honor them. Study them. Learn from them. "I may not get there with you . . ."

You will be like ravens. Free to pick and choose, beautiful, raucous, difficult to control, both trickster and avatar. *Y'all ain't gonna let nobody hold you down. Hold you down. Hold you down.*

Did you know, once upon a time, Black folk could fly? Or so it has been said. A hidden truth. A metaphor. A way of looking at yourself and at the world. Remember that when you think you are stuck in the mud.

Your loving godfather,
Randall
Garrett

PART I
COMFORT ME

1

Scuppernongs
and Beef Fat

SOME THINGS ABOUT THE WOMEN
WHO RAISED ME

You don't eat it because it's good for you.
You eat it because it's good.

I forget the exact cause for the occasion, but I remember it was a Saturday night in the 1970s. l remember we were at the Camp Lejeune marine base in Jacksonville, North Carolina, where she worked as a cook, "she" being Clementine Whitley, one of the women who raised me.

Saturday nights in those waning days of the Carter administration were marked by too much television viewing for me. TV of the mildest, most innocuous sort: *Hee Haw, The Lawrence Welk Show, The Love Boat, Fantasy Island.* Sundays were even more boring than Saturdays, which at least held a mythical promise of some type of weekend thrill—something *could* happen. These imaginary joys never materialized out in the deep woods and swamps of eastern North Carolina, despite my cousins' intense anticipation of such.

Imagine a "party" of sorts down on a military base, with lots of food, some dancing. (Perhaps it was Independence Day, perhaps it was some military promotion celebration; it could have even been a wedding reception—I do not now remember the reason for the gathering.)

Without a doubt I was the youngest person there. By most standards, then or now, this was a rather ordinary affair: the enlisted men with their dates; rhythm and blues and soul music playing; socializing of the loud and back-slapping type, which—to the eyes and ears of a fourteen-year-old country boy—is as attractive as the prospect of oral surgery. And there was the food, which to me was the most special part of the special occasion. And though the fare was rather ordinary—fried chicken, potato salad, slaw, hushpuppies—I remember having recently been introduced to the grown-up and somewhat decadent charm of grilled beef. We are speaking specifically of sirloin and rib eye and the mischievous T-bone, something in which a boy can delight, considering its direct and gruesome anatomy lesson as well as delectability. T-bone steaks were fun and still are fun to eat.

Those hearty and fun-loving marines spared no expense when it came to the food and selected the most capable and gregarious cook they knew to helm the event, that being my aunt Clem. My being her sidekick in the kitchen that Saturday night meant I could eat my belly full. That is to say, steak galore!

I was not exactly a glutton. But the fact is, fourteen-year-old boys exist for very few things on this planet, and eating is very near the top of that brief list. Curiously, at the same time, I had somehow come under the trance of "eating right." Probably by public service messages interjected in and around Saturday morning cartoons, or school nutritionists visiting classes. However it came to me, I had digested the notion that animal fat was BAD. While chomping down on a juicy steak cooked by Aunt Clem, I sliced off the fat and pushed it aside with some contemptuous comment about eating fat and how fat wasn't good for us, delivered with all the sagacity a self-righteous, greedy fourteen-year-old can muster. To which she replied by picking it up and popping it in her own mouth, saying, "You don't eat it because it's good for you. We eat it because it's good."

Family lore has it that I spent my first night in my ancestral home of Chinquapin, North Carolina, in Clementine Whitley's house located on a bend of the Northeast Cape Fear River. Clem—Clementine—was one of my great-aunt Mary's best friends, and in truth my cousin.

Clem was descended from a very large family. Her mother, Viola, was at the time one of Chinquapin's oldest matriarchs. The family originated from and lived in what local people referred to as "The Quarters," for upon the land where her home sat was where the enslaved people of the long-gone Chinquapin Plantation lived. Miss Viola had many children, so Clem had a vast arena of brothers and nephews and nieces and cousins galore. This was exactly the web of family into which I was born. For, indeed, I was related to both Clementine (via her mother) and her husband, John, or Chicken (via his mother). Chicken drove a bus. Clem worked down on the marine base in Jacksonville. By the time of my birth, Clementine Whitley had grown small-town famous as an outstanding cook. Women who themselves were not slackers in the kitchen held her food in high esteem. My connection to her was a powerful thing.

It was into this world of taste and hardheaded common sense that I became conscious of the world.

MAMA. CLEM. NELLIE MAE.

Mama was my great-aunt, who took care of me directly. The night after I was brought down to Chinquapin by the twenty-year-old woman who bore me, a love child, I was taken to where I had been requested, my father's parents' home fourteen miles away. This had been the overarching plan: for this illegitimate but now-acknowledged boy-child to be raised by his grandparents in the railroad town of Wallace, North Carolina.

My paternal grandfather, at that time in the mid-1960s, ran a prosperous dry-cleaning establishment, and his wife, my grandmother, was a popular and busy seamstress. My father had led a somewhat privileged life compared to most of his Black boy contemporaries. My future was so bright I should have worn shades.

I was recently reacquainted with the woman my grandfather hired in those days to be my governess. She told me I was a rambunctious baby who fought to get out of my crib. And that I actually succeeded on a few occasions.

Perhaps my grandfather's sister, Mary Fleming, recognized this spirit in me and liked it. She would spirit me away on weekends to the ancestral home in Chinquapin, the first village in which I'd slept. This weekend absconding continued and continued until, one sad day, her husband, Redden, died. My grandfather suggested my great-aunt keep me, to keep her company on the farm. This is how Aunt Mary became Mama to me.

Nellie Mae: She was a substantial woman of substantial proportions and the spirit of a mighty thing. Her hugs were crushing, enveloping, as genuine as heavy rain. She too worked down at Camp Lejeune as a domestic for a high-ranking marine officer. She spoke of that family as if she had been a true member, something for which Mama and Clem upbraided her, saying: "They don't care about you, woman."

And yet this was Nellie Mae's spirit, the purest example of agape I've come in touch with. Her laugh, her smile, her cooking, her generosity with time and things exuded a largeness of spirit, a positivity, a joy. Nellie Mae had a vast green Pontiac Bonneville, circa early 1970, when cars had more in common with whales than with the combustion engine. On Saturdays Mama, Clem, Nellie Mae, and I would take trips down to Wilmington, about a two-hour drive in those days before the interstate. The backseat of that sturdy automobile was my playground. We would stop en route at Paul's Place for one of their famous hot dogs. The first stop in Wilmington would always be Hudson Belk department store, where I would endure a couple hours of watching these women browse through dresses and shoes, my penance for a quantity of minutes downstairs in the toy department, ogling toys we could not afford. But I could afford a coloring book.

Coloring books! With my Crayola 64 box and my coloring book, I would be a child free in his own universe.

Back at Nellie Mae's house I would go down in front of the television, coloring. The women would be enjoying themselves, gossiping and cooking, and I would employ my burnt sienna crayon and sky blue and crimson to make a blank world real.

One story from that time I heard into my teenage years, I still remember vividly, though the retellings have probably polluted the event.

It was a humid spring day; the dogwoods had done blooming. I was hot and sweating down on the floor with my coloring book. The women were sitting about Nellie Mae's den around me. I became frustrated with the heat and declared loudly, "I'm having a hot flash," something I had heard my womenfolk exclaim quite a bit in those ten years, all being women of a certain age. All three roared with laughter, much to my confusion. It would be another decade before I understood their amusement.

At the risk of being self-aggrandizing or simply tedious, I include here a passage from my first book of fiction in which I wrote one of the most honest passages I've ever written about my great-aunt:

> He remembered his grandmother's hands to be small and firm, also callused from hard work, but still soft in a womanly way. People called her Retha. Aretha Davis Cross. A mother

of the church. His mother. Hers were the hands that were his beginnings: In the beginning were hands, and hands were the beginning; all things that were made were made by hands, and without hands was not anything made that was made. In her hands was life; and the life was in her hands. Her hands reached through the darkness. Her hands lifted and supported. Undid and did up. Comforted. Scolded. Fed. Clothed. Bathed. Her hands did the teaching, the sending, the receiving, the mending, the strengthening. Her hands spoke and listened, smiled and encouraged. (*A Visitation of Spirits*, "1:15 A.M.")

THE GREATEST GIFT: FLOPSY, MOPSY, AND PETER RABBIT

Mama had been a professional cook, a domestic, a graduate of NC College (later NC Central University), and, by and by, a kindergarten teacher.

That she taught me to read at the age of four is not a curiosity. But sitting with her, looking at Beatrix Potter's bright watercolors, imagining Peter Rabbit and that sinister farmer, Mr. McGregor ("Why don't he leave that rabbit alone?"), introduced me to the keys of the world. I remember not only that book (ultimately written all over by this engaged child, who did not imagine the story could ever end) but also the pads with the blue lines, three in which to capture the print. The *R*'s and the *T*'s and the serpentine *S*'s. A life-long fascination with the word. "In the beginning was the word, and the word was God."

But more, for some peculiar reason, on the Christmas of my fifth year, Mama gave me a children's adaptation of *Moby-Dick*, full of lurid illustrations of the great whale and the doomed captain, and dramatic seas and thunderous skies. My mind was overstimulated, and happily so. In short, I was hooked. Soon would come *Treasure Island, Kidnapped, The Swiss Family Robinson.* (To this day I am slightly ashamed of my obsession with these blond kids marooned on a tropical island. Like Nellie Mae, my heart was just too damn large.) All this due to my great-aunt Mary Fleming, my mama, her need to grow things, to give.

And so, as always, there are three things: a love of food, an instinct toward compassion, a love of words and story. To me these all work together, bind each other, make wonderful sense, make life *life*. How could a fellow not wax in gratitude recognizing the seeds of his life.

The three things these women gave me: love of food, love for my fellow human, love of reading.

———————

MAMA'S GARDEN: We were, per course, cash poor and land rich. Mama's ingenuity and resolve and green thumb made us wealthy when it came to nourishment. In fact, she grew enough to share with many of the neighbors and church fellows.

We are talking a garden of over an acre. She grew sweet corn, sweet potatoes, tomatoes, green beans, butterbeans, carrots, radishes, beets, red potatoes, white potatoes, mustard greens, cabbage, collard greens, okra, okra, okra. She canned; she pickled; she blanched and froze. As a boy, I took all the work and time and energy to accomplish all this bounty for granted; now I look back in wonder.

But I write about childhood. Relations, connections, negotiations . . . adulthood brings different imperatives, different emotions. When one is a child, one sees older folk, perforce, as fixed and unmoving in time. Experience helps us see our mothers on a continuum that gives us insight, inspires remorse, tenderness, and awe. Old age (Mama died at eighty-nine) engendered another type of sensitivity. Indeed, enough material for a roman-fleuve.

ONE OF MY MOST PRECIOUS MEMORIES: GATHERING GRAPES IN FALL

The scuppernong grape is one of the few grapes indigenous to North America, one of the muscadine family. They are plump spherical things, with a mighty thick hull, and a mucus-like sweet interior with obnoxiously large seeds clustered at the center. The hull is acidic and the pulp, when ripe, sweet like candy. Mr. Proust had his cookies; I have my grapes.

My dear friend Allan Gurganus once said to me regarding scuppernongs: "They are so *entertaining* to eat!" Which I have ever since recognized as the precise truth of the matter.

Come late September, just before the leaves commence to turn, the grape arbors grow heavy with ready grapes. In our county many arbors would invite folk in to pick their own grapes. My memories of those afternoons picking (and eating) grapes comfort me and keep me buoyed. The pop in the mouth, the sweetness, the early fall sunset, my Mama's laugh.

Mama would make wine from these mischievous berries, barreled in the fall when the grapes were plentiful, tended through the winter, and opened in early spring. I remember my first taste of this home-made wine. It was harsh, it was sweet, it was bracing. I remember the very character of it to this day, though no one seems to understand how to make it in this fashion today, despite my home county's boom in wineries and distilleries and grape growing. This method, this special witchcraft, left the earth with my mama in 2007.

You don't drink life because it's good for you, you drink life because it is good.

2

The Rooster, the Rattlesnake, and the Hydrangea Bush

When I was a little bitty boy, no more than four, I carried on a feud with a rooster. This rooster had no name, nor was it a colorful bird. Dun white it was, with a set of vivid red waddles which provoked within me a rather reptilian revulsion. I would chase the rooster, and in turn, the rooster, letting out a chanticleer squawk, would chase me.

My childhood was not exactly idyllic, but I wouldn't trade it for Mark Zuckerberg's billions. Sustenance surrounded us, demanding industry and thrift. We might have been poor but we were never hungry. My cousin Norman and his wife, Miss Alice, lived directly across the dirt road from our house. I remember every divot and rise and slope of their emerald front yard where I'd run back and forth with this maniacal bird. I remember the great and ancient oak tree at the very edge, too big to climb, with its gnarled above-the-earth roots straight out of a Grimm brothers fairy story. I remember the barn and pigpen to the east and the orchard to the west. It seems in those days every farmer with his own land had an orchard of some design. Cousin Norman's contained: a peach tree; a number of pear trees; and a multitude of horse apple trees, the little green apples essential to making the tartest, most magical apple pies over which a boy might dream and drool; tall and productive walnut trees; pecan trees aplenty. Cousin Norman's farm sat on a bend of a branch or creek that snaked off and to the Northeast Cape Fear River. A grape arbor grew mighty close to the water. In autumn that grape arbor produced the plumpest, sweetest, purplest scuppernongs known to man or beast. Grapes weren't the only thing that brackish branch produced.

The truth is I remember this day largely the way one remembers a Polaroid picture one took in haste. It became one of those stories told and retold so often the tellings are mixed with what actually happened. Unbidden, a cousin recounted this story to me at our last family reunion. I know he was in New Jersey at the time. Nonetheless, this much is true:

Cousin Norman and Miss Alice were sitting on their high concrete front porch. Miss Alice liked to dip snuff, and she would spit on occasion with great accuracy off that porch, often into this vast hydrangea bush to the east of the porch. Front-yard hydrangea bushes are not uncommon, even something of a standard in the South. But I recollect these bushes, like that oak tree, to have been of legendary proportion, not unlike those monstrous cabbages one only sees at the state fair. As soon as I walked into their yard, the rooster came flying at me, its powerful thighs pumping, its talons clawing at the earth. Had I eaten one too many of his children?

Not to be undone, I puffed up my chest, Tarzan-like, and rushed the feathery juggernaut, causing it to turn tail and make a mad dash for the hydrangea bush.

Fairly swiftly a mighty ruckus ensued. The great bush commenced to shimmy and shake, its green leaves to tremble earthquake-like (though at age four, the idea of an earthquake would have been as foreign to me as a credit default swap). The rooster ejected itself from the bush rather like a white cannonball and made a beeline toward the smokehouse. The hydrangea bush continued to shake and rattle. At this stage, both Cousin Norman and Miss Alice were standing, agog. Indeed, Miss Alice was hollering. Foolishly I moved closer to investigate. She was hollering at me to get away. Cousin Norman had gone into the house and would return soon with a shotgun. What I could see, only in flashes, was a diamondback rattlesnake, coiling itself round and round the base of the hydrangea bush, causing its entirety to shake in this indecent fashion.

I did not see Cousin Norman dispatch the reptile, for I had made my greatest imitation of a chicken I would make in my brief life.

———————

THIS WAS IN rural Duplin County, North Carolina, once the epicenter of tobacco, currently the epicenter of pigs and poultry. My home, my world, was always edible. A moveable feast.

———————

ONE OF MY earliest memories is the death of Great-Uncle Redden when I was three. We were out grading flue-cured tobacco, and he succumbed to a blood clot on the porch of a house used to prepare the cooked bright leaf and pack it up into bails wrapped and secured by large burlap canvasses. Grading—separating quality from trash, smoothing them for market, one by one—was a tedious job, and largely done by women.

I don't remember the specific women there that day, though I suspect I do, for I remember their faces surrounding my great-aunt Mary (whom I called Mama, the woman who raised me). What immediately followed would be something I'd witness for the rest of my growing up: people showing up heavy-laden with food to the homes of the recently deceased. Hams, fried chicken, oven-baked barbecue chicken, pork chops smothered in gravy, dirty rice, Spanish rice, potato salad galore, slaw, sweet potato casseroles, candied yams, hushpuppies, cornbread, soup, chopped pork barbecue, collard greens, pound cake, chocolate cake, coconut cake, pineapple cake, red velvet cake, sweet potato pie, lemon meringue pie: my mother's lemon meringue pie was both performance art and sorcery—it enchanted everyone who looked upon it and who tasted it.

The idea here of course being that the immediate family would not have to think about cooking or where to find food. Everything was taken care of. There is a lovely passage in one of the early editions of Emily Post's *Etiquette*. She instructs us not to ask the bereaved if they would like something to eat, rather we should make a warm bowl of broth and put it in the bereaved hands with a spoon.

("We gather with food because food is the ultimate and final expression of how we love and the culture of our community. . . . The laying out of the dead and the laying out of the food pulls me closer and closer to that vortex of all things familiar and comfortable." See Jaki Shelton Green's food story, "Singing Tables," in *The Carolina Table: North Carolina Writers on Food*.)

In the end we are talking about expressions of love; not the sentimental, Hallmark-card version, but material, immediate, unambiguous demonstrations that you care, that you are there. It is practical, it is flavorful, and it is real.

When you grow up in a small rural community, it seems everyone is related to everyone, somebody is somebody else's cousin. Everyone knows everybody else. It seems like a lot of people are dying because you are acutely aware of every death—you probably ate Sunday supper with that person at one point, you probably visited their sick bed, went to school with them, certainly went to church with them.

———————

IT IS DIFFICULT to look back on these dire gatherings without just a little mirth. Despite the somber setting, there was still a party-like atmosphere about the proceedings. Usually relatives would come from far and wide (New York, Washington, Detroit), a sense of homecoming like a family reunion. Or as Lyle Lovett once sang:

> I went to a funeral,
> And Lord it made me happy.
> Seeing all those people
> That I ain't seen
> Since the last time
> Somebody died.

Here's the Coca-Cola, here's the lemonade, here's the sweet ice tea, here's the fruit punch, here's Uncle Roma's mason jar full of bootleg moonshine, or a jug of homemade scuppernong wine. Here it is because we are all human. And as it says in the Good Book, "Man cannot live on bread alone."

———————

CERTAIN OF US sons and daughters of the South have a chip on our shoulders about stereotypes regarding the American South. Portrayals, clichés, misconceptions about what it means to be a Southerner in the twenty-first century, in North Carolina, can be worrisome at best. Friends of mine I presume to be more secure than I don't give a flying rooster what people in New York or Los Angeles or Paris, France, think of them, and they ask me, "Why do you care? You have no investment in this North versus South silliness." Nonetheless some of us still smart as if by hornet sting at the residue of the implication that *Southern* means backward,

ill-educated, lazy, superstitious, unhygienic, and dumb. But I suspect, at bottom, my aloof friends do care, but just don't care to talk
about it.

One thing I've learned as an adult is that not all super-
intelligent people are necessarily reflective about themselves and
about the world.

Foodways are too often lumped in with all the other overarching folksy, old-fashioned, technophobic, churchified photocopies of
Mayberry and the General Lee. Things get even more complicated
when the element or icon in question holds a special place for the
Southerner. (Andy Griffith, grits, okra.) Yes, many of us adore fried
chicken; yes, a great many of us have strong feelings about barbecue,
and sweet ice tea. That does not mean everything we eat is fried (from
turkey to Milky Way bars to butter—though some do—and it is true
that in my mother's hometown, Rose Hill, you can find the world's
largest frying pan, used each year to fry a record-breaking amount
of chicken during the Poultry Jubilee), or that vegetables are of little
import and are meant to be boiled into shameful, tasteless mush,
if not fried. Historical nuance is rare in these too-frequent carica-
tures. A great many Southerners aid and abet these visions of the
Old North State and its environs. So much so that sometimes railing
against stereotypes feels quixotic at best; futile even on a good day.
Nonetheless, we find ourselves, like William Faulkner's young Quen-
tin Compson, having to state the affirmative with a denial. "I don't
hate it. . . . I don't. I don't! I don't hate it! I don't hate it!"

———————

WHY FOOD?

So let me tell about the South. Let me tell what do they do there?
How do they live there? Why do they?

The serious study of food and foodways in the academy is still a
relatively young discipline and is still having a hard time gaining

the respect it deserves. Eating is something we must do in order to live. I know people who think of food as merely fuel for their body. Something to stave off hunger. To them thinking overmuch—and surely writing—about food is pure decadence, the stuff of gluttony and the idle well-off. For so long gastronomy (the technical name for food writing) was the province of the elitist gourmands with money to burn and no concern for their health or waistline. In conjunction with those who actively disrespect food writing and the study of foodways are those who don't think of food at all, beyond chomping down on a Quarter Pounder, finding the cheapest Chinese buffet lunch, or scarfing down Buffalo wings and fries while watching the NCAA tournaments.

Speaking of fancy French words, the guy who came up with the idea of a dedicated discipline to writing about food and who gave us the word *gastronomie* was a Frenchman named Jean Anthelme Brillat-Savarin (1755–1826). His masterwork, *The Physiology of Taste*, is often quoted, in particular this line: "Tell me what you eat and I will tell you what you are." There, truly, is the rub.

History, geography, business, culture, science, demography, labor, narrative, myth, and folklore, even music, all intersect in the world of food. Can there be a North Carolina without sweet potatoes, blueberries, and cucumbers? (Do most North Carolinians know that our state produces more sweet potatoes than any other state? This represents 50 percent of the United States' supply. Or that our still youngish wine industry brings in over $1 billion a year; but more, that our industry grew on the backs of the muscadine, which is one of the few grapes indigenous to North America and prolific in North Carolina?) These connections are neither vague nor frivolous but central to our state's character and the character of its people, even those who sincerely believe their lives are untouched by food they don't put in their mouths. Very serious stories like the crisis among Black farmers losing their farms, the

ecological damage caused by industrial hog farms, and food insecurity in Southern urban areas (ironically), all embrace economics,
the environment, race, social justice, health, and so much more.

We contain multitudes.

―――――――

THERE IS A place in Atlanta I insist on visiting every time I'm in
town. The Dekalb Farmers Market. Few places—especially in the
American South—bring together so many cultures, so many foods,
so many people, from around the globe. I like going there not just
for the grains from Ethiopia, the nuts from Israel, the fruits from
India and Malaysia, the fish from Europe, or the vegetables from
Venezuela—foods you won't be finding at the local Food Lion or
the Harris Teeter—but also to see the people, this polyglot, multiethnic, multicolored parade of humanity coming together over
one thing: food. People from warring backgrounds, people who
are sworn enemies, gather together peacefully in a foreign land.
Israelis and Egyptians, the Japanese and the Korean. To me this is
a more practical United Nations, and effectively so. This represents
the power of food, more than to stop hunger, more than to feed
gluttony, more than sales and business.

Of course I recognize that this is a naive daydream of a world-
besotted professional dreamer. I know that food cannot accomplish
what politics, mighty armies, crushing economies, and slick science
can achieve. Though I do know that all generals and senators eat,
as do business moguls and geneticists.

Nowadays places like Carrboro and Durham and Raleigh and
Charlotte and Asheville and Wilmington are becoming more like
the Dekalb Farmers Market. It is a gradual thing. Incremental. And,
to be sure, some of my fellow North Carolinians harbor a lot of
anxiety over that change. What will happen to the old ways? they
mutter. They see falafel as a threat; cactus pads as enemy combat-

ants; sea cucumber as an arch invader. I hasten to remind them that in London and in Toronto, two of the world's most multicultural cities, you can still easily get spotted dick, Welsh rarebit, and poutine. Barbecue and fried chicken are not going away anytime soon. (Today salsa outsells tomato catsup in every state in the union. Yet the Constitution still stands. Meanwhile taco trucks are blossoming all over our state like cherry blossoms in Washington, DC, in April. And we're the better for it.)

Some folk see the American South as a bug trapped in amber; others see the South as an integral part of the great American Experiment—still aspiring to get it right, to make it better; an ongoing thing—rich with contributions, opportunities, and possibilities.

I do dream and wonder about our state's culinary future. What will newcomers bring and support, what of our past will they adopt, what blends and hybrids might occur, what new crops will we begin to grow, what new uses might we discover for sweet potatoes and tobacco plants and pine needles and the humble butter bean?

3

Greens

A MESS OF MEMORIES ABOUT TASTE

Spring, circa 1968, Chinquapin, North Carolina

I am cursed with too good a memory. The foods of my first years haunt me like ghosts. They remind me, make me. "Remember what it tasted like?" they taunt me. "Remember that taste?"

In those days, when tobacco was still king in eastern North Carolina, tobacco beds were planted in the early months of the year. Long, rectangular patches, sheltered by thick plastic tarp, propped up by mighty reeds bent into deceptively strong hoops, lancing up and over the dirt like a series of bell curves, creating a knee-high canopy over the bare and prepared earth. Each bed entire had the dimensions of an Olympic swimming pool, sometimes even longer. Tobacco seed was sowed there, covered by the plastic, with inches of air above, and within weeks the burgeoning seedlings were ready to be thinned out, gradually, till the time came, usually post-Easter, when the stronger seedlings were pulled from the gentle earth of the bed and replanted in the fields—these select survivors now destined to become the human-sized bright leaf of icon.

It was common practice to reserve a patch at the far edges of the beds for greens—mustard and collards and turnips, primarily. Green like tobacco, they sprouted, were cropped periodically. Unlike the tobacco, which had many weeks of growth ahead till it was relocated and primed, these tender leaves were ready for consumption after a few short weeks.

The day I remember, particular and specific, had to have been before I was five, but after my great-uncle's-death when I was three. (I remember that day vividly as well, for he died on a multicolored quilt meant as my playground, on the porch of an old house used to grade cured tobacco leaves. This occurred right before my eyes in September of 1966.) My great-aunt, my grandfather's sister, now a widow, kept me, raised me as her own. I called her Mama and she was.

The day of which I speak, this day of green and greens, Mama and I had gone with two cousins to the tobacco fields, and they had lifted up the plastic at the edges of the beds to reveal all that newness. The earth, dark and loamy, smelled not of fertilizer and chemical products, but of rainwater, dead leaves, earthworms, and something like peace. The leaves of the mustard greens—and for some reason that year there was only mustard greens, so vibrantly bright green they almost glowed, vibrated in the sun—were snipped by fingers, so delicate they were, no knife was needed.

Mind you: we are speaking now not of salad greens to be eaten raw, with oil and vinegar dressing and the addition of chopped vegetables—tomatoes, onions, cucumbers—but rather the greens that love heat, not unlike tobacco, and need heat to find their greater essence. The liquid, the liquor.

Mama had not gotten a new washing machine yet, and she did our laundry in a 1950s Speed Queen with an external ringer ("THE MOST CLOTHES WASHED *CLEAN*, PER HOUR, PER DOLLAR"). The great-bellied tub ("one big, beautiful, double-wall, bowl-tub agitator-type") troubled the clothes in soapy water, then again in clear water, after which each garment, one at a time, was run through the hand-powered ringer, a laborious task that seemed to take hours, not to mention all the trips back and forth to the clothes line.

WHAT I REMEMBER from age four: returning home from the tobacco beds and Mama carrying the freshly picked mess of mustard greens in a galvanized bucket, overflowing at the top. Watching her clean the baby leaves, rinsing them, putting them in a big pot on the stove to cook. The day not too hot for late March, mild, alive with the atmosphere of new growing things, azalea bushes and dogwoods making blooms. Watching Mama, having started the greens, haul on the laundry. Being warned over and over: "Don't touch that wringer, boy!" Feeling more and more, by and by, such dread knowing it could crush my small fingers. Me so very wary of it! Me watching her, with great effort, sliding the clothing into the greedy maw of the thing, her spinning round the crank, by hand, round and round and round again, pressing the water from the underwear and shirts and pants and sundresses and socks, grunting some, sweating much. The clothes now clean and ready to be hung in the breeze.

Finally, all the clothes finished and swinging in the vernal air, me and Mama going into the kitchen. Her ladling out a great mound of the stuff with a great big spoon. For us: a bowl full of mustard greens. (Was there even salt?) Mama feeding me by her fingers one dripping, green leaf after another, like strands of spaghetti. Me opening my mouth like a bird to receive each bite. Gulp. I gobbled them down not with greed but with a sweet and clear delight, a wonder even. I don't remember being at all hungry, but I remember being satisfied. She grinned at me with approval, continuing to feed me the slender emerald strands, salty, bitter, alive. Her amusement at my eagerness to eat. We both laughed and giggled. I remember the taste of mustard. Peppery. Not unlike a savory candy. A particular goodness. A satisfaction as rich as a cool drink of water yet going toward the center of something more rare and more nourishing.

Many decades later I would ask Mama if she remembered that day, and she gave me this look as if to suggest that there was no way I could remember such a thing from four years of age (though I remember so very much more from even younger); as if to say this memory held such tiny, oblique, minor significance that it could not be of much worth at all; as if to question my sanity; as if to wonder if I were joking. I was quite serious indeed.

"Boy, what you talking 'bout?"

I myself have often wondered why this green memory, out of such a cornucopia of powerful, indelible, life-altering, and formative memories, sticks with me so powerfully. I suspect it was the very simplicity of the act—and the fact that it had no true ulterior motive other than the sharing, the maternal gesture, and the witness of taste. This thing, this moment, was more than about eating, it was about experience, about sharing in a free and simple way we rarely achieve as we frow older. I give, and you receive.

Ain't it good?

Ain't it good?

Ain't it good?

It is.

An initiation into the flavor of the world.

4

Swine Dreams

OR, BARBECUE FOR THE BRAIN

I like pigs. Dogs look up to us. Cats look down on us. Pigs treat
us as equals.

—Sir Winston Churchill

The rural North Carolina world in which I grew up has largely
gone. Farms were small and plentiful, and country boys like me
learned so much about life from livestock—especially, in North
Carolina, from hogs.

My cousin Norman lived directly across the dirt from my mother
and me. Along with his other farm concerns—tobacco, corn, soybeans, chickens—he raised scores of hogs, killing a number in
December for their meat, and selling the prized ones a bit later
for cash money. An old man when I was born, he had the air of an
Old Testament figure, and seemed to know everything there was to
know about coaxing plants from the ground and the feed and care
of animals. His grandsons, Harry and Larry, were daily fixtures on
his farm, and my best buddies in the world.

Then in high school, they were a few years older than me, and
they were my educators about all those things grown-ups were

never going to explain to me. Grown-up things. The birds and the
bees sorts of things. Subterranean, hidden things were our major
topics, after basketball and comic books. So much of the good
stuff about adult human society seemed off limits to me, which
made me even hungrier to know about it. The world was an end-
lessly fascinating, alluring, deadly, promising place, and they had
the vocabulary to describe it all, and the opinions to make it make
more sense. They had a knack about making the salacious seem
routine, yet still somehow magical. As far as I was concerned, they
knew everything.

Their grandfather kept his hogs in a two-story barn: It held corn
in a great room and had an open cavity where the tractor slept.
Above that was the tall, wide room with the large double doors in
front—the belfry, where the dried tobacco was stored. To the south
were stalls for the hogs. Their pens extended from their wooden
chambers out into the fenced-in cornfields where they rooted and
rutted and went about their hog business.

One early spring afternoon after school, we awaited the arrival
of a particular hog star the way a crowd of fans awaits the arrival
of the UNC basketball team after winning an away game. There
was much talk of what would occur betwixt the boar and the sow—
between the boar and many sows in fact, one by one. About how that
boar was a right lucky fellow: a true stud. I had a vague notion of
what was about to happen: a boar hog was to impregnate each sow
so that Cousin Norman could have more hogs to raise and butcher
or sell. This part made sense. The fuzzy part, in my eight-year-old
mind, was the act itself. Thanks to Harry and Larry's impeccable
tutelage, as well as the R-rated films they took me to, I had learned
about the congress between a man and a woman. But the mechan-
ics of hog sex boggled my mind. I kept trying to figure out how it
was done, and I was too proud to ask the right questions: What went
where? Does the boar ask permission? This was an event I had to

witness to complete my education as a North Carolina farm boy. For my cousins—well, this was basically country-boy porn.

The headliner boar hog arrived in a massive wagon towed by an oversized truck. The hog itself did not disappoint. When the slats were removed, he lumbered out like a creature from a nightmare. He was huge in every direction, dark brown and much hairier than the workaday porkers I slopped in the twilight after supper. I've never seen a hog that big. He stood taller than me, almost as tall as a grown man. The wideness of him, the heft of him, the length of him . . . he was a real-life monster. His head was the stuff of horror movies; its giant size was matched with mean eyes and the woolly mammoth tusks. (Who knew that domestic hogs grew tusks?) I'd never seen such a thing. His cavernous mouth dripped white, frothing ropes of drool. When he snorted I could see the air, like steam but thicker, heavier: the hog looked like pure evil. And, yes, his testicles were outrageous—mighty, pendulous, bulging, spherical things, clearly potent.

But he did disappoint with his seeming indifference to his first intended. A few attempts were made—now I saw how they did it: The impossibly large beast clambered on top of the female hog, herself no sylph, his hooves insistently drawing his great weight across her back, and then his red business attempted to invade her red business. The entire activity was clumsy yet riveting to behold. Suddenly the word "hump" had an entirely new meaning. Piglets were to be the outcome, by and by, by some mysterious process that I still accorded to magic. How else could you explain it?

We leered. Me, Harry, Larry, Cousin Norman, who had the most interest in seeing that the deed was done, for what seemed several hours, until boredom overtook us, and we retreated to watch something far less titillating: *Charlie's Angels*.

But all night my curiosity pricked at me like fire ants. Are they doing it? What does it look like?

The next morning, while everyone else chewed their bacon, I slipped outside. I couldn't stand it anymore; I had hog sex on the brain: I had to see. I walked across the road, under the great oak, to Cousin Norman's big barn, past the tractor and corn crib, to the rear stall where the great boar hog entertained his hog lady—wow! He was atop her. Penetration had not only been achieved but was occurring right before my prepubescent eyes. His sighs and grunts sounded like the air being slowly released from a great engine. And the motions he was making were, frankly, obscene. Like a shot I ran back across the road, into the house, into the dining room—the eight-year-old herald of pig fornication.

"They're doing it!"

I ran back to the barn followed by two horny teenagers whose interest in the matter held different curiosities than my own. We witnessed. Larry made some nasty, Rudy Ray Moore–like observations. Harry told me something then that I did not believe but have come to learn is true: male hogs have a corkscrew-shaped penis, and their sex act goes on longer than most mammals'. And for me, something momentous had occurred. My mind had been expanded in some mysterious way. I was seeing through a glass a little more darkly.

We sauntered back across the road to finish breakfast, our eyes and ears satiated by having witnessed something primordial, something that felt even forbidden to have beheld.

My mother stood on the porch. Arms akimbo. A look upon her face: I imagined Jack's mother looked the same when he told her he had sold their only cow for some dad-gummed magic beans.

"Don't you ever—ever—do something like that again!" she said. I had never, nor have I since, remembered her so close to apoplectic rage. Her fury seemed to loom above her like a towering phoenix afire, her tone like a pissed-off biblical prophet. "You just don't do things like that! You don't talk about such things! Have you lost your mind?" Her disappointment, her disapproval, bewildered me, and

I felt dirty and ashamed. "That's not information you broadcast to people. Polite people don't speak of such things. What kind of person do you want to be?" She retreated into the house to get ready for school. Harry and Larry slapped me on the back and laughed.

"Don't worry about it," Larry said to me. "It's natural."

WHEN I STUDIED playwrighting in college, I remember distinctly my first encounter with the great American writer Sam Shepard, for that was the first time I didn't need anyone to tell me that what I was reading was great. His subject—the American male—was fundamental and ready to be re-thought, re-invented, de- and re-mythologized. I almost came to worship those plays, for they felt so new and vital and alive. One of my favorites was *Curse of the Starving Class*, and in particular a fairly famous speech in that play.

In the scene, a character, who once shepherded lambs, tells a younger man the story of castrating lambs. Of how one day he absently threw the detached glands up on an old tin roof, and of how an eagle that had been eyeing him would swoop down and snatch up the lamb testicles. The eagle eventually gets into a tangle with a greedy cat that covets the balls equally. They both perish, eagle and cat, crashing from the sky. That speech always haunted me and goes to the core of what makes Shepard such a powerful artist: he captures something about Americans and manhood, indelibly, with organic nuance, understanding the vulnerability bound up in testosterone.

I knew and felt that experience personally. Not from lambs, but from hogs.

In my teenage years, on certain spring days, Cousin Roma would recruit me to help him geld the shoats. He did it with a razor blade and an aerosol can of some type of disinfectant. My job was to hold the few-months-old (or younger, I don't really remember at what age the violence was committed) pigs by the legs; they weighed less than 50–60 pounds at the time. Poor things. Uncle Roma would razor out their sacs and spray the violated area amid the unholy squeals. Each year I helped, now older, now gleaning more deeply the mystery of porcine fornication and impregnation of the anatomy and the imperative that moved both the hogs and us humans—though aspects of that mystery are still coming into focus, still growing, still being added onto.

I looked down upon what I was doing, what my uncle was doing to the shoats, and my first response was always a squeamish empathy, thinking how painful such a thing must be to endure. Even then, years before I came upon Sam Shepard and his parable of lamb, eagle, and cat, I envisioned something priestly about the act. Something that went to the soul of men and hogs, to the root of us.

So much of it all remains a mystery.

5

Chinquapin

ELEMENTARY PARTICLES

1

THE THERE THERE

The Kenan Family Farm; Chinquapin; Duplin County; North Carolina; United States of America; Continent of North America; Western Hemisphere; the Earth; the Solar System; the Universe; the Mind of God.

34.8 degrees N latitude. –77.82 degrees W longitude. 39 feet above sea level.

The Northeast Cape Fear River. Creeks and brooks like lacework across the land, defining fields and forests. The northernmost edge of the Angola Swamp—home of Venus flytraps.

Longleaf Pines and oak and sassafras. Maple, sweetgum, cedar. Laurel, magnolia, myrtle. Shortleaf pine, pitch pine, pond pine, Eastern white pine, loblolly pine. Sycamore. Cottonwood. Chokeberry. Hemlock. Elm. Pecan and walnut trees. Orchards: apple, pear, plum, scuppernong grape arbors. "Weeds" and wildflowers and grasses. Poke salad. (The American chinquapin tree was practically wiped out by the chestnut blight between 1905 and 1940.)

Raccoon, opossum, squirrel, field mouse. Insects. Frogs (tadpoles). Crayfish (crawdaddies). Lamprey eels. Catfish. Bats. Rabbit. Deer. Bobcat. Muskrat. Black bear. Alligators.

Chicken snakes, Rattlesnakes, king snakes, black racers, coachwhips, hog-nosed snakes, green snakes, garter snakes, coral snakes, milk snakes, corn snakes. Cottonmouth moccasin.

Corn. Soybeans. Cotton. Cucumbers. Strawberries. Sweet potatoes. Peanuts.

Hogs. Cows. More hogs. Lots of hogs. Chickens. Turkeys. Even more hogs. Indeed, more hogs than people. Mules (already so few by now, in the 1970s).

Tobacco. Tobacco barns. Tobacco packhouses.

Tractors. Combines. Plows. Discs. Trucks. Truck beds.

The billboard: "You Just Missed It!"—1/2 mile back, Miss Sally's Diner.

Churches: First Missionary Baptist Church. St. Lewis Baptist Church. Sharon Baptist Church. Chinquapin Presbyterian Church. St. Mark Church of Christ. Mt. Horeb Pentecostal Church. Church of Deliverance and Restoration Pentecostal Church. (Known affectionately as "Holy Rollers.")

Cemeteries . . . and sparrows and thrushes and robins and cardinals and the occasional egret or heron. Quail/bobwhites. Hummingbirds, hawks, bluejays, mockingbirds. Woodpeckers. Turkey buzzards.

Stores: Speaker Thomas's Grocery Store. Billy Brinkley's Grocery Store. Parker & Sons' General Store and Supply. M. L. Smith & Sons (at Mills Swamp), known by everyone as "Luther Jim's."

The glorious ruins of a nineteenth-century train station: two stories, paint gone and dun and slowly falling down, the top balcony stubbornly holding on, defying gravity, the physics of collapse . . . burned down by the Chinquapin Volunteer Fire Department in

1981. The long-abandoned rails of a train created to haul lumber at the turn of the nineteenth century. Rusty, overgrown, yet still there, even now . . .

Bank: United Carolina Bank. (Closed in 1987.)

United States Post Office.

Schools: Chinquapin Elementary #1 (formerly the Black school); Chinquapin Elementary #2 (formerly the white school). Football. Basketball. Baseball. (Mascot: the Indians.) 4-H Club.

My mother's garden: snap beans (Kentucky Wonders), pole beans, butterbeans, field peas, okra, cabbage, collards, mustard, Irish potatoes, carrots (sweet, sweet, sweet like candy; best straight from the earth—the dirt is good for you!), beefsteak tomatoes, cucumbers, onions, garlic, cayenne pepper, bell pepper, sweet corn, beets. Watermelon. (Begonias, wandering jew, dahlias, zinnias, geraniums, roses, sunflowers/black-eyed susans, snapdragons, azaleas . . .)

. . . THERE IS MORE. Much, much more. Scents and tastes. The color of things. The sounds of laughter. The sound of dirt landing upon coffins. Hymns. Pop tunes on the radio. First loves. Vacation Bible School in June. Murders and talent shows. The time the carnival came to town . . . and for me *Star Trek* and Charles Dickens and Batman and *The Swiss Family Robinson* and Spider-Man and *Treasure Island* and *The Hobbit* and the intense desire to be elsewhere. (How could I have forgotten blueberries?) And yet a funky good allegiance and gratitude. "Chickenpen, Nawf Cackalacky—smile when you say that, fella . . ."

Memory is a Polaroid.

"Location pertains to feeling; feeling profoundly pertains to place; place in history partakes of feeling, as feeling about history partakes of place," Eudora Welty writes in "Place in Fiction."

2
STRUCK BY LIGHTNING

Her: There was something about her that rubbed me the wrong way. Maybe it was the way she looked at me. Maybe it was the dip of snuff that never, ever, never left that place between her bottom lip and her gums; the way she spat the brown juice like a laser beam with enough accuracy and force to bisect a horsefly in mid-flight.

I got along with her sons; one was a grade ahead of me in school, one was a grade behind me. One was out of school. One was a lap baby. Her daughter, Trisha, my age, never had a good word to say about me, and teased me without mercy. Her older daughter, Anne, looked upon me as if I had escaped from the pound, and wondered where the hell the dogcatcher was when you needed him most.

But with Miss Ella, it was a matter of indifference, impatience, disregard. Maybe I wanted her to like me, and, once I sensed I was beyond any sort of such affection, I retaliated by disliking her more.

She was a large woman. Dark of skin. Lips large. Eyes deer-round and sad. She fancied sundresses of the brightest hue. She complained often of the pains in her oversized feet, sandal-shod, toes painted fuchsia.

Their family was the poorest of the poor, which was mighty poor indeed in Duplin County. Tobacco season was the only time, truly, when they could augment government cheese and garden food with more store-bought food, when everyone could get day wages and the light bill would get paid. And everyone in the family worked. The baby was more often than not at the workplaces along with her. I don't remember much, if anything, about her husband. He never came to church. I wonder now if I ever laid eyes on him. Not that she ever came to church too often, except on those occasions when they served fried chicken, barbecue, slaw, potato salad and ice tea afterwards. She never seemed to miss a funeral.

Nonetheless, when it came to tying tobacco, she was highly prized and sought after (also as a grader of cured tobacco). Her skills resided in her speed and in her accuracy. When she handed tobacco—a deceptively simple activity: three or four good-size leaves, the stems evened out with a pat of the heel of the palm, and backhanded to the tier—she accomplished the feat with Henry Ford–like automated precision, always the fastest hand in the South. When she tied—standing over a stick, suspended on a wooden and spindly "horse," grabbing the backhanded bunch of leaves, looping them in cotton twine, once, twice, and over, onto the stick, snug, one packet of bound leaves tight against the next, and the next, until the length of the wooden stick was full and tied off at the end: pop—she became a blur, a musician: zip, whir, zip, whir, zip, whir. God help you if you made her wait too long. And when the stick was complete, loaded down with big bunches of green leaves like oversized praying hands pointing downwards, she would grunt, "Stick!" This was my cue to come grab the done-thing and take it to a pile, which grew from nothing in the morning into a rectangular mountain of emerald by the end of the day. Her contempt for my slowness (or at least by her standards) was one of the burrs between us, when she would spit out the brown juice and say, "Come on, boy. Ain't got all day. You slow as Christmas coming. Where you at? Ham mercy."

I had been raised to respect my elders, to be courteous and gentle with all, to never sass back, and all that good Gospel Jazz. I did not enjoy the company of this woman.

That fateful day we were putting in tobacco for my cousin Seymour, who owned a small farm, but who also leased a great many acres from the bigger landowners. This certain field was remote from his farm, and the original barn there had long ago burned down. So we went about our toil on the edge of a copse of trees on the edge of this particular fifty acres of bright leaf. Under longleaf pines and oaks. A tarp had been strung over our heads to keep out the sun and the rain, but more important to give some protection to the stacked tobacco. It was a fairly flimsy setup, and the ground beneath our feet was uneven and rough and root-interrupted and grass-jagged and leaf-strewn. As much as I hated working in tobacco, not being under the proper shelter of a tobacco barn made this adventure even more hateful.

When the fields had been primed, we would load the pile of tied tobacco sticks onto a flat-bed and haul it to one of Seymour's flue barns and hang it all there, high in the rafters, ready for firing—a hard day's work.

There was no Doppler radar or Weather Channel in those days. For all of us, the day had begun before dawn, so not even Cousin Seymour had heard a weather report, not that anything short of a hurricane would have stopped the day's work. Cropping tobacco went on regardless the temperature or precipitation. The show must go on.

The workday began bright and hot and blue skies. Sweat and dirt and black tar hands and tractor fumes and mosquitoes and snakes and plump, neon-green tobacco worms. Zip, whir, zip, whir, zip, whir. The workday was gossip about soap operas and whose husband was cheating on whose wife and who was in the hospital ailing with what and who had just lost his job and who was pregnant and who was moving back to North Carolina from New York. Zip, whir, zip, whir, zip, whir, zip, whir. The workday was aching backs and sore feet and dirt everywhichaway and sweat and bugs and dreams of sleep and supper and more cool water to drink.

I remember the clouds gathered with a breathtaking suddenness. All had been clear. Now the shadows grew and engulfed all. Dramatic enough to make all pause and take notice and comment: "Hmmm, child. Look like a storm is coming up." Day practically turned to night before the rain began. The wind already gusting.

When the water droplets—fat aqueous pods to be more accurate—began to fall, at first vertical, and very soon horizontal, there was no time to retreat. Lightning crashed. Thunder truly rolled.

The makeshift tent failed promptly. We huddled, dark in the dark, torrents drenching, at the base of the largest, friendliest oak, wrapped up in the fallen, plastic blue tarp, the wind howling. I don't remember being afraid at all. Merely amused. After all that hot, it feel good to be wet, as if in a pool, all of a sudden. A number of us younger ones were giggling, snuggled up, after a fashion, in the dark and wet.

Lightning first, then thunder. You could hear the bolts striking in the distance. That's what creates the thunder. It is God's hammer slicing through the sky. The earth rocks. Graves shake. Hearts and time stop. The sound of over three million volts of electricity lancing down from the sky is a different sound. Thunder booms—the sound of electricity-cleaved air rushing back together. But lightning resounds more like an obliterating zap. Jove is angry. Ozone is in the air.

No wonder the old ones always made us young ones hush and be still every time a thunder cloud came up. They understood more about that terrible power than we could.

I don't remember the sound when it hit us, only that the insides of my eyes lit up. And the tell-tale tingle of electricity running through my being's fiber. Does sinew and muscle know it is being shot through with an abundance of electrons? What did Frankenstein's monster think when he was jolted back to life? How does the soul respond to electricity? Do androids ever dream of tobacco? I remember the pause before everyone hollered. Screamed. Shouted. I remember all us hauling ourselves up, running ourselves to the trucks and cars. I remember fleeing in the rain and dark. I remember sitting in the car, everyone talking at once. "Jesus!" No one was dead. No one seriously harmed. The lightning had hit the oak;

the energy flowing down into the earth, through us. We had been made, briefly, part of a circuit. I remember a soaked Miss Ella, sitting in the backseat of a Chevy Nova, moving her head, slowly, from side to side, and saying loudly, "Lord, Lord, Lord, . . ." breathing heavily, as were we all.

"God was looking out for us," Cousin Seymour later said.

The next day I rode with him in his truck to see the sight. A great part of the oak tree was split, its whitish greenish-tan, vulnerable, wounded-looking innards exposed. Some sear on its bark. ("It resembled that perpendicular seam sometimes made in the straight, lofty trunk of a great tree, when the upper lightning tearingly darts down it, and without wrenching a single twig, peels and grooves out the bark from top to bottom, ere running off into the soil, leaving the tree still greenly alive, but branded."—Herman Melville, *Moby-Dick.*)

The next evening, after a long, long, long day of work, I remember returning home. I was bone-tired, recollecting powerful things for which I had no words, the feeling of electricity, the flash behind my retinas, the odd sense of camaraderie I shared with the fellow workers ("Did you feel that?"), thinking and wanting school to return in a few blessed weeks, when work would be done, and hot, dirty fields would be a hateful but necessary memory. I remember I was watching a Marty Feldman special on TV (*Marty Back Together Again*). I heard a car drive up and stop in the yard. I went to the door to see who it was. Miss Ella.

My mother greeted her on the front porch. Miss Ella said hey to me, pleasantly, but I stayed behind the screen door. I said hey back. She had brought my mother tomatoes and collard greens. My mother ooohed and aaaahed her appreciation at the quality of the produce, and thanked Miss Ella, and they sat in the white rocking chairs and talked. Only a few minutes, less than a full smoked cigarette in time. Just catching up. A wee touch of gossip.

"Well, I better get back," Miss Ella said, rising.

"Wait a minute," Mama said, and went to fetch some freshly picked okra for Miss Ella.

"Why thank you," she said. "Looks good."

For some odd reason I came out onto the porch to say bye.

She spat a hyper-fast snuff shot off the side of the porch, onto my mama's pansies. "That was something the other day, won't it?"

"Yes, ma'am," said I.

"Now you can tell folk you been struck by lightning." She let out an inky dark, earthy, loud, unrepentant witch's laugh. The very sound of it and the look on her face made me grin. She winked at me.

I watched as she got into her beat-up old Galaxy, a dull and unpolished metallic silver it was, and I watched it roll on down the dirt road, gaining speed as it went, dust rising up into the approaching-twilight air.

Those days of rattlesnakes and wild electrons were not lived, for me, like a character in a children's book, with warming hues and wonderful narrative arcs, and gentle old men walking me to the fishing hole imparting gentle wisdom about how to live a gentle life. More often than not there were mosquitoes and roadkill and spiteful gossip and raunchy tales I should have been spared. Neither were those days free of pettiness and bitterness and down-right hatefulness and illness and rounding death. Those days were largely filled by a sense of lucklessness and a heavy dose of hard work, and seeing others work harder. In truth, Miss Ella treated me not much differently than she had before the lightning strike. Her life had not been altered much at all, but I knew mine would be. Such knowledge is at once a separation and a binding. What I did not know at the time was how indelible were those moments, those characters—people—that place, all of which would follow me all the way down my Yellow Brick Road.

Eudora Welty writes, in "Place in Fiction": "Where does the mystery lie? Is it in the fact that place has a more lasting identity than we have, and we unswervingly tend to attach ourselves to identity?"

A thing happened. A thing you shall never forget. It happened here, in a place that has known you and will always know you. By that knowing you are made.

LATER THAT VERY summer, not the same day, but from the same porch, I would see the aurora borealis. Such a sight so very rarely seen so far south. Filling up the sky. Ghostly. Multicolored yet largely, vastly green. Moving slow and yet not moving at all and lazy and with power beyond glory. Electrons spilling into our atmosphere. Above Cousin Norman's house, just across the road, above his barn, above the great oak tree that had lost its great twin in 1957, above the soybean field, above the forest and deer, above us all.

According to astronomical records, that day was July 6, 1974. I was eleven years old.

6

Ode to Billie Joe

And Papa said to Mama as he passed around the black-eyed
peas,
"Well, Billie Joe never had a lick of sense; pass the biscuits,
please"

—Bobbie Gentry, "Ode to Billie Joe"

This is *Romeo and Juliet* set in post–WWII rural Mississippi. Romeo is played by Robby Benson, 1976's version of the Jonas Brothers all wrapped up in one; Juliet being a doe-like Glynnis O'Connor, whom the camera loves. The picture: *Ode to Billy Joe*, being Max Baer Jr.'s second movie. (He being the son of the heavyweight champion boxer Max Baer, and once Jethro Bodine of *The Beverly Hillbillies* fame in his youth.) Based on the hit 1967 song by songstress Bobbie Gentry. Baer's first big hit, the first of a short run of memorable movies about the Dirty South, tinged with erotica and nostalgia, a far cry from the Clampetts yet not quite Walker Evans and William Faulkner either . . . unless you count his notorious *Sanctuary*. . . .

I saw it at a small theater in Wallace, North Carolina, when I was but thirteen. It is a painfully simple story: small-town boy courts and sparks a small-town girl; they fall in love; boy falls, by wicked external influence, into a night of debauchery (an act only hinted at on camera); he cannot forgive himself, and, like some Protestant American martyr, ends his life, leaving his beloved to ponder and spin and wonder. ("Today Billie Joe McAllister jumped off the Tallahatchie Bridge.")

It was the first movie I remember haunting me and actually causing a mild depression. Melancholy. I was too young to have a sense of surety (What did Billie or Billy Joe McAllister do to cause himself so much pain?); my notions were inchoate, and too vague even for a premonition. I probably knew the word "homosexual" but its meaning was but an urge in my pants and far from any reality. Yet what I am certain of now is the sense of dread, the Signs in the Sky, the warnings and omens, the prefiguration of doom: Beware all ye who enter here. There be dragons there, y'all!

But what hateful dragon could smite the lovely Robby Benson? (I sometimes jokingly say Robby Benson made me gay.) Shame on that damn dragon! The penultimate scene in the woods— overwritten and overacted, and embarrassingly powerful exactly for that reason; so true to the adolescent spirit, lacking in all taste or any sense of proportion; so in love with its own melodramatic knowledge of being alive and of having feelings—the scene where a cast-away Billy Joe, all sweaty and mottled with dirt and peat, comes upon his lady love, in a glade, after having foraged for days alone in the wood: here he confesses, at the same time, of his profound lust for her, and of his now-corruption, obviously beyond Christian redemption, all this before running off to jump his young life away into the Tallahatchie River. To this day that humid scene still shatters my heart, despite Max Baer's clumsy but well-meaning hand. I felt naked when I watched it, revealed, and feel naked even now when I see it.

7

Comfort Me with Barbecue

Though it is the blessed chicken I probably remember most from that night, the hog was the Alpha and the Omega. Amen.

In those days the fire and rescue squad in tiny Chinquapin, North Carolina, was all volunteer. Every other weekend—and almost every weekend during the summer months—the tradition was to have a benefit Saturday barbecue sale at the station.

The station was white, two stories, and church-large, housing the fire truck and ambulance. The kitchen upstairs, restaurant quality, all white and stainless steel, and the women who looked after it kept the place spick-and-span.

Out back was the barbecue house. Made of brick. An anteroom for storage and stacked with cords upon cords of wood, and a narrow long room containing mostly a brick-lined barbecue pit, able to hold at least four grown hogs at once. There was a wide, sturdy table for the main post-roast activities.

This being eastern North Carolina, when a person said "barbecue" they meant, quite specifically, whole-hog barbecue. (Of course barbecued chicken was a thing, but the good people of the lowlands would never confuse the two.) The barbecue meat is then chopped into fine chunks, and sauced with a vinegary, peppery mixture oft guarded by pitmasters with guile and wit.

Usually a deacon from our church, First Baptist Missionary Church, would show up with the donated hogs, late on Friday afternoon. Most often it was my cousin, Seymour, a well-regarded farmer, who had also won high praise for his skills around a barbecue pit. His job was to get the fires going. His job was to supervise the laying-on of the hogs upon the metal screens suspended high over the fire. His job was to season and anoint the roasting meat with his special secret sauce. His job was to stay up all night making sure there would be good and plenty pig-meat to satisfy an entire community of less than one thousand. The atmosphere was quite merry, even festive. And I loved it so very much when my mother would allow me to spend the night at the fire house, "helping."

My cousin's husband, Mr. John Brown, was a "Yankee," a former resident of Harlem, who moved to his wife's home after having worked for the city of New York for over twenty years. This was very like a Black and white version of *Green Acres*, with this dapper African American gentleman learning the ways of the descendants of the Confederacy. Luckily he had a high emotional IQ and a raucous sense of humor, so these sitcom encounters tended to end on a happy note. Having been a civil servant, he felt it a responsibility and almost sacred duty to become a member of the fire and rescue squad soon after he arrived in town. The Friday nights he would stay on call at the fire house were the nights I'd be right there with him, like a mascot and barbecue aid.

There were two firemen/EMTs on call that night, ready to hop in the readied ambulance for a call. And despite the level of accidents and trauma most Friday nights engender, the incidents in this wayback, rural community were luckily few. So I would sit around, often with other folk visiting, other folk caught up in the fun of an all-night pig roast, sitting in the common room of the station, lying and laughing and watching silly shows on the black-and-white TV. This was my chance to feel important, to feel a part of things, to be an eyewitness to the vital stuff of life. I wasn't even old enough to get a driver's license.

On one particular night, I shall never forget, Mr. Brown had a notion to cook a chicken on the flaming coals that cooked the hogs. He brought from home a fryer hen and went about seasoning it with salt and pepper and a quantity of the vinegary sauce he got from Cousin Seymour. We wrapped the chicken in aluminum foil. Then more aluminum foil. And yet more aluminum foil. We didn't want the chicken to burn, but we wanted the heat to get in there and do its thing. We put the aluminum football in a corner of the furnace, and we covered it with coals, and we waited.

Not very long after that, at around 8:00 p.m., the alarm went off. Good gosh! The dispatch spoke the name, and it was one of my schoolmates. Of course, I couldn't go along on the ride, shouldn't have if I could have. I remember watching the ambulance pull out of the garage in a great zip, the lights flashing, the siren hollering. I had seen this sight many a time on television—the opening of *Hill Street Blues*—but this was not entertainment. This was life and death.

One of the men hanging out at the fire station that evening was literally an old salt, a former merchant marine, well advanced in age, whose wrinkles were a thing of fascination: Mr. Easter. He had a complete set of ill-fitting false teeth and would sometimes try to spook me by poking them out like a vampire. "Boo!" I think it amused him more than it amused me.

Imagine a seventy-year-old, retired white sailor from Massachusetts, of all places, trying to comfort a fifteen-year-old African American lad who'd just learned that his classmate had been shot in a hunting accident. Mr. Easter took me into the den and talked with me, not like a man talking to a child, but the way I figured men spoke to men. Mr. Easter had been everywhere—literally—and seen everything. He possessed a depth of knowledge and wisdom and sensitivity that most folk overlooked. He taught me an old rhyme:

> There is so much good in the worst of us,
> And so much bad in the best of us,
> That it hardly behooves any of us
> To talk about the rest of us.

In my romantic mind, I like to think of him as a character straight out of *Treasure Island*. To me, he was.

By and by the ambulance returned. My schoolmate had not survived, and I watched Mr. Brown, quite sad and solemn, wash the blood from the ambulance. The tale of the happenings were at once ordinary, cautionary, bleak, and grim.

But there was the chicken: We retrieved it, we unwrapped it, and somehow the amount of time—hours roasting on the coals—was perfect. The meat was so tender it melted upon the tongue. The flavors, quite simple, yet amplified by the wood-heat, and the wood-slowness, had imparted something rich and penetrating in a way no marinade could approach. We speak often of comfort foods, but some foods, at some times, do more than merely comfort. Beatific.

After our singular meal, the tone now somber, Mr. Brown and his comrade slept. Mr. Easter had gone to his home across the street. But I could not sleep, I did not want to sleep. I stayed up the rest of the night, alone, watching *Creature Feature* on Channel 12: *I Walked with a Zombie* (1943). A ghoulish but odd fit.

Sunrise brought a difference. Sunrise brought taking the hogs from the fire. Sunrise brought witnessing Cousin Seymour disarticulate the meat from the bones—and by now the meat was so very tender and so very cooked that it largely slid off like honey. Like a kitchen dog in a medieval kitchen, I got to munch on the bony parts, the meat seasoned to a fare-thee-well, robust, smoky, deeply satisfying.

Witnessing then, the meat, now in white buckets, being taken to the upstairs kitchen, past the red-and-white checkered serving tables, into the hospital-clean kitchen. The chopping. The seasoning. The tasting. The mounds of delectable pork made ready for the serving, for the sale, for the benefit, for the good, the good of us all.

And by noontime the people came, Black, white, young, old, Yankee and good ole boys and girls. We all got heaping helpings of spicy goodness—along with cole slaw and potato salad and baked beans and hushpuppies, that old, crunchy, North Carolina classic. It was not fancy, but it was indeed fine. Community was an experienced thing, not simply an idea.

8

Ghost Dog

OR, HOW I WROTE MY FIRST NOVEL

I.

I never saw the ghost dog, but I can see it, nonetheless. Some said it was actually a wolf, grey with flashing red eyes. Some said it was a very large "sooner" (a Southern term for mongrel or mutt, meaning "as soon this breed as it is that breed"). But in the majority of accounts about ghost dog sightings, people remarked that the dog was white, ghostly so, and more often than not a shepherd, the kind with a keen nose and pointy ears. Noble. Resolute.

In every account I heard as a child the dog was always helpful: my great-great-aunt had a story of how the dog had led her out of the woods once when she was lost. I heard a lot of such stories when I was growing up. There was even a long story featuring my own great-great-grandmother, a storm, a mule, a broken-down cart and the heroic ghost dog. One woman reported being set upon by a pack of canines and how this beautiful white dog leapt to her rescue, appearing out of nowhere, and escorted her safely home. When she turned around in her doorway, the dog had vanished.

The sightings always occurred along a particular stretch of asphalt highway—once a trail for Native Americans, then a dirt road for horses and wagons, and, by the time I was a boy, a main route to the beach. Highway 50 cut through an astounding forest of old-growth timber (which was clear-cut only a few years ago). Oak. Poplar. Pine. Especially the majestic, soaring, massive-limbed long-leaf pine that has recently become endangered. For me, as a child, this forest was truly primordial, ancient, full of mysteries, dangers, witches, and goblins, and all manner of wonders I had read about in Grimms' fairy tales. And that amazing white dog. The dog I had never seen. But he lived in my imagination. He still does.

It makes perfect sense to me, now, that one day I would write about that ghost dog and that world of southeastern North Caro-lina. Duplin County. Chinquapin. A town of only a couple of hun-dred souls. Farmers, poultry-factory workers, marine-base laborers, largely. But that seeming inevitability was not so obvious to me at the time.

II.

I recently saw an interview with the late, great scientist and science fiction writer, Arthur C. Clarke, inventor of the telecommunication satellite and author of *Childhood's End* and the story that was the basis for *2001: A Space Odyssey*. He said: "The mark of a first-rate scientist is an interest in science fiction. The mark of a second-rate scientist is lack of interest in science fiction." By that logic, I should have become a first-rate scientist, but alas, that was not meant to be. When I first left my small, ghost-haunted North Carolina town, I matriculated at the University of North Carolina at Chapel Hill, the nation's oldest public university, a bastion of classical thinking, progressive social thinking, high art, and most important for me at the time: scientific thought. My goal in those days: to become a physicist. My interest in science had been provoked by my having gotten lost for hours in space operas like Isaac Asimov's *Foundation* and Frank Herbert's *Dune*, in *Star Trek* and fantasies about alien cultures and faster-than-light travel, black holes, worm holes, and cool ray guns. (I'll never forget the day my physics advisor said to me when I was a junior: "I think you really want to be a science fiction writer, my boy." When I took umbrage, trying to explain away my C in differential calculus, he quickly said to me, "There is no shame in being a writer. More scientists," he said, "would be writers, but they can't write. So be grateful you can," he told me. He himself moonlighted as a writer about fine wines.)

Truth to tell, my interest in science fiction—I had already scribbled, on lined notepaper, two or three seriously dreadful SF novels, thankfully lost to time—led me to study creative writing, and studying writing led me to the study of literature. But we are taking about the highfalutin, canonical type of literature, Charles Dickens and F. Scott Fitzgerald and William Makepeace Thackeray. It became clear to me early on that there was an orthodoxy at work here. Being in the American South, and at a premier Southern American university, Southern literature was king and queen: Thomas Wolfe. William Faulkner. Flannery O'Connor. Richard Wright. Eudora Welty. Southern literature meant social realism. These were the iconic figures held up to us aspiring young Southern writers. Any penchant for the fantastic or the phantasmagorical was met with discouragement. Ridiculed even. Real writers, good writers, wrote about the world as it was. "Write what you know" was the mantra of the creative writing courses nestled in the bosom of the English department, and my major, by my senior year, was no longer physics but English. I was writing what I knew. I knew about ghost dogs.

III.

Ten things about Chinquapin:

1. Soybean fields
2. Two Black Baptist churches

3. Rattlesnakes
4. Turkey houses
5. Cucumber fields
6. Deer
7. Summertime family reunions
8. Tobacco barns
9. September revival meetings
10. Cottonmouth moccasins

IV.

When I arrived at Chapel Hill in the fall of 1981, the percentage of African Americans was in the single digits—around 4 or 5 percent. Yet those hundreds among thousands made their presence known. For whatever reason, most of my closest friends were fellow African Americans. Was it a need for familiarity? A sense of bonding? The comfort of kin? To be sure, I had many good, close, and true white friends—and Japanese friends and Hispanic friends and Indian friends, and with many of whom I am still close—but the gravity of African American culture fascinates me. I wrote for the Black student newspaper. I sang in the Black Student Movement Gospel Choir. I was a founding member of the Carolina Comic Book Club which was, not by design, but refreshingly, thoroughly integrated and dominated by Black guys, curiously enough.

I never felt any actual pressure to "write Black." I had great respect for the Gospel of Social Realism and its canon, and I knew it well. But for every autobiographical story I turned in to workshop, I would also pen a story featuring a root worker (a practitioner of African American folk magic) or a space station or a talking dog. Moreover, by that time, I had encountered three writers who gave me what I like to call permission.

The best training any writer can receive is reading, reading, and more reading. Even more than writing, this is also essential. And though I drank down the aforementioned canonical writers of the South with great alacrity and added to that mix a deep investigation of the Great African American Book of Fiction—Ralph Ellison, James Baldwin, Gwendolyn Brooks—I would stumble upon writers beyond those garden walls who had enormous impact on the way I looked at the world of prose fiction. Isaac Bashevis Singer. Yukio Mishima. Anthony Burgess. Writers who were not, at first glance, the obvious heroes of a young Black man from rural, southeastern North Carolina.

It was Toni Morrison, already popular, but years before *Beloved* and the Pulitzer Prize and the Nobel, who taught me something of mind-opening importance. With precious few exceptions, African American literature fell under the umbrella of "protest" literature, going back to the nineteenth century and the plethora of famous slave narratives. Even as late as 1970, the year Morrison's first novel was published, most important African American novels dealt largely with issues of civil rights and social justice for Black people. But Morrison took as her primary subject matter Black folks themselves, not racism or politics. She instead chose to focus on personal and family dynamics, matters of the heart and soul. In her world, the perspective of white folk could go unmentioned for hundreds of pages. For my eighteen-year-old mind this was a revelation.

The writings of the great Colombian author Gabriel García Márquez were my first introduction to what has become popularly known as magical realism. I would never be the same again. (In his Nobel lecture, García Márquez stressed that there is nothing truly fantastical about his work; the world he writes about is uncompromisingly real. I understood right away exactly what he meant.) Here was a writer who wrote about ghosts and a town suffering from mass amnesia and storms of butterflies and women flying up to heaven with the same matter-of-fact language of social realism—in fact his three favorite writers are Faulkner, Ernest Hemingway, and Virginia Woolf.

Zora Neale Hurston, whose long-neglected works were just beginning to be rediscovered when I was in college, hit me like a neutron bomb. Here was this trained anthropologist, this Floridian, this African American, who seamlessly integrated folklore with folklife, social realism with the fantastic. Like Morrison, who learned much from Hurston, she did not put the politics of race above the existential essence of Black culture.

Song of Solomon. One Hundred Years of Solitude. Their Eyes Were Watching God. It was as if they were collectively saying: Go write ahead, boy. Do your own thing.

For my honors thesis I turned in several chapters of a proposed novel set in a small North Carolina town very like Chinquapin called Tims Creek. It featured a young lawyer, a native son, who had become a successful Washington, DC, lawyer. But one fateful summer when he returns to Tims Creek full of a certain emotional turmoil, he runs across a root worker who curses (blesses?) him, and the next night, in the full moon, he becomes a werewolf! I called it "Ashes Don't Burn."

Mercy, mercy, me.

V.

Imagine what it is like to have as your first job out of college working for the publisher of two of your literary heroes. Alfred A. Knopf. New York City. The long-time publisher of Toni Morrison. The new publisher of Gabriel García Márquez. 1985. I would soon become the assistant to the editor of the author of *Love in the Time of Cholera.* For an aspiring writer, this was like studying at the feet of Merlin.

But there was another education afoot for me. I would come to spend years living in Queens and then Brooklyn. I was now rubbing shoulders daily, in the subways, on the streets, in the stores, and eventually in homes, with Black folk from all over the African diaspora. I got to know Black people from Ghana and Trinidad and Haiti and Toronto and Houston, Texas. This exposure challenged all those closely held notions of what it means to be Black and made me look back at the world in which I had initially grown up with brand-new eyes. Suddenly the fish fries, the out-of-tune church choirs, the hours spent toiling under the sun in tobacco fields, Vacation Bible School, hog killings, and stories of ghost dogs became important somehow, important to be written about. This urgency was over the connections of my very specific rural South to the larger African cultures, but I also saw the uniqueness of the world in which I had come of age. This new apprehension felt very like a mandate to not only write about that world now lost—for Duplin County had changed dramatically from the time I had been a boy, just like so much of the rural American South—and to write about it honestly, with that honest mix of the seen and the unseen which was integral to capturing the world that had shaped those lives, my life.

"Ashes Don't Burn" had one fundamental flaw, and, in hindsight, I thank my teachers back at social-realism-saturated UNC for helping me to realize that roadblock. The impediment had nothing to do with lycanthropy. Simply put: I was not a thirtysomething lawyer going through a crisis upon returning home. I was not writing what I "knew." But I had been a boy in that same home, so, by and by, the narrative I had been laboring over changed. I kept the supernatural cast that I'm sure inhabited those dark woods. The landscape did not change at all; in fact it probably richened and deepened, partly from my nostalgia for it, and as a response to the six-billion-footed city, dreaming of the woods and the deer and the cornfields. But I cannot think about the forests of my boyhood without imagining some inexplicable presence lurking, just behind that great oak tree, meaning ill or good. You must pay attention.

The story I scribbled at doggedly, in the evenings, on subways, on the weekends, would ultimately be published in the summer of 1989 as *A Visitation of Spirits*. There are no ghost dogs in it, amazingly, but plenty of other ghosts and creatures, spirits of the world and of the mind, mingled in with a healthy dose of social realism as I had been scrupulously taught, and which I respect with great admiration.

For me, now, this approach seems inevitable. Right. The only way for me to do it. Yet the path toward that fictional vision was neither straight nor easily achieved, but worth every twist and bend and cul-de-sac.

I hope to return to lycanthropy one day soon. There is something in that mythology that fits well in Tims Creek, in Chinquapin. And of course, soon and very soon, I hope a ghost dog will make an appearance in one my stories. Leaping to the rescue only to vanish again into the imagination.

PART II
WHERE
AM I
BLACK?

9

Come Out the
Wilderness

... I can hurt
You with questions
Like silver bullets.

—Yusef Komunyakaa, "Venus's Flytraps"

"You North American Blacks, you make me so angry," she was
saying. "You set yourselves off from the rest of the diaspora. As
if your experiences were somehow *better*. 'We suffered more.' When,
in fact, the slavocracy of the Caribbean was much more brutal."

We were in a cafe in Greenwich Village, arguing over coffee about
the nature of Black America. "But you miss the point entirely," I said.

She was African. In fact an Ethiopian princess, a direct descendant of Haile Selassie, now studying anthropology at the University
of Colorado. Her mother worked for the United Nations and she
had spent a great deal of time at their family estate in Antigua,
where they were watched over devotedly by Rastafarians, who consider the last emperor of Ethiopia to be their Messiah. Moreover,
her family had married into an old Black North Carolina family—
thus she felt more than qualified to declaim on African Americans.

"What you say is true," I said, "but what separates us is not just the psychological shackles of slavery, but the extent to which our bloods have intermingled . . ."

"Bullshit." She laughed and shook her head in disbelief. "You think that there was no other rape and that there aren't Creoles throughout the world? That doesn't make you different, make you *better.*"

"No one's saying we're *better.* Just different."

"But you all act that way."

"What? I don't think American Black people think they are any better than Africans or West Indians, but we do recognize that our experience has been markedly different. Look," I said, "we've become a part of this country in a way that no other Black group has become a part of their country. I mean, we made this country. We still do. Why was slavery instituted here in the first place? Free labor. And look what that labor has created, materially, for better or worse. Moreover, we've contributed to every aspect of American life, scientifically, legislatively, militarily, artistically . . ."

"Oh, God, I don't want to hear any more about Black music . . ."

"It's not just Black music. It's everything. Hell, we are America. We have more claim to this country than anyone other than the Native American. We've been here for over three hundred years, for Christ's sake. I don't mean to disparage the diaspora, but how can we ignore our blood-and-sweat connection to this land? This very land here?"

"What I'm talking about is just that attitude, that your experience is somehow better . . ."

"Not better, different . . ."

No one won the argument that warm spring evening. Yet the discussion haunted me for years afterwards, not because I had not thought of these ideas before, but because I had not realized how deeply I felt about being an American, an African American. Nor was it the beginning of a search for my identity, but a turning point, a turning point which led me to the decision to explore firsthand the idea and the reality of what it means to be Black in America. To question what it means to be an African American.

———————

WHAT DOES IT mean to be Black?

In discussing Black America, on whatever level, be it politics, economics, music, food, I often use the word "we." Aside from the necessity of sometimes making broad generalizations about broad groups, the more I think about African America, the more I cannot help but question what I mean by "we." I'm not the only Black person who does this. All through my growing up, my relatives did it, my teachers, my ministers; in school, at work, whenever or wherever I encountered Black folk talking about Black folk—even when speaking to non-Black folk—the word "we" was used.

Do we mean race? Do we mean culture? Do we mean skin color? The more I thought of it, the more problematic the idea became— even as I persisted in using the word, becoming ever more uncertain of what I—what "we"—meant.

Did I mean race? If I did I was a hypocrite, because I don't believe in "race" as a fact of nature. Biologically speaking there is only one human species, and though tremendous amounts of time and money have been spent on the classification and subdivision of human beings, classifications that go beyond mere skin color, no one has succeeded, scientifically, in demonstrating any significant difference between people who look different from others. Consider cats: A Siamese, a calico, and a tabby are actually of different genus—that is, they have specific genetic codes (even though they can mate); whereas Koreans, Botswanans, Apaches, and Swedes are all within the same genus. We humans are all calicos, despite visual persuasions to the contrary. But as a rule, human beings don't think that way. Since the time the noted anthropologist Franz Boas wrote, "Where is the proof of the development of specialized hereditary capacities? Where is the proof that such capacities, if they exist, are recessive? How can it be shown that such specialized characteristics in selected mating will be bred out? Not a single one of these statements can be accepted," no one has presented any compelling evidence to the contrary. Where race is concerned, I feel very much like Henry Adams when he wrote: "And yet no one could tell the patient tourist what race was, or how it should be known. History offered a feeble and delusive smile at the sound of the word; evolutionists and ethnologists disputed its very existence; no one knew what to make of it; yet without the clue, history was a nursery tale."

Race is better explained by what historian Barbara Jeanne Fields calls "an ideological construct and thus, above all, a historical product." As a great many historians have noted, "race" is far more a mythology than a reality, brought about first by the proponents of slavery as a way to create a caste system in the United States. It is a melding of class with pseudobiology in such a way as to make and maintain an inferior, unequal group of people, a people both socially and economically on the lowest rung of the ladder. "During the revolutionary era," Fields writes, "people who favored slavery and people who opposed it collaborated in identifying the racial incapacity of African Americans as the explanation for enslavement."

For two centuries "race" has become more and more deeply ingrained in the American imagination, and in some cases has taken on a life apart from its original intentions. Today the word "race" has profound currency. Be it in politics or mass culture, the buzzword "race" elicits for the American ear a panoply of meanings or "realities." Polls are tallied in terms of "race"; the US Census Bureau divides people by "race"; on television talk shows and news broadcasts, on the front pages of newspapers and on the covers of magazines, the word "race" is used with great surety and finality, as if it were a scientifically quantifiable trait. Americans know what they think they know, and in that knowing lies tremendous power.

As Lorraine Hansberry has a character in her play *Les Blancs* say:

> Race—racism—is a device. No more. No less. It explains nothing at all . . . I am simply saying that a device is a device, but that it also has consequences: once invented it takes on a life, a reality of its own. So in one century, men invoke the device of religion to cloak their conquests. In another, race. Now, in both cases you and I may recognize the fraudulence of the device, but the fact remains that a man who has a sword run through him because he refused to become a Moslem or a Christian—or who is shot in Zatembe or Mississippi because he is black—is suffering the utter *reality* of the device. And it is pointless to pretend that it doesn't *exist*—merely because it is a *lie!*

In that same way, to be an American is to be shaped by the "device" of "race." Whether one believes it to be reality or mythology, whether one is white or Black or something entirely other, to live in the United States is to be shaped on some level by "race."

Yet race is only one element of being Black, only one side of the multisided rubric of understanding who "we" are.

MY FIRST CONCEPT of what it meant to be Black came from Chinquapin, North Carolina, 1963 through 1981, in the years, as James Agee so aptly put it, "that I lived there so successfully disguised to myself as a child." It would take me years to truly appreciate the plain yet endless beauty of the lowlands of North Carolina. The fields of corn and soybeans and tobacco; the forests bisected by narrow dirt roads, full of oak and sassafras and long-leaf pines, brimming with squirrels and possums and wild cats. Here were the men in coveralls on tractors and the women with snuff tucked deep in their bottom lip. Here was a land little changed since the 1950s by the time I went to high school. Here I inherited a vision of being Black.

What did it mean to be Black? In the beginning of my life, in my mind, it meant a pointillism of culture. Collard greens. "Amazing Grace, how sweet the sound." Grits and tote. Quilts and pigs' feet. Thundering preachers and prayer cloths. It was head rags and chitlins, "Chain of Fools" and "Swing Low, Sweet Chariot." Ultra Sheen, Afro Sheen, neck bones, cornrows . . . These signs and symbols were the air I breathed, the water I drank, the ground upon which I walked. Rituals, cuisine, fashion, music, language . . . Oh, the rhetoric and the vocabulary, the syncopation of old men at the barber shop, the women at the tobacco barn—this was music in itself—all formed my culture, unbeknownst to me. Culture, for the insider, is wound round about and worn daily; unless one leaves a culture, one never really sees it for what it is: the blueprint for living. Culture says: Live this way. Moreover, for me—and I'm certain this is true for anyone in any culture—these particles of being were a portrait of endurance, of strength, of love, of community, and of respect. On many levels one could witness this affirmation, bold and subtle; hear it in the reprimands and the pet names; see it in the old women's stitches and the old men's whittling; taste it in my mother's pound cake and in my uncle's scuppernong wine; smell it in the sweat of men working in the fields—or this was my assumption, spurred on by the talk and the subtext, the slip and the grip of this world in which I grew.

We were never given to define or dissect our Blackness. And for what reason would we? Being Black—or Negro or colored—was something taken for granted. When my great-great-grandaunt Erie or my cousin Norman told stories of "the old days," of the difficulty of breaking new ground with nothing but an axe, a shovel, and a mule and plow, of community barn raisings, of dealing with the KKK through stealth and steely will, of old-time revivals that went on for days at a stretch, of midwives and pickled cabbage—I took for granted that this tapestry, this ever-reaching-back fabric was what being Black was all about. To think in terms of being authentic or unique, for me, as a child, was utterly inconceivable, for the perception was the reality. Why would it be otherwise? Indeed, in my youth, if I had met a Black Nigerian or Rwandan or South African, the idea that he or she did not think exactly as I did would have been shocking—and I am certain it would have been so to most Blacks in my hometown as well.

Moreover, this perception of what it meant to be Black was mysteriously corroborated by watching *Sanford and Son* on TV or reading *Ebony* magazine when it arrived in the mailbox each month; by those textbooks that, every February, served up those timeworn heroes of every God-loving Black American—George Washington Carver, Booker T. Washington, and Harriet Tubman. (Did any of us children suspect there could have been Black male insurrectionists? How dangerous a notion—to teach Black boys about Gabriel Prosser or Nat Turner.) When I was a child, even *Superfly* and *Dolemite* came to the local movie theater. This was Blackness we knew, we accepted, we understood, we celebrated: Black was seamless, undifferentiated, defined—as far as we were concerned. Whether you were in New York City or Chinquapin, North Carolina, Chicago, Illinois, or Savannah, Georgia, there was only one Black culture, from Mary McCleod Bethune to Martin Luther King Jr. We had the same icons, the same language, the same food, the same politics, the same beliefs. And we were certain that all Black folk felt the same as we did; if, indeed, they were Black. If they thought otherwise, then, of course, their Blackness was highly suspect.

This was the fallacy; this was the lie. A persuasive Black-think, a monolithic sameness, a we-ism. This was the ideology which, in my late twenties, I had dashed against the brick wall of reality.

———————

WHAT DOES IT mean to be Black?

Indeed, who is Black? In the United States, for well over a century, "a black is any person with any known African black ancestry," writes F. James Davis in *Who Is Black?* "In the South it became known as the 'one-drop rule,' meaning that a single drop of 'black' blood makes a person black." Or "one Black ancestor" or a "traceable amount." The fact that the definition of what it means to be Black is still on the law books is enough to give any thinking person pause: Where does genetic heritage end and cultural heritage begin? What do we mean when we invoke "Black culture"? Does Black culture belong to anyone who is genetically defined as Black?

Many people who hold with the idea of a Black race also hold with the notion of an essential Blackness, an inherited culture embedded within the genes of every Black man and Black woman. An essentialist view of Blackness goes hand in hand with the idea of race as a fact—where defining culture becomes inextricably bound up with the idea of a "race." The cultural critic Michael Eric Dyson has defined racial essentialism as "black intellectuals oppos[ing] the strangling of black culture by caricature, offering instead cultural standards to help define racial authenticity." Others have traced the idea back to the mid-nineteenth century, noting it in the writings of Langston Hughes and W. E. B. Du Bois as being an appeal to sentimental tribalism, something to do with mystery, primitivism, and soul. Indeed, this view of essential Blackness is in no way limited to intellectuals, for too many times have I listened to people testifying to the inherent "soul" of Black people, exemplified by, but in no way limited to, soul music and soul food. One part propaganda, one part mysticism, this view of Blackness, especially when used in a positive light, is seemingly irresistible; this view appeals to an unspeakably attractive connectedness, solidarity, a larger-than-human consciousness, Jungian in its telepathic zeal. Truth to tell: I thought this way for much of my life, saw my Blackness as irreducible, inalienable, inherited.

To be sure, many people might view my dismissal of essentialism as blasphemy; my rejection of race as treachery. In fact, the first person to get me to see otherwise was a Black woman at college who, as a founding member of SNCC and a sociologist, could not have been more committed to African American culture. It was Sonya Stone who first got me to see how powerful a thing culture is; how rhythms are philosophy, ritual is history, language is art. How, in fact, the idea of a biological explanation of "race" diminished the human achievement of culture. In fact, she was the first person who told me I should become a writer.

"Cultural evolution," according to scientist and writer Stephen Jay Gould, "can proceed so quickly because it operates . . . by the inheritance of acquired characters. Whatever one generation learns, it can pass to the next by writing, instruction, inculcation, ritual, tradition, and a host of methods that humans have developed to assure continuity of the culture."

Culture. But what exactly is African American culture? Much ink is spilled yearly trying to pin down that ever-moving, ever-self-defining phenomenon. From condemnation in attempts to pathologize Black culture by using it to explain away crime and single-parent births, to celebration in attempts to propagandize Black solidarity or uplift Black morale by praising Nobel Prize–winning fiction, scientific invention and jazz, Black culture has a way of being many things to many people. But the one perplexing question for which I found no satisfying answer was: With so many people spread over so vast a continent, can there be one Black culture anymore? Has television and technology and expansion robbed Black culture of any inherent meaning?

INITIALLY, FOR ME, this problem of perception, of apprehension, of acceptance, had to do with real estate.

I first came to New York City in 1985, fresh out of college, the prototypical country boy a-loose in the big city. I was intimidated, ambitious, and eager, and I found a job with a major publishing house fairly quickly. After living for six months with relatives in Newark, New Jersey, I moved to the Upper West Side. Then Queens. Then Brooklyn. Then the West Village. Then Hell's Kitchen. For ill-paid editorial assistants, finding a place to live in New York occupies an inordinate amount of time and energy. Much of the decision about where I lived had more to do with my wallet than a choice of neighborhoods; with sublets that fell through; with rent going sky-high.

Moreover, there was a social consideration. Coming to a large city, knowing no one, means that your social circle will be largely dictated by who you work with. For me, this meant that most of my associates were white. Over time, my circles grew and my friends were Black and white and Indian and Japanese and Native American—a polyglot potpourri of multiculturalism. To better partake of this cross-world living, I tried to live as close to the nexus of work and social fun as I could: I very much enjoyed living in New York.

Except when I complained to my family about rents and having to move so often. Their response was: "Why don't you just move to Harlem? Surely you can find a nice cheap place up there." Many of my relatives had lived off and on in Harlem from the early '20s until the mid-'70s. As a child I remember visiting a grandaunt who had an enormous apartment on Edgecomb Avenue, or Sugar Hill.

Why, indeed, did I not just move to Harlem? Ah, the secret, silent monsters in us all! . . .

It took me years to admit to myself that the question made me uncomfortable, that it picked at a psychological welt I would prefer to avoid. I had visited Harlem on a great number of occasions; regularly visited the Studio Museum; attended the Abyssinian Baptist Church, the Apollo, the Schomburg Library; visited friends on 135th and 149th and all over; tutored kids in East Harlem. The history of the 1920s Renaissance or Cultural Revolution resonated in my bones; all my cultural heroes, from Duke Ellington to Zora Neale Hurston to Countee Cullen to Alaine Locke, dwelt within the historic aura of the Cotton Club and the Negro Ensemble and the Theresa Hotel. Yet deep within me welled a strong resistance to the idea of living in Harlem in the 1980s. This resistance resulted in a hidden feeling of guilt and shame.

I had logical reasons, I told myself. The few apartments I found—when inclined to look there—were, when nice, unaffordable; and when affordable, far from nice. Unspoken were fears of crime and concern about distance from work and my social life. Perhaps even a fear of stigma. In my early twenties I had begun to deal with a social reality that I had successfully kept at bay till then.

My academic world had always—except for kindergarten—been integrated, and from high school on, more often that not, I was the only African American in my classes. At college, a predominantly white school where the Black population was around four percent, this continued, and I countered it by attending Black church services on campus and off, singing in the gospel choir, taking Afro-American history classes. Though, perforce, I had white friends, my closest friends happened to be Black. Even then—though I did not realize it, had no way to realize it—I was struggling to be a "real" Black person. I feared that so much contact with white folk, studying so much European culture, living with, eating with, and sometimes sleeping with, white people, would in some way put my Negro "soul" in danger.

Ironically, in my moving here and yon in the New York metropolitan area, I had lived in an all-Black neighborhood in Newark; a veritable slum in Queens; in Spike Lee's neighborhood in Brooklyn; and, in 1991, just before this crisis of identity came to a head, in Hell's Kitchen, which, if I had taken the trouble to research, I would have discovered to once have been the heart of Black New York at the turn of the century. To be sure, my discomfort had little to do with the reality of my living situation and more to do with the *realty* of my mental state, with the real estate of my mind; the unspoken fear that the farther I lived from Black folk, the farther I lived from my own Blackness; that, ultimately, I was assimilating. Growing up I had been taught to always be proud of being Black, and to be ambitious and committed to my work. Somehow in this New York, the two were clashing. Though in no overt way, one seemed to be pushing out the other.

Looking back, I now see how ill-founded was my fear, personally; how much youth and insecurity and life choices, present and future, were in play. Yet, how real the possibility had been; how precarious a thing is identity. However, at the time, I had to keep asking myself: What is Black identity?

————

WHAT DOES IT mean to be Black?

In the 1970 movie *Cotton Comes to Harlem*, based on the novel by Chester Himes, a leitmotif is the recurring question: "Is this black enough for you?"

Is this Black enough for you?

Much of the tumult in the social revolution of the 1960s and early '70s, amid the civil rights movement and the demand for economic equality and opportunity, was the internal definition, or redefinition, of what it meant to be Black. In this period the phrase "Black is Beautiful" became popular. (Though Du Bois had said it decades before.) Afrocentric garb and hair became popular. Radical became chic. The Black middle class—which had initially led and underwritten the civil rights movement through all the preceding decades—had become supplanted in the public eye by Afro-crowned and dashiki-wearing young men and women, from all kinds of economic backgrounds; the idea of middle class or bourgeois values, long a part of the very fabric of the African American community from Los Angeles to Atlanta, became suspect. (And in those days, due to segregation, no one had to question what an African American community was or meant.) A profound shift in identity, politics, and social thought took place very quickly, dovetailing with the overall youth-engendered rebellion against the status quo: to be Black was to be poor, disenfranchised, to live in an urban slum (or what became "the ghetto"), to distrust "the man," and to be very, very angry. Of course this is a rank oversimplification and disturbing distortion of what really happened to African American culture during the '60s and '70s; yet it speaks to the larger American perspective, to what it means to be Black in America at the turn of this new century; it speaks to a perception affecting both Black and white alike.

Though the Black middle class, economically speaking, grew in historic numbers in the intervening years, and though doctors and lawyers were graduated, good marriages were made and kept, and businesses flourished—the image of Black identity in the popular media never overcame the trauma of riots and assassinations and marches of the past decades. Nor did the Black middle class successfully come to terms with that time; as more African Americans rose above the poverty level, they abandoned the old neighborhoods—or so the new mythology reads today.

Moreover, the idea of being Black and middle class (or upper class as some would have it) has always carried an element of stigma within Black communities. Historically, to be middle class was to have some ostensibly "white" blood, i.e., light skin. This circumstance was another of slavery's many legacies, the caste system within a caste system that awarded privilege to the lighter and more hardship upon the darker, just as the house-slaves of the antebellum myth and reality were the mulatto offspring of miscegenation and the "field niggers" were the darker, more African-looking men and women. After Emancipation and Reconstruction a society of light-skinned privilege emerged; those with lighter skin had education, professional jobs, their own cotillions and balls and clubs. Neither white nor Black, they were a Creole society suspended in time.

Or at least this vision of the Black middle class, the Black middle class before the civil rights movement, became a galvanized force in the American imagination. In reality, though some of this version of social history is accurate, it ignores the larger question of what most African Americans held as goals and ideals, how they defined themselves, and what their values were. A great many dark-skinned African Americans became doctors and bank presidents and college professors; and not every light-skinned Black person was born with a silver spoon in his or her mouth. Moreover, what most Americans deemed "middle-class" or "bourgeois" values were as much a part of poor families as of the well-to-do: For my own grandfather and great-grandfather and great-great-grandfather and no doubt his father before him, family came first, then God, then the community, and then economic prosperity. They were churchgoing—how otherwise could the African American church have become such a powerful force?—and largely "conservative." Which is not to say their politics was anything like that of the neoconservatives of our day. They were also unable to vote, sent to substandard schools, relegated to the back of the bus, lynched, and partitioned—their conservativism was a form of survival, both physical and spiritual, a combination of common sense and shrewd logic. Religion had more to do with how they lived their lives and how they thought than we now could ever really imagine.

But after the necessary and largely successful battles for civil rights, though the reality was not replaced, the image of what Black identity consisted of was forever altered. (Ironically, Martin Luther King Jr., the scion of a well-to-do family, was of dark hue; Malcolm X, son of a minister and sharecropper, was light-skinned with reddish hair.) "Is this Black enough for you?" and "Black Power" were slogans of positive affirmation; dark men and women were not only in vogue, but their beauty, long a mark of derision, became a sign of affirmation. To be Black became defined by "the struggle" and if you weren't down with the struggle, who were you? And though Gil Scott-Heron declared, "The revolution will not be televised," in the end it was. Televised, broadcast, filmed, photographed, written about. The most curious manifestation of this "revolution"—far from the type of Marxist revolution dreamt of by the Black Panther Power Party—was the blaxploitation films of the '70s. These films—*Shaft*, *Superfly*, *The Max*—exemplify, if not typify or even account for—a strange collusion between African American culture and the mass culture. Being Black no longer arose from the reality of day-to-day existence, and upon dreams of equality, and health, and education, and a reasonably good life. Being Black—no longer colored, no longer Negro—Black, came to consist of a deluge of images, largely negative, of violence and drug dealers, prostitution and poverty. And though no one would argue that these elements existed, their preponderance and intensity far outweighed the actual numbers of decent working folk, quietly working, voting, raising their children. These images of glorified gangsterism clutched not only the African American imagination, but also the American imagination as a whole, especially in places where despair could take hold. Though, in truth, a great many factors entered into the equation—economic policies, the slow collapse of the industrial base and modernization, eroding urban infrastructures, chronic unemployment, rising tuition, etc.—as far as identity and perception of what being Black is composed, media affected fashion, language, music, food, personal relationships, religion, and education in extraordinary ways.

From the natural to Jheri curls to shaved heads; from break dancing to rock; from platform shoes to Reeboks; from large church congregations to empty Sunday schools; from Jack and Jill to the Bloods and the Crips; from Shirley Chisholm and Jesse Jackson to Al Sharpton and Colin Powell; from Motown to Def Jam Records; from *Good Times* to the *Jeffersons* to *In Living Color*; from *Soul Train* to *Yo! MTV Raps*—these outward manifestations have become signs of the ways African Americans perceive their culture, themselves. To ask in 1886 or 1966 or 1996: *Is this Black enough for you?* would yield a profoundly disparate set of inferences and commonalities, implications and significations, becoming more and more uncertain, inexact, curiously diffuse—even as mass culture assumes it understands the question and knows the answer, as if the answer were not only self-evident, but also, in many ways, inevitable.

Is this Black enough for you?

———————

WHAT DOES IT mean to be Black?

Upon first reading James Baldwin's *Notes of a Native Son,* I was deeply disquieted. Intellectually I understood exactly what he was talking about, and the language, the language of the Bible and its prophets, rang in my head; yet on a gut level I felt, ironically, alienated from his vision. Baldwin grew up poor and struggling in Harlem, harassed by the police as a young man, convinced that the American Republic was hell-bent on his destruction. Though he was a prophet of love, race pervaded his writing. I, on the other hand, had grown up on land that had been in my family for five generations; my grandfather was a successful businessman and my cousins were college professors and colonels. I had known racism of the most visceral sort, but nothing as hellish as what Baldwin had encountered, nor were my scars anywhere near as painful.

I spoke at length with my brother-in-law who had grown up in Harlem, and with friends, and with teachers. Despite having grown up in what Baldwin himself referred to in "Nobody Knows My Name" as the land of "this dreadful paradox" where "the black men were stronger than the white," I felt in some way not Black enough, somehow—ridiculously—inauthentic; that, because of his struggles, James Baldwin was somehow closer than I to being a real Negro.

By and by, I came to understand, intellectually, how wrongheaded and stupid I had been. Nonetheless, I became more and more preoccupied by the idea of Blackness; by what people said, what people meant, and how things were. And perhaps more importantly, where I fit in amid the fantasy and the reality. When I came to New York, my confusion over how to define my own Black identity simply mounted; especially as talk in the media and even in conversation threw the words "race" and "Black" about with such reckless abandon, as if they were saying "apple" or "salmon."

Perhaps the most arresting definition I would find of what it means to be Black came from Ralph Ellison's essay "The World and the Jug":

> It has to do with a special perspective on the national ideals and the national conduct, and with a tragicomic attitude towards the universe. It has to do with special emotions evoked by the details of cities and countrysides, with forms of labor and with forms of pleasure; with sex and with love, with food and with drink, with machines and with animals; with climates and with dwellings, with places of worship and

places of entertainment; with garments and dreams and idioms of speech; with manners and customs, with religion and
art, with life styles and hoping and with that special sense of
predicament and fate which gives direction and resonance to
the Freedom Movement.

He went on:

More important, perhaps, being a Negro American involves
a *willed* (who wills to be a Negro, I do!) affirmation of self
against all outside pressures—an identification with the group
as extended through the individual self which rejects all possibilities of escape that do not involve basic resuscitation of the
original American ideals of social and political justice.

"*Willed* affirmation." "Perspective." "Identification." These words
were powerful, yet I still had to ask myself: Affirmation of what?
Perspective on what? Identify with what? Though Ellison made
supreme sense, I still felt that the country, the world, had under-
gone such dramatic changes since the segregated 1950s that it was
important to rediscover those countrysides and cities, to revisit the
places of worship and entertainment, to see afresh the manners
and customs. Before I could affirm or identify, I had to go beyond
my narrow world and see Black America. Then I ran across a passage in an essay by Zora Neale Hurston:

The realistic story around a Negro insurance official, dentist,
general practitioner, undertaker and the like would be most
revealing. Thinly disguised fiction around the well known
Negro names is not the answer, either. The "exceptional" as
well as the Ol' Man Rivers has been exploited all out of context already. Everybody is already resigned to the "exceptional"

Negro, and willing to be entertained by the "quaint." To grasp
the penetration of western civilization in a minority, it is necessary to know how the average behaves and lives . . . For various reasons, the average, struggling, non-morbid Negro is the
best-kept secret in America.

Though she wrote this in 1950, I felt more than forty years later it
still spoke the truth. In fact, considering what I was seeing on television, reading in the newspapers, hearing on the radio, the need
was even greater in 1991. And even though she was speaking to the
majority culture, I felt a personal need to discover this "best-kept
secret" for myself. To calm my soul, I needed to set out, to see for
myself, as I wondered about the nature of my own Blackness, to take
my question on the road. For, according to the US Census Bureau,
African Americans live all over this country. I wanted to know what
they thought, what they felt about these questions; I wanted to see,
in Minnesota and Maine, how Black folk lived; I wanted to understand, in Alaska and Arizona, how Black folk defined themselves,
what they felt their culture was. If, indeed, they felt they had a culture. If "we" were "we." Perhaps even to witness ways of being African American that I had never dreamed of.

Mindful of Du Bois's admonition "to car window sociologists, to
the man who seeks to understand and know . . . by devoting the few
leisure hours of a holiday trip to unraveling the snarl of centuries,"
I decided, just the same as he had done, to travel the country, with
the intention of devoting nine months to a year to the endeavor.
My plan was to trust in fate and serendipity, to plan little and find
what I found, to avoid the obvious places, the places written about
ad nauseam; to look at the map and follow my curiosity—little did
I know it would take years.

Preparing for my journey, I noted with intimidation that in the
year of my birth, the estimable novelist John A. Williams had set

out on a similar task. "Late in September, 1963," *This Is My Country Too* begins, "I set out in search of an old dream, one that faded, came back into focus, and faded again. The search for my America." Reading his account, from Syracuse to Seattle, from Arizona to Louisiana, I—so much the product of integration, affirmative action, the "New South," a Child of the Dream—could not help but be awed and terrified by how he, a man of African descent, was viewed and in turn viewed the United States of America; how he was treated miserably, refused service in restaurants and hotels, witnessed some of the most outrageous discrimination in housing, jobs, education; how perniciously strong were the soon-banished Jim Crow codes. Reading his account, for me, was like reading about another planet, a planet remarkably transformed in the space of my lifetime. But how much had it really changed?

For me there was only one way to find out. With all these questions in my mind, and in my heart, in the summer of 1991, I girded up my loins and my wits and my courage, and packed my bags and books into a quintessentially American jeep—that I named Bucephalus, for though I am not an egomaniac, I am not unambitious—and, heading north on I-95, set out to discover for myself what it meant to be Black.

10

Where Am I
Black?

OR, SOMETHING ABOUT MY KINFOLKS

Cyberspace, North Carolina

During the academic year of 1994–95, I was honored to be a guest lecturer at my alma mater, the University of North Carolina at Chapel Hill, and its perpetual academic rival, Duke University. It was a bracing experience. Or, to paraphrase Marianne Moore, I laughed too much and was afraid of snakes.

Many revelations presented themselves to me that year, and some were daunting, and some were tender, and some I would like to forget, but probably never will, not without work. I became reacquainted with my family in a way that geography heretofore had made not possible; and I became reacquainted with a young Black man, really a boy, ten years in the past, who made the first important move of his life, when he left a small village on the coastal plains of North Carolina, and matriculated at a major university, in an area later described by the national news media to be among the most civilized in the country. And not the least of all my discoveries and rediscoveries was my fervent return to the computer.

———————

THE REASONS I never got any good at basketball are fourfold: (a) I didn't really have a place or anyone to play with; (b) I didn't play and practice when I had the opportunity; (c) I was so pitiful when I did attempt to play that I was roundly discouraged and ridiculed; and (d) I really didn't care. Actually I did, but it helped me deal with the fact that I was so bad, by feigning indifference until that feigning became real. In fact, not playing basketball gave me as much identity as it gave those Black teens who did. If they were to become superb dribblers, slam dunkers, passers, shooters—I would become superb as something other. Or that's what my twelve- and thirteen-year-old mind told itself. My being drummed out of the corps of future NBA wannabes was so draconian. And it is for a great number of Black males. Mine was in junior high school during school tournaments. We had a varsity high school player as a coach for a week. I was at the bottom of the lineup. I played for two shakes of a dog's tail near the end of the game when the outcome was inevitable, and even then I got laughed at and eyes rolled at by fellow players. For a while, I carted around something like contempt in my heart for all athletics, seeing supreme hypocrisy operating under the guise of sportsmanship. And being a boy, I could not get my mind round the conflation of commerce and recreation and "education" and, let's just face it, fun. I had not yet developed the ability to see and think on more than a few levels and could not understand how a particle could contain the truth and a lie and remain whole. I was a sensitive lad.

Now many will say that this trial by fire, as harmless as it is, ultimately builds character, not unlike what some folk say the military will do for adolescents. I don't know about that. But I will weigh in with the observation that to be a young Black male in the public school system is to experience a weird, outsized pressure to excel at this now-national pastime. Young boys such as myself are weeded out of the process early. Most, unlike myself, try and try again, and deepen their affection and admiration for the sport and for the Michael Jordans and Dennis Rodmans and Horace Grants of the world. And, to quote B. B. King: "I'm not saying it's wrong; and I'm not saying it's right." Suffice it to say that today I watch my fellow schoolmates from UNC burn up the court and amaze the world (and draw down huge checks) with the rest of them. I cheer the Bulls and lament the Knicks. I see the game whole and for what it is. No longer is my ego bound up in my sorry inability to put a big orange ball through a metal hoop.

It was on this very subject that I would stumble upon what was to be my penultimate inquiry into the nature of Blackness: haphazardly and unexpectedly, a discussion of basketball on the Internet.

SOMEONE SAID IT takes a village to raise a child. I do not doubt that piece of West African wisdom. But in my case, it was largely done by four people, with a village to back them up.

I was born illegitimate and male and Black to a poor woman in Brooklyn, New York, in 1963. Luckily for both of us, my father acknowledged me as his issue, and he happened to possess a kind-hearted father, who offered to raise me with his family in Wallace, North Carolina. My grandfather had been born in 1914 and had by the early 1960s built himself a thriving dry-cleaning establishment; his wife was a seamstress. From the very beginning, they doted on me. I came to live with them at the age of six weeks.

My grandfather's sister, Mary Fleming, still lived in my grandfather's hometown, just fourteen miles east of Wallace, a village called Chinquapin, unincorporated and rural, largely tobacco fields and cornfields and hog farms.

My great-aunt Mary took a shine to me straightaway and would often take me from Wallace to Chinquapin on the weekends, to spend time with her and her husband, who ran the family farm. I'm not certain how many weekends she did take me back to Wallace, but one weekend she simply didn't bring me back, and there I remained. My grandfather, who drove one of his own delivery trucks, came by Chinquapin every Monday, so he saw me each week.

Three years later, on a mild September day, my great-uncle Redden died of a blood clot. I remember this vividly, for he died right next to me, on the porch of a packhouse, where my great-aunt and other women were grading cured tobacco. My grandfather suggested, now that my great-aunt Mary was a widow and alone, that I remain with her, which I did for the next fifteen years. I did, and I continue to call her Mama.

It took me years to appreciate the accident of my winding up in a place like Chinquapin during my developing years. For in many ways, Duplin County, fairly remote, off the beaten path from any metropolitan area of consequence, forty miles from the ocean, rich with history, was in a time warp. During the years that I was learning the English language, and figuring out the basic realities of the world, the United States was going through some of its most tumultuous events: Vietnam, Woodstock, Watergate, rashes of assassinations, civil rights marches and boycotts and sit-ins, the Black Panther Party, free love, flower children, Kent State, Jackson State, men walking on the moon, the Great Society. In Chinquapin, all those events could have been happening in Thailand. Not to say that folk were ignorant of the goings-on in the wide world; rather, folk were simply focused on more pressing matters: getting crops in, getting their children fed, grown, and married, caring for the elderly, going to church and trying to be good, with occasional missteps. Chinquapin from 1963 to 1981 could have been Chinquapin in 1920, with the exception of a few welcome new gadgets. Mama had an old Admiral television set, which was situated in a handsome walnut cabinet, the screen about the size of a letter; a set which broke down before my uncle died. She didn't get a new one until I was in kindergarten—something on which I always blame my addiction to print, although she, who worked in kindergarten, taught me to read when I was four.

Moreover, I was surrounded by folk who had been on the planet for the entire century, and their view of the world began before any of these newfangled machines were even invented. There was my cousin Norman, who lived right across the dirt road from us, who was in his seventies when I was born. He knew an awful lot about the land and raised hogs and chickens and had an admirable orchard adjacent to his and his wife Miss Alice's house. There was my great-great-aunt Erie, who was the youngest daughter of my great-great-grandfather. (Only years later did I discover how rare it is for a person to know a great-great aunt. Indeed, both my maternal great-grandmothers were living when I went to high school.) Aunt Erie had over ten children, most of whom were away, but all were colorful people, and they would descend on Chinquapin during the holidays and the town would feel like a festival. There was my aunt Lillian, who lived in a big two-story house down the road, and her multitude of daughters, and her sons, Herman and Irving, who had worked to send many of the girls to college, and Herman's nine children with whom I went to school . . . and that's just one limb on one branch of one side of the tree of the extended family in which I grew up, surrounded by stories and antics and foibles and gossip and artifacts and something like love, though the many feelings engendered by life in a small town are much more complex and tangled than most people who've never lived in one, belonged to one, could ever imagine.

There was church. Two churches in fact. First Baptist and St.

Louis. Both Baptist, and to this day I cannot say why Chinquapin never had an AME church. My mama was zealous about my going to church, and I remember too many sermons to be in my right mind, and the pastors Hestor and Lassiter the younger, who succeeded Lassiter the senior. There were revivals in September and Vacation Bible School in June, when the blueberry season came, and Sunday school each and every Sunday—even on fifth Sunday when nobody had church services. Church remained an indelible mark on my growing up and, no matter how far or how fast I run, the lessons of Baptist Protestantism and Southern Calvinism will be etched on my brain—probably my soul—the way circuits are hardwired to a motherboard.

There was school, which I truly enjoyed. And all the Black women who taught me (I actually had more Black teachers than white teachers before I went to high school), women who had known me and my mother their entire lives; women who watched me and all the other Black boys and Black girls like sentient hawks, and who would report any crime or misdemeanor with the rapidity of lightning. Getting away with wrongdoing or occasional mischief was doomed to fail. I remember feeling completely watched, and always felt that was one of the many reasons I couldn't wait to say goodbye to the hamlet. Not that I wanted to do anything particularly evil; I just didn't want my business known to every Myrtle, Blanche, and Willie Earl.

I will not be romantic about Chinquapin. From as early as I can remember, I always wanted to get the hell out of there. After all, it was what it was: a very small backwoods North Carolina village. The schools were not desegregated until 1969; a great many roads were unpaved; medical care was twenty-five miles away and then not particularly competent; water was pumped from private wells, and many folk had no running water. As soon as I could read newspapers and magazines, I had a clue that the world was wide and far different from what I had seen day in and day out in Duplin County,

and something like resentment grew in my breast. I resented people who were elsewhere. Though I would not know the phrase for
decades to come, like Milan Kundera's poor artists in the novel *Life
Is Elsewhere*, I figured real life was going on somewhere else.

Of course that was a boy thinking, feeling. And though I think
that this feeling, inchoate and arch, was the origin of my wander-
lust, I now see those elements of Chinquapin that were so fundamental in making me a fairly good citizen, a fairly decent person, a
fairly respectful human being, and, probably, a writer. Though, in
truth, all those years, there was nothing I wanted to do more than
become a scientist.

IN 1994, PARAMOUNT COMMUNICATIONS launched a new television
network called UPN, and one of their flagship shows was *Star Trek:
Voyager*. Apparently the success of their cash cow franchise was so
irresistible—after *Star Trek: The Next Generation* and *Star Trek: Deep
Space Nine*, and the string of movies—that they couldn't resist the
moneymaking urge.

The remarkable thing about this new series was not the fact that
this super-duper new starship had been flung to the other side of
the galaxy, and that it would take its crew more than their lifetimes
to get home—no. What I found arresting was that the security
officer was a Vulcan, one of those pointed-eared, green-blooded,
utterly logical aliens from the planet Vulcan, whom Mr. Spock had
made a part of American pop culture, and he was Black. Mr. Tuvok,
played by the actor Tim Russ, was the logical, honor-rigid, emo-
tionless embodiment of all of Gene Roddenberry's peculiar psycho-
sexual hang-ups about the id and cognition, which, as the young
folk say, blew my mind. This series was clearly made to address all
the cultural, ethical, ethnic bugaboos that had been haunting the
franchise since the 1960s. The captain was a woman, the first offi-

cer was a Native American, the science officer was a Korean, and the chief engineer was a woman—half-Klingon.

Too much can be made of this minor historical development, I am well aware. But, for a while, what Paramount had unwittingly done—in a sheer and utter and bald attempt to pander to people like me—made me ponder many a thing.

A Black Vulcan. For me, in high school, besotted and beset by science fiction, and watching the original *Star Trek* religiously, and fantasizing about being on a starship, it was not imaginable—or at least I did not imagine—the convolution or the notion of "race" in conjunction with alien life, let alone on the planet Vulcan. Moreover, this purely monetary gesture on Paramount's part was rife with a huge cultural irony which tickled me no end.

Vulcans, for those who don't know, are a species who, centuries ago, decided that emotion was a bad idea, so they essentially eradicated it from their society. In emotion's place, they elevated the philosophy of logic, to which they subjected everything. This premise, the notion of a "humanoid" without the petty, messy, irrational baggage of feelings, was what made Mr. Spock so compelling for so many folk. He became a built-in device for examining emotions in a new way—in a way that only science fiction, really, can successfully achieve. Moreover, Vulcans are bound by rigid codes of honor; filial piety is paramount, as are duty, dedication to science, and they only mate once or twice in their life, and that act is seen as something of an embarrassment and is shrouded in solemn ritual.

The irony comes when you consider the image of the Black man in popular media, indeed, long before popular media existed: emotion-less? logical? honor-bound? sexless? One could take this cultural juxtaposition as a joke. But, in 1994, when this new media phenomenon was presented, blatant and subtle in its various permutations, and admittedly minor in the scheme of things, it nonetheless made me wonder. Was our society finally, so close to the turn of the century, coming round the bend? Were we ready to begin to reimagine our deepest prejudices, and come closer to that Martin Luther King and Rodney King vision? Were we starting to climb to the mountaintop and get along?

Always keep Ithaca fixed in your mind.
To arrive there is your ultimate goal.
But do not hurry the voyage at all.
It is better to let it last for long years;
and even to anchor at the isle when you are old,
rich with all that you have gained on the way,
not expecting that Ithaca will offer you riches.
Ithaca has given you the beautiful voyage.
Without her you would never have taken the road.
But she has nothing more to give you.
And if you find her poor, Ithaca has not defrauded you.
With the great wisdom you have gained, with so much
    experience,
you must surely have understood by then what Ithacas means.

—C. P. Cavafy, "Ithaca"

In 1994, Chinquapin had finally been thrust—more like yanked— into the heady whorl of the postmodern era. The ambulance was state of the art. The town had city water. There was cable television and a supermarket and two convenience stores, at which one could rent videos of movies that had, in some cases, been released in the last six months. Less than twenty miles down the road was Ellis Airport, with a landing sleeve and a rotating luggage belt. Interstate 40 had been completed only a few years before, which effectively created a line all the way from Barstow, California, to Wilmington, North Carolina, and, for the good folk of Duplin County, cut an hour off the drive to the Raleigh/Durham/Chapel Hill area, which in that year had been assessed by *Money* magazine as the most livable place in the country. My grandfather now used a microwave and cultivated a taste for *Die Hard* and *Lethal Weapon*, while my mother watched *Montel* and *Oprah* and was receiving medical care that, in 1963, would have been essentially the stuff of science fiction.

To be sure, these things seem minor to most folk in the country, but the way they changed the complexion and the quality and the quantity of life bewitched me. For in my mind, Chinquapin was still backwoods and out of step, yet, thanks to satellite dishes and faxes and email, was not so far away from the rest of America, and not so quaint and *Tobacco Road*.

Nevertheless, for me, Chinquapin was very much a land of specters, so many of the people I had known as a boy now dead and gone. I could not help but hear their ghosts about the rooms and fields and barns, now empty and relic-like. And, as sentimental and shamefully nostalgic as it may sound, groups of folk no longer sat about on porches and just talked; now they watched HBO and Cinemax. Most farms had been bought out by larger farms; church congregations seemed sparse. The old folks who remained seemed older, more frail, halting, almost ethereal, some from Alzheimer's, some from neglect and being forgotten. My running buddies were practically all gone, like me.

All of which is not to say that any of these changes are in and of themselves bad, and I am the last person on the planet Earth who will lament the passage of an era. Chinquapin did, and probably still does, abound with a multitude of hateful truths, dirty laundry, murders, substance abuse, strife of every manner, small-mindedness, racism, boredom, and downright inertia.

During my year back home, I could make the drive in less than two hours, go from Chapel Hill's squeaky clean, high-tech, PhD-laden opulence, to Chinquapin's postmodern present, where hog farms were running riot, and the chopped barbecue was good, and I could get chitlins and run from snakes and attend the Daughters of Zion's annual event at the church, and go home and watch BET, and check my email after calling a friend in Japan.

I was not so much bothered as disquieted by the changes that were occurring in Chinquapin, for in a way, those changes were at the foundation of the changes that were taking place in America. Chances were that the young folk in the elementary schools and the high schools of Duplin County were not having the same sorts of experiences that I had had in school. In fact, their experiences were probably very close to those of young folk growing up in Alaska or Maine or Wyoming or Arizona. Yes, there was a local flavor, a local color, but the information they were receiving, there in no-longer-quite-so-remote Chinquapin, was not very different from the information being received by kids, Black kids, in Seattle and Madison and Salt Lake City and New York.

More to the point, those things that I had taken so for granted about being Black, which had come from my mama and my grandfather and Uncle Roma and Aunt Lillian and Aunt Mildred in third grade, and Reverend Raynor and Miss Ruth, were now being dictated by *Martin* and *Moesha* and Snoop Doggy Dogg and Dr. Dre and Russell Simmons and *Vibe* magazine and, yes, Paramount. Chinquapin was becoming more like the rest of America. It was being absorbed by the vast cultural soup of consumeristic we-think.

The problem, as I saw it, had to do with the idea that Blackness was not so easily beamed through a satellite or through an optic fiber. After all this travel and bother, I had, in many ways, arrived back in Chinquapin with the same question: What is Blackness?

> I have argued that Internet experiences help us to develop models of psychological well-being that are in a meaningful sense postmodern: They admit multiplicity and flexibility. They acknowledge the constructed nature of reality, self, and other. The Internet is not alone in encouraging such models. There are many places within our culture that do so. What they

have in common is that they all suggest the value of approaching one's "story" in several ways and with fluid access to one's different aspects. We are encouraged to think of ourselves as fluid, emergent, decentralized, multiplicitous, flexible, and ever in process. The metaphors travel freely among computer science, psychology, children's games, cultural studies, artificial intelligence, literary criticism, advertising, molecular biology, self-help, and artificial life. They reach deep into the popular culture. The ability of the Internet to change popular understandings of identity is heightened by the presence of these metaphors.

—Sherry Turkle, *Life on the Screen: Identity in the Age of the Internet*

I had a revelation one day in the library in Phillips Hall, the math and science building, back when I was a junior: sentences are very much like equations.

Why did I want to become a scientist?

People in Chinquapin considered it, me, a little weird or just plain strange, my pursuit of science. But then again, in Chinquapin, in general, I was considered a fairly strange child.

I always believed the desire stemmed from my fundamentally intense sense of magic and the supernatural. From a very early age I had been fascinated by tales of ghosts and vampires and werewolves. Witches, sorcerers, wizards, warlocks, to my preteenage mind, were the ultimate. Perhaps it was the ability to affect matter, to change the world. (Psychologists might say that such a strong interest in what can only be called magic actually comes from a deep-seated dissatisfaction with regard to the way things are, a desire to actually change a world one feels powerless to change. That may also be so.)

Nonetheless, somewhere about third grade or so, the more I learned about the world, and was able to distinguish fact from fiction, I settled on the notion that the real, modern-day sorcerers were those men in white lab coats who sent people into outer space, and designed lasers, and made experiments into the nature of atoms and electrons. They could affect the physical world, change it. I don't know if I made the connection, though I probably did, that "witch" means a wise woman, or a person of knowledge, and "science" means knowledge. In both cases, knowledge meant power. For a poor colored boy living on a dirt road, with an overly fertile imagination and strange ideas, the concept proved to be irresistible.

Thus science fiction, thus *Star Trek*, thus notions of teleportation and warp speed and solar-powered cars and gravitational fields and Maxwell's equations; thus the ambition to become a Black Arthur C. Clarke or Isaac Asimov, a PhD in the physical sciences and a writer of science fiction—for I had always written, knew I always would write; thus Chapel Hill, on a track for a BS in physics; thus computers.

When I came to Chapel Hill in 1981, the personal computer craze was essentially in its infancy. Apple had yet to introduce Macintosh, and kids like me, who were weaned on BASIC in high school, were dying to learn the more sophisticated, more powerful languages. As a physics major, I was required to take a course in numerical analysis in my sophomore year. The professor was an experimental nuclear physicist from New Zealand who wore khaki shorts and boots and socks, and who essentially made us learn FORTRAN on our own, for that was, in his opinion, the best way to learn it. I remember staying up for thirty-six hours, most of that time in Phillips Hall, creating a program that would translate Kepler's laws of planetary motion into a graph. All this was done on a big mainframe computer. In the laboratory where I reported as a work-study student, the physicist who worked with the microbiologist there was going to teach me the latest version of PASCAL, which was one of the hot new computer languages.

Most of my comrades-in-arms in those heady and headache-provoking years were from backgrounds of a little more financial substance than my own, and a few had their own personal computers. They knew much more about hardware and wiring and circuitry than I, largely due to the fact that they had had a head start. I had only been able to work on a computer when I attended North Carolina's Governor's School in 1979. Duplin County high schools had no computers in those days. (And some still don't.) Nonetheless, I had no intention of letting any of that stop me. I was well on my way to becoming a computer geek in the grand, nerdy fashion. (Back then, the word "geek" was not as widely used as it has become today. Science folk were known as "nerds," but a "geek" was a badge of honor: it meant you knew machine language, the stuff of the future.)

Somewhere in my sophomore year, my designs went badly astray: I got distracted by literature and writing. I found a mentor in a kindly and loveable old curmudgeon named Max Steele, who was then the head of UNC's creative writing department. And he wasted no time in informing me that most of the science fiction I so deeply regarded was essentially trash. I bristled with resentment. He said that my background was rich and fecund and just made to be written about, and that I didn't know what I was wasting if I neglected it. He suggested I read some real literature. Fully intending to prove him wrong, I did just that. I discovered he was right; I also discovered something that I can only describe as vital about the process, and the danger and the possibilities of writing. I came to know the work of James Baldwin and Richard Wright and Alice Walker and Toni Morrison. I fell in love with Isaac Bashevis Singer and Yukio Mishima and V. S. Naipaul and Henry Dumas and a man named William Shakespeare.

The truth is, I would have made a dreadful scientist. I was a disaster in a laboratory, a bit too dreamy. My academic advisor told me this. I took more and more English classes; Gaussian matrices annoyed the hell out of me; and thermodynamics, as fascinating as they are, made less sense than Buddhist koans. By the summer of my senior year I was hell-bent in the pursuit of language; differential calculus and I said goodbye.

To this day, I feel that I've failed in some way by not pursuing my original goal. To be sure, we all have such naggings in the back of our heads, though I am happy with my choices. But the relevant thing here is that, after 1985, I not only turned my back on science but I also turned my back on the computer. I would come to tamper with computers and programs in the most innocuous way after the personal computer revolution, but only with games and word processing.

Ten years later, however, back at Chapel Hill, the computer and I became reacquainted.

———

MY GRANDDADDY IS one of my heroes.

He was born on his father's farm in Chinquapin, and his mother was the local schoolteacher. He worked at various jobs as a young man, including shipbuilding down in Wilmington, but in 1942, he and another man bought the equipment to open a dry cleaner. When he began, he would walk to people's houses in the community of Wallace, and ask if they needed anything cleaned, and he would tote their clothing to and fro. By and by, he bought his partner out, his business grew, and he was able to build a two-story red-brick house, with a lovely terrace in the back, and next door was his cleaners and my grandmother's seamstress shop.

He sent his youngest son to college and paid for it himself. His older son joined the air force. By the time I was in high school, my grandfather's routes went into three counties, and for a time, he employed a number of delivery trucks. My grandfather also sold clothing and bought houses that he would fix up and rent out, and for a time even dealt in scrap metal.

My uncle, George Edward, suffered from epilepsy and other ailments, and came to live with my grandfather and grandmother after he had been discharged from the military and needed to be looked after. I remember this period as a particularly troubling time, and I helped my grandfather on his route, down to Maple Hill and Beulaville. I would sometimes drive his truck through those narrow highways and secondary roads. What struck me and stuck with me long after was first of all how hard he worked, and secondly, how many people he knew and how much he was trusted and respected. Even at that age, it never occurred to me how difficult what he had accomplished must have been for a poor boy from Chinquapin, North Carolina. Indeed, all the products of his labor I essentially took for granted; to me, my head full of stuff and nonsense, my grandfather was a wonderful man, but nothing about what he did made him remarkable. He was simply a small businessman.

My grandmother died when I was in college, and for a time, my grandfather was understandably depressed. They had been married for almost fifty years. I still miss my grandmother. In the mid-1980s my family had a rash of trouble. My mother's house, the ancestral family home, burned to the ground; my mother's son-in-law, who had become very like a father to me, came down with a mysterious ailment that almost caused him to die; and my grandfather suffered a horrible burn accident.

I then lived in New York, and I flew down straightaway. He was in the Burn Center at Chapel Hill's Memorial Hospital. Initially, the doctors said his chances were grave; he was not expected to live, he had been burned on 75 percent of his body, much of it third-degree burns. We would make the trip from Chinquapin to Chapel Hill each day, and to watch him in such pain was enough to make us despair. At one point, he told his sister that he wished he could just die.

My grandfather remained in the hospital for three months. He was, at the time, seventy-four. Each week, his prognosis got better and better, and, much to the doctors' amazement, he recovered enough to go home. He was not 100 percent, as he would say, but he was alive. The doctors suggested that, though with therapy they could help him regain his full walking capacity and the use of his limbs, he would never regain the full quality of his life. He went through months of painful therapeutic exercise and changes of dressings.

Within two years, not only had my grandfather recovered almost completely, not only had he regained his ability to walk unassisted by a cane, not only had he gone back to his six-day-a-week, fourteen-hour-a-day schedule, and gone back to tending his massive garden of peas and collards and mustard greens and okra and sweet potatoes, but he also, at seventy-eight, married a woman ten years his junior.

> John educated himself so fast that within a few months after he bought his modem, he was on track with the other MOD [Masters of Deception] boys. For one thing, John figured out that some rules are the same, whether you're on the street or in cyberspace. If you want to get ahead, no one is going to just *let* you. You have to take what you want and get there yourself. He played a little game sometimes. He called it Let a Hacker Do the Work. Like the time he called a hacker named Signal Interrupt in Florida, and sweet-talked the kid out of all *kinds* of information, just by claiming to be a member of the Legion of Doom.
>
> Another way cyberspace was like the street was that it helps to have friends.
>
> —Michelle Slatalla and Joshua Quittner, *Masters of Deception*

John Lee was essentially a poor Black boy from Brooklyn, who, with a $299.00 Commodore 64 computer, became one of the most brilliant and most notorious hackers in the country. He had been a member in good standing of a group of boys who called themselves the Masters of Deception, a high-brainpowered bunch of bad boys who were breaking into private computer files, rewiring phone lines, stealing a look at the credit histories of the rich and famous, and other crimes that had the FBI nervous and frustrated, and AT&T hopping mad.

Interestingly enough, the Masters of Deception had been formed in response to another group, the Legion of Doom, whose members were well-heeled white boys from all over America. The Masters of Deception were the sons of blue-collar folk, largely living in New York.

In their book of reportage about these fancy goings-on, *Masters of Deception: The Gang that Ruled Cyberspace*, Michelle Slatalla and Joshua Quittner write about one fine day in 1990 when several hackers were yakking on-line:

> "Yo, dis is Dope Fiend from MOD," the newcomer says in distinctly non-white, non-middle class, *non-Texan* inflection.
>
> One of the Texans (who knows who?) takes umbrage.
>
> "Get that nigger off the line!"

Needless to say, John Lee did not take the comment without offense. In fact, the MOD and the LOD "waged war," which led to all sorts of high-tech shenanigans, involving security companies and serious offenses, and an FBI sting operation that showed the old folk how the new folk were changing the world, with bytes and bits and data gone mad. At one point, an entire grid of AT&T's Eastern Seaboard service went completely down. These boys were trouble, but a new kind of trouble.

John Lee appeared later on magazine covers and on *60 Minutes*. He wore dreadlocks, and had gold capped teeth, and appeared "down," as they say in the "hood." And he was indicted and ultimately sentenced to a year in jail and three years of suspension, and two hundred hours of community service and a fifty-dollar fine. By this time, he had been a student at Brooklyn College and seemed, in many ways, unrepentant. Who can say?

Nonetheless, I followed the news reports of these guys I had left behind, or who had left me behind. (Who knows? I might have become a hacker had I remained in the wonderful world of computers; I certainly had the interest and the inclination.) It struck me how the cause of this "war" between these two groups of pubescent hotshots had been precipitated by the onslaught of a very low-tech ideology, something that Texas hacker had inherited from a country almost three hundred years old, and a culture over four hundred years old, where a boy with the intelligence to bulldog multinational corporations and government agencies in cyberspace was reduced to being just another nigger.

———————

THE TERM *CYBERSPACE* actually had been invented in, of all places, a science-fiction novel, published in 1982. *Neuromancer*, by William Gibson, was a departure from most science fiction of its day, which had, over the decades, become dominated by space operas of little green men and postapocalyptic danger-scapes. In truth, the late Philip K. Dick had been the prophet for the sort of writing that Gibson would almost singlehandedly create, called cyberpunk. But it was Gibson's crystal-clear vision of a world not destroyed by the bomb but overrun by international conglomerates that have gobbled one another up, and megalopolises that covered entire coasts, and of the gap between rich and poor becoming a chasm, and of artificial intelligent life, of the hacker-like specialists called "cowboys" who "jacked" into an electronic world of data where information was in some way seen, and where one could lose one's life. This man-made world of the data-stream Gibson dubbed "cyberspace," and the phrase stuck.

Nowadays it is hard to find someone who has not heard of cyberspace or Vice President Al Gore's information highway; hard to find someone not impacted by personal computers and Windows and Macintosh and email and the Internet and the World Wide Web; hard to find someone who is not, as William Gibson had been, more than a little skeptical about the whole evolution of technological might.

I particularly like the phrase created by cultural critic Scott Bukatman, "Terminal Identity." Image addiction, mediascape, virtual space. Already most Americans live most of their lives virtually: through television, or through a screen, or at a terminal, or over the phone. This way of living is not new news, it is self-evident; moreover, these modes and manners are reshaping what it means to be American, and, in some ways, what it means to be human, and yes, what it means to be Black.

Call it Terminal Blackness.

> William Jordan Jr., an electrical engineer, and his brother, Rodney, a software designer, wanted to test their concept of "the uncut black experience"—blacks marketing to blacks and controlling the experience.
>
> And what better way to do that than to use the Internet's World Wide Web? It offers small black businesses an inexpensive way to market goods and services to a vast audience of blacks and others. An estimated 10 million to 30 million people worldwide use the Internet.
>
> —"Black Businesses on the Internet:
> A Market that Was 'Invisible Until Now,'"
> *New York Times*, September 4, 1995

For many Americans, the expanding universe of computers lies somewhere in the imagination between Buck Rogers and "Mr. Rogers' Neighborhood." Wondrous and neat. But if you happen to be an African-American, the same gadgets may evoke less benign images. Try racially segregated schools, back-of-the-bus seating and town halls buzzing with angry white males.

Farfetched? Well, consider this: blacks spend several billion dollars a year on consumer electronics, but relatively few plunk down for computers. As PCs rapidly rewire the ways this country works, plays, learns and communicates, blacks are simply not plugging in to what feels like an alien, unwelcoming place. Certainly economics and education are also powerful handicaps to computer ownership. The average household income for blacks is $25,409; for whites, it is $40,708. But dollars and diplomas don't fully explain why some black professors let their university-issued computers gather dust. There are other important causes of this computer gap, reasons that are rooted in African-American history, culture and psychology.

—"CyberSoul Not Found," *Newsweek*, July 31, 1995

What, some will ask, does this have to do with being Black?

There exists a company called It's a D.C. Thang that sells T-shirts with "an African American flavor" over the World Wide Web. There is Carlos A. Howard Funeral Homes, "the first funeral home on the Internet," whose owners are Black. There is Melanet and there is NetNoir and there is Sphinx Communications and Black News Network and Afrinet and AfriTech and the African American Information Network, and an entire host of other local bulletin boards and forums. Many of these online companies belong to what is known as the BPON, or Black Pioneers of the Net network. Organizations like the National Urban League have set up training centers across the nation to teach Black folk computer literacy, as have mammoth computer firms like AT&T and Microsoft.

The truth of the matter is that the cost of a computer, for a family, for an individual, in the last few years of the twentieth century, is affordable. Indeed, most poor folks in the United States own a car—for it is a necessity in most parts of the country, and the cost of a computer is a fraction of a used car. Moreover, libraries and schools make access to computers easier and easier every day. The question then shifts to the user: Does a person value the machine enough, and the learning and the skills needed to use one? Already, people I know who work for any large corporation or university or college or library or museum or bookstore, etc., communicate through email and record invoices. What are we saying when we dismiss that percentage of African Americans who do value the power of this Brave New Cyberworld? Are they any less Black? And, according to all the numbers, they are getting more and more company, day by day.

I am not eager to say that any of these new ways of existing on the planet are bad, nor am I quick to say that they are all good. A person always runs the risk of being either a reactionary or a booster, when the prosaic truth usually runs somewhere towards the middle.

All that said, I nonetheless find this development not only tantalizing, but at the heart of my original question(s) about identity. This thing we call being Black, does it exist outside of our bodies? Where, indeed, am I Black? On my skin? In my mind?

ORIGINALLY I DID it for writing.

I wrote my first novel out in longhand, and then typed each page up on an IBM Selectric typewriter, and then entered the final copy onto an old Xerox computer. My second book was also written first in longhand, on yellow legal pads, but I then entered the changes on a secondhand IBM knockoff that had no hard drive. In 1991, I purchased what was then a state-of-the-art portable computer on which to write and take notes. One day, three years later, out of the blue, this computer gave up the ghost, and I was forced to buy a new one because I had become habituated to the damned thing functioning as a fancy typewriter. This new computer was a sleek laptop that amazed me with its elegance, its small size, its speed, its Windows operating system; I was slowly seduced out of my stance as a pseudo-Luddite.

I returned home, to Chapel Hill, the year the media machine discovered the Internet. TV shows, magazines, books practically yelled about the new "computer revolution." In ten years, what had been essentially the province of geeks and scientists and hackers had become, in the words of politicians and marketeers, "mainstream." I was then in North Carolina's triangle, Raleigh/Durham/Chapel Hill, one of America's most congenial brain trusts, the area situated between the University of North Carolina, North Carolina State, and Duke University, known as Research Triangle Park, the gift of North Carolina's forward-looking, long-time Democratic governor James B. Hunt, who created this enterprise zone to lure large corporations to build laboratories and factories, taking advantage of the atmosphere, the forests, the universities, and the PhDs.

At dinner parties, everybody was talking about the joys and hardships of email; friends were telling me about staying up all night surfing the Net; I was hearing strange things about being "on-line." After a while, I was beginning to feel left out, and intrigued.

Ten years after I had thought my computer use was going to be minimal at best, and I would never again learn a computer language, I was back in Chapel Hill, owning yet another computer, this one faster than fast, with massive storage, a modem and three Internet accounts; I bought loads of books that told me all sorts of information about FTP and Gopher and Veronica and Mosaic and Listservers and Usenet and Telnet. I sat amazed, for this was far from the days of a monochrome screen, with awkward, unattractive type flashing at your bewildered retinas at 3:00 a.m. No, this was a multicolored world of pictures and images and bells and whistles and information, information, information. I was fast becoming drunk with the stuff.

Presently, I found myself on-line, and what an amazing world that was, all fresh and new and cyber-wonderful. I explored, I lurked. I visited chat rooms, my eyes aflash with curiosity; my mind afire with the possibilities of this humming new mechanism. Here I was in my room in Carrboro, North Carolina, talking to folk in New Zealand, in Nigeria, in China, in Passaic, New Jersey. I say talk, but what we were doing was typing at one another; who they were, who I was, was largely immaterial; in truth, at the time, I deeply believe we were all, essentially, in love with the concept. We were netizens.

One fine night, I found myself on America Online, chatting with a man who said he was Black and living in Los Angeles. We fell into a typersation about this and that. By and by, why I don't now remember, we began to discuss basketball. I allowed as how I was no good at the game, and probably went on too long about my feelings of insecurity, especially after having gone to a basketball-crazy place like UNC. Without preamble or warning, this cyberNegro typed: "Well, I got to get outta here and git wit some real niggas." And blipped off on his merry way.

Now objectively there is nothing remarkable about this minor incident. Folk on the Internet tended, and still tend, to be ruder to folk than they would be face-to-face; there is something about the electronic anonymity engendered by the beast that makes people insensitive. No, the thing that got my goat, stuck in my craw, angered the hell out of me, was the content of his aspersion. Here, after years of seeking out the nature of Blackness, after talking to so many Black folk, after reading, discussing, debating, investigating the nature of Blackness, here I was being accused of not being Black. That stung. That hurt.

But what fascinated me—after I realized how silly it had been to allow my feathers to get ruffled by somebody I did not know—was how quicksilver and fast was my reaction; how subjective the idea had been on the one hand; and how, on the other hand, the very nature of what this cyber-fellow expected to be Black had fallen into question. Indeed, how could you be Black on a computer screen? To be sure, he meant more than skin color, but how, qualitatively, could anyone adjudge how Black you were or even if one were Black? This silly incident led me once again, like a snake chasing its tail, right back to my original dilemma. What is Blackness? Where does it exist? How can one person be more authentic in his being than another?

———————

MY GRANDFATHER IS now eighty-four. He rises each morning between six o'clock and seven. Most months of the year he first goes out and tends his garden, which is almost half an acre. He still works six days a week, and his hobbies are still renovating houses and restoring furniture, and he cleans carpets sometimes on the side. George Washington Kenan seems to have more energy every year.

He owns a 1964 Park Lane Mercury, which is red, has less than one hundred thousand miles on its odometer, and runs like a dream. That car is one of his most prized possessions.

I enjoy sitting and talking with my grandfather for hours, and he seems to enjoy waxing nostalgic. I was surprised to learn a few years ago that he almost regrets not having become a farmer; he learned many things about farming as a teenager and knows in his soul that he could have produced bountiful crops. Once, in the 1950s, he owned a farm for twelve years, and farmed while he ran his business. He sold the land at a profit in the 1960s. (Ironically, that land is now the site of a new luxury housing development.)

My grandfather tells me stories of his father and his father's father, of his days working at the shipyard, and of building his business from practically nothing; he talks of Chinquapin, which, in his day, was home to more people than it is now. Much of today's technology baffles my grandfather, and he coexists in a world with it, paying computers and faxes next to no attention. Air travel astonishes him, and new cars amaze him, but he knows his old Park Lane remains something special; and he only flew on a plane once when his older brother was sick and dying, and otherwise has no real use for flying.

I remember once discussing nursing homes with my grandfather, who remains grateful that at his age he has maintained his independence. He marvels at the paradox of how much medical science has done to prolong life; and yet, once when a member of the family fell sick, he or she became the focus of an entire family, not the nuclear family of the 1950s television dreams, but of uncles and aunts and cousins. He remembered when his own father fell ill, how people would take turns sitting by his side, the women taking care of him.

"No," he said, "it ain't like it used to be. People just don't seem to care about people the way they once did."

The truth is that I am very different from my grandfather, and we both know this for a fact. I can no more imagine such a world as he describes, than he can imagine jacking into cyberspace. I am a creature of network television and books and music and cyber-dreams; I am the inheritor of not only his vision but also of the ultimate dream of the American: individualism. I am not surrounded by family and bound by codes of caring and closeness. At the age of thirty-four, I am as itinerant as the fabled Wandering Jew. I have changed my address more in one year than my grandfather has in his entire life. I could easily live in California or Brazil or Japan or Ireland or South Africa. My friends come from all over the world, and some of my closest friends I have not seen for years, though we keep up over the phone and through the computer.

In this way, in many ways, I am emblematic of my generation. Despite my rural background, I am now a netizen, a paradoxically rootless American whose home is reluctantly the world. We have exchanged the village for the globe, yet, despite what Mr. McLuhan predicted, the global village can be a cold, impersonal place.

And whence Blackness in this strange happenstance we find ourselves? After this long march across the country, I now see that the era in which I came of age was the era in which the concept of being Black or Negro or African American changed indelibly. During my grandfather's time, the construct was at once political (Jim Crow), cultural (language, food, clothing, music), and spiritual (Black Baptist). Now Jim Crow is no more, one can bridge the distances between Protestant, Catholic, Islam, and agnostic, and this thing called culture, once specific to so many regions, has become a postmodern amalgam of this and that, borrowings and findings and newfangled creations like Kwanzaa, and media manipulations of street lingo, innocent of its origins and only interested in style, newness, the expression of being other, being Black. But what is Black anymore? Who is authentically Black in a country, within a culture, where one's very existence has always been the shifting identity of survival?

Black American culture was always a Creole culture, a mixture of remembered African ways, of European impositions and influences and inflections, of Native American wisdom, and of the stubborn will to survive. Long before the term was coined, Black culture was a postmodern culture; folk made it up as they went along. Therefore, who can be authentically Black, when every Black person holds the codes and the blueprints of that Blackness?

NOT ONLY DO I march to the beat of a different drummer, but some-times I fail to make out the beat. It seems at times I'm making it up as I go along. I think of those Black folk in the 1860s who had none of the modern baggage my contemporaries and I lug around. As deprived as they were, they were also lucky. They knew exactly who they were. There was no jangling television set, no blasting boom boxes, no candy-colored magazines, no Walmarts, Tower Records, web pages, billboards. Marketing had yet to be invented, and con-sumerism was a mere glint in Rockefeller's eye. We—Black, white, indifferent, but American—must now disentangle ourselves from the garbage of the Information Age; we must pioneer a new way of seeing ourselves; we must reinvent humanity.

Who I am and who the world wants me to be will not jibe. So much of this disease is caused by peer pressure, the perceived notion that one is not "Black" enough; the hints and clues that somehow I, he, she, wishes to be other than other, and therefore a traitor.

Traitor. A strong word. But a traitor to what? Traitor to the race? Most countries punish treachery by the most severe means avail-able. But how do you betray that which has yet to be truly defined?

Going back to Chapel Hill resurrected a great many of my per-sonal specters, many of which I was certain I had laid to rest years ago. But walking down the halls of the English building, down the long green mall, down Franklin Street, into the massive Davis Library, I was accompanied always by the kid from Chinquapin, ten years before, and, like those patients of charlatan psychotherapists, I began remembering those things that I didn't want to remember.

After polyglot and polycolored Brooklyn and Queens and Man-hattan, it struck me how homogeneous and largely white Chapel Hill was in 1994, and how much more it had to have been in 1984. All those Scots, Irish, English, and German faces, blond, brunette, and red hair all seemed to weigh on me more, and I wondered then how I had coped with that sea. I remembered how often I joined groups of Black folk out of the sheer need to see Black folk; how I volunteered at soup kitchens and tutored Black kids, perhaps more out of a personal need than out of a desire to help.

I remembered incidents of being singled out as a Negro, like the time I was almost ejected from a frat party, being the only Black person there; or the time the police stopped me while I was running down Rosemary Street near a number of sorority houses, because I "fit the description" of someone who had mugged a woman the day before. I remembered trying to express my outrage to my white housemates at the time, and their baffled inability to say anything at all, which made all of us feel inexpressibly worse and alienated from one another.

I remembered, as a freshman, having gone to a mixer at one of the tony North Campus female dorms, and being introduced by one of my roommates to a young lady friend of his. She asked me where I was from, and I said, Chinquapin. Her eyes grew wide, and she exclaimed, "Oh, you mean in *Africa*?" Everyone laughed, primarily at her profound ignorance, but somehow I felt the laughter aimed at me. I felt marked.

Perhaps, most damningly, the thing that came back to me with such a wave of psychic force was the remembrance of how very much I disliked myself. I was not white, rich, socially in; I felt excluded, and subconsciously unacceptable.

I never wanted to be white; I never felt ashamed of being Black. Indeed, until my school had been integrated in the first grade, it never occurred to me that anyone was any different from me and my folks. Over the years, increasingly, as I watched more television, read more, thought more, became exposed to more and more of the insidious social microcosm of high school, I did become more and more dissatisfied with my own personal lot. I believed everything my family told me about what one had to do to succeed in this world, that, as a young Black man, I had to make certain my house was in order, that I had to eschew the more frivolous activities my white contemporaries indulged in; I had to hit the books; I had to prove myself.

By college, I remembered ten years later, this pressure had become acute. Often, in those years, I was not only uncomfortable but depressed. I now remembered that I did not often have a good time as an undergraduate. I felt myself on the outside looking in.

Many of the Black guys I knew in those years made a fetish of whiteness. They coveted white women, and cultivated white attitudes, white clothing, white manners and mores. Was I one of those misled young men?

Sometimes I think I was; sometimes, most times, I know I was not. This conundrum being, at its base, the basis of my questioning. The question becomes not whether I, a young Black man, an "affirmative action baby" (whatever that means), a child of the dream, wished to shed my skin, exchange my nappy head for blond tresses, expunge my chitlins-and-collard-greens past, and adopt a New England clenched-teeth speech, eradicate all folkways and knowledge of the Veil, and blissfully slip into a country-club future unhampered by the shadow of the Other. No, the question becomes: Did I, in my attempts to learn and to experience another world, somehow lose, divest, mitigate, or disavow who or what I was? Did I, in mingling and comingling with white folks, dilute or pollute or weaken my legacy as a son of a son of a son of a son of slaves stolen from Africa?

By 1994, I had moved a long way from that way of thinking. Like Lorri Hewett, I had come to realize that being Black is not something to grab; like the Reverend Swift in Utah, I understood that being Black was more than love, peace, and hair grease. I had remedied the confusion of politics, economics, social class, and skin color; I had come to understand that other people's notions of me could only influence me as much as I allowed them to do; I had come to the unshatterable conclusion that being Black was indeed a willed affirmation, a recognition of my past, my beliefs, and my most secret dreams.

> We Americans have lived in a country that's been very success-
> ful technologically, and we instinctively think that every prob-
> lem must have a technological solution.
>
> —I. F. Stone, National Public Radio, April 12, 1983

I met Richard Elias Wimberly III the first day I arrived at Chapel Hill as a freshman; he roomed right across the hall from me, in one of the older dorms on what is called the North Campus of the university.

The first Black student was admitted to Chapel Hill in 1951, to the medical school; in fact, Chapel Hill was the first Southern university to voluntarily accept Black students, though it did not gracefully tear down the barricade for most Black folk for decades. In 1981, most of the eight hundred or so Black students (out of twenty thousand) lived in what was known as South Campus, at the southernmost edge of the school, where four of the newest, high-rise dorms had been erected. It was understood that South Campus was where the Black folk were largely housed, and those who chose to live elsewhere were considered somehow different. And though it was not an instant badge of Oreo-dom (for instance, Michael Jordan and most of the other basketball players lived on a special floor of a privately owned and operated "dorm" called Granville, north of North Campus), one was open to being suspect. Or, to be more specific, folk would wonder where you were at.

When I chose Grimes Dormitory, I was blissfully ignorant of all these territorial imperatives; it merely seemed logical to be close to most of my classes. There were a number of other Black guys in my dorm, twelve or fifteen out of about a hundred students. It took me a while, but gradually I came to realize what some of the folk on South Campus thought of the Black folk who lived on North Campus. The truth is they were right about a number of those people; that is to say, some of those Black men and women who sojourned on North Campus did so because they wanted little if anything to do with other Black folk, while for some there were other reasons; and some, like me, had given it little, if any, thought.

For many people on South Campus, the few who knew him, Richard Wimberly fell into the former category. Richard was from a prosperous upper-middle-class family from Raleigh, which belonged to one of the oldest and most affluent Black churches in the state; his father owned his own business, and Richard had gone to one of the more competitive high schools in the state capital. Richard was beautiful, athletic, articulate, a gentleman and a preppie; funny, good spirited, a history major. Richard enjoyed playing basketball and was good at it. He had an eye for the ladies and loved pepperoni pizza, and Richard was deeply, deeply religious.

Richard had white friends, Richard had Black friends, Richard had Chinese friends, Richard had Japanese friends. And fairly quickly, the two of us became fast friends. I often wonder if the proximity in which we lived for a year was the basis of our friendship, plus the fact that being Black together, surrounded largely by white folk, forced us to seek one another out. And of course, the answer is partly yes. However, we had so much in common that I feel it was inevitable that we would get along so famously. Our interest in history, sociology, and in Dungeons & Dragons led us to spend hours just talking. And yes, our interest in *Star Trek* and science fiction, as well.

In the fullness of time, we spoke more and more about our specific circumstances, about the speculations folk had made about him, about us. One of our mutual friends actually told Richard to his face that for months he had assumed Richard to be an "uppity nigger"; one who didn't want anything to do with Black folk; one who thought he was better than other Black folk; one who had few Black friends by design. This friend later asked for Richard's forgiveness, saying, after getting to know him, that Richard was "all right." These ideas intrigued both Richard and me, and we shared our feelings of insecurity, of doubt, of the possibility of self-hate, of the doublethink that goes on in one's own mind when people who don't know you cast aspersions about your inner self; the second-guessing that breeds discontent. These ideas led us to ask questions about Blackness. What is it?

I remember one night in particular, one which seems too good to be true, though it is true nonetheless. Richard and I had started talking after studying late; somewhere around ten or eleven, we were in the hall, on the landing, talking. At one point, we looked up, and the sun was peeking up. Neither of us was tired. We talked about many things that night: personhood, faith, history, economics, Hegel, Martin Luther King, sex, death, manifest destiny.

At one point, Richard said something to the effect of:

I would love to just travel all over the country and study Black people. Try to figure out what exactly it is we talk about when we talk about Blackness.

I remember, as the sun came up that morning, as we said good night and went to our own beds, agreeing with him, thinking, somehow, I would try to do just that.

Richard went on to Duke Divinity School, and then on to become an ordained minister, and then chaplain at Central Prison in Raleigh. When I told Richard my plans, to do what he himself had suggested, he was perhaps more excited than I. I suggested that for the final chapter, I would go with him to the prison and interview him and some of the inmates. He thought that would be a grand idea.

Richard married a beautiful Black woman named Denise in the summer of 1993. He died almost exactly a year later of cancer.

Life, love, work, service, death.

I remember most fondly how fervently Richard Wimberly applied his mind to the conundrum of being. The issue of being Black was no singular, isolatable question for him. He saw it always within the context of faith, of humanity. It never mattered to Richard what others thought of him; rather, it mattered what he thought of himself. He refused to allow himself to be dictated to about what or who he was, for, like Ralph Ellison's Invisible Man, he stubbornly examined each and every particle of his life; he questioned it, not on the basis of what he was supposed to think about it, but on the basis of what he actually thought of it. This, of course, is a wearisome, tiring, frustrating exercise, and when anyone questioned him or became impatient with his dogged analysis, he would just smile his infectious smile, and say, "Now just bear with me . . . "

Now just bear with me . . .

> Now you've been told, so you ought to know. But maybe, after all the Negro doesn't really exist. What we think is a race is detached moods and phases of other people walking around. What we have been talking about might not exist at all. Could be the shade patterns of something else thrown on the ground— other folks, seen in shadow. And even if we do exist it's all an accident anyway. God made everybody else's color. We took ours by mistake. The way the old folks tell it, it was like this . . .
>
> —Zora Neale Hurston, *Dust Tracks on a Road*

11

Blackness on
My Mind

New York, New York

There's a crow flying   I took the ferry to a highway
Black and ragged   Then I drove to a pontoon plane
Tree to tree   Took a plane to a taxi
He's black as the highway   And a taxi to a train
That's leading me   I been traveling so long
Now he's diving down   How'm I ever going to know my home
To pick up something shiny   When I see it again?
I feel like that black crow   I'm like a black crow
Flying   Flying
In a blue sky   In a blue, blue sky

—Joni Mitchell

During this sojourn in America, I came to develop a strange romance with the motel. To be sure, it was not a part of my original intent, but this romance became, in the end, part and parcel of my journey.

The sun-splashed bed and breakfasts, too quaint for comfort; the tawdry and broken-down rooms ghosted by truck drivers, prostitutes, and johns; the hunting lodge with the black-and-white TV; the depressing, dull dungeons on the edge of a megalopolis, like something out of a Fritz Lang nightmare; the happy inn run by the Indian family on the shores of Lake Erie. The coffee shops. The laundry rooms. The front desks. The sunken beds. The corporate logos. The free books of matches.

I understand that the filmmaker David Lynch made a documentary about American motels. I have not seen it. But, from what I gather, he concentrated on the kitsch and the unusual, which is abundant and interesting enough. However, I am compelled by the quotidian and the lackluster, and the vague promise of rest proffered the wayfarer. But, in truth, what can the motel offer? A warm, clean bed. A safe and convenient place to park the car. Shelter from the elements. A place to bathe and rest your suitcase. Fresh towels. A boob tube. Fresh towels. All well and good, but how far these several things are from home; how far they've come from providing actual rest. As Frederick Douglass once said, "You may not get what you pay for in this world, but you will certainly pay for what you get." My question, then, perhaps: What price is home?

Whether I like it or not, my time in motel rooms is as much a part of my years of travel as the people and the landscapes and the histories. For there is something about living in motels, about being in an *American* motel room, that is an experience in itself. I find that in a motel room, I become a person apart from myself. I have entered a strange limbo, a quasi-world, ruled ruefully by corporate demographic studies, stingy owners, American tourist demands, and the American psyche of what it means to be a human being away from home. Home, that ever-elusive intangible mythology of self and place. I found it difficult, if not impossible, to write about these experiences without taking myself back to that room in Atlanta where I scribbled notes, or read articles and books; that place in Lafayette where, after a day of chasing this person, this book, this fact, this lead, I would return with a sigh, and reenter a beige or off-white womb of sorts, with a newly made bed, and a freshly vacuumed carpet, and a clean bathroom; this place in Anchorage where I sat waiting for a confirming or a returned phone call, and picked up that most benign but universal of habits, television watching, after having gone over eight years without owning a television set. (I became so addicted to CNN that I would seriously think of passing up a motel when I discovered that they did not carry that monotonous station.) For there is something about being in a motel room, alone, with that big cubic receiving device, a device you know hums and glows and flickers with pretty pictures and multifaceted sounds, with just a snap of a switch, that makes it a necessity: this illusion of company, this promise of connection; this unflagging desire to mitigate loneliness. Impossible, yes, for me to think of these days abroad in my own land, without thinking, fondly, of my times in these sundry homes away from home. For as I left other people's homes, I could not but acutely think about the idea of what composed, comprised, configured a home.

So it was, that when I finally returned to New York, when it had hit me like a boulder that this trip of trips was indeed over for me, that I reemerged from this period of intransigence, and began again slowly to think of myself as a person who was of a place, and in a place, and able to make a home. And in many ways it was fitting for me to think of New York, and not North Carolina, as home, for, in the most basic of senses, it was my home. It was the place where I was born; it was the place where I had made my living and the bulk of my life for the last eight years; and it was a place I mysteriously, deeply loved. And though I was not a true New Yorker, having been stolen away at six weeks old, and having grown up a true country boy, New York could bewitch me as it never could someone for whom the asphalt and the concrete and the noise and the grime were commonplace. Like Thebes for Oedipus, who had to rediscover his heritage, beyond his heritage, New York seemed to hide secrets and dreads and conjurations wherein I might find

some lurking truth about myself. But that is, of course, the myth of
New York, from the dancers on Broadway to the investment bankers
on Wall Street, from the Israeli cab drivers to the Hungarian wait-
resses. The monkeys in the zoo, and the pigeons, too, New York,
New York, they all want you.

> And then the voyages, the search for the happy land. In his
> moment of terrible vision he saw, in the tortuous ways of a thou-
> sand alien places, his foiled quest of himself. And his haunted
> face was possessed of that obscure and passionate hunger
> that had woven its shuttle across the seas, that had hung its
> weft across the Dutch in Pennsylvania, that had darkened his
> father's eyes to impalpable desire for wrought stone and the
> head of an angel. Hill-haunted, whose vision of the earth was
> mountain-walled, he saw the golden cities sicken in his eye, the
> opulent dark splendors turn to dingy gray. His brain was sick
> with the million books, his eyes with the million pictures, his
> body sickened on a hundred princely wines.
>
> And rising from his vision, he cried: "I am not there among
> the cities. I have sought down a million streets, until the goat-
> cry died within my throat, and I have found no city where I
> was, no door where I had entered, no place where I had stood."
>
> —Thomas Wolfe, *Look Homeward Angel*

I know I romanticize New York. I always have and I probably
always will. I feel sorry for people who are not in love with the place
where they live. For many people, sadly, such a happy marriage of
geography and emotion is not possible. I count myself among the
lucky.

Trey Ellis once told me he believed that certain folk were born
hard-wired for certain cities. He knew two brothers, he told me; I
think he said they were twins. One brother was laid-back, sybaritic,

open, fun-loving—he wound up in Los Angeles. The other brother was an A-type personality, driven, neurotic, constantly on the move, frantic, busy, busy, busy—he lived in New York.

Utterly un-American, deceptively kind, beset by blizzards and exploding towers and the worst traffic in the nation; home to the Irish, the Jewish, the Indian, the Pakistani, the Haitian, the Senegalese, the French, the German, the Dutch, the Italian (ah, the Italian), and the highest concentration of Chinese outside of China, not to mention the Greek and the Spanish, which includes Puerto Rico, Honduras, Ecuador, El Salvador, Belize, Costa Rica, Mexico, et al., and don't forget Spain.

North Carolina's favorite native-son novelist came to New York. Thomas Wolfe wrote a story, "Only the Dead Know Brooklyn," that will probably always do the city proud. One of this century's most influential writers of prose, Joseph Mitchell, was also a North Carolina boy. As was the roving Charles Kuralt, and so many others. Call it tradition, call it coincidence, call it what you will, but I believe in some strange and mysterious link between my home state and the place I now think of as home. True, the great city draws folk from all over the world, yet curiously Carolinians seem to love it most by writing about it.

> One may well ask at once whether a travel book is an appropriate place for an investigation into the heart of a region. In some respects, travel writing is a shallow form of serious literature, the only form in which ignorance is pure bliss. W. E. B. Du Bois once wrote scornfully, perhaps quoting someone, about "car window sociologists," who view their human subjects mainly from a comfortable distance, then write about them with confidence and, no doubt, consequence. No matter how long he or she lingers in any one place, filling notebooks or tape cassettes, the travel writer must surely be most often a

> car window sociologist, a car window psychologist, and a car
> window writer, however plentiful or intimate are the interviews
> or chats with members of the native population.
>
> —Arnold Rampersad, "V. S. Naipaul: Turning in the South"

At one point, after I knew it was over, the traveling, the talking, the searching; after transcripts and notes and diary entries were organized and placed in order, I looked at a mound of over 5,000 pages of stuff, words upon words, undigested, needing digestion—and I panicked.

The manuscript-to-be was my bone; I had to chew on it.

There was a horrible psychological terror involved with bringing this project to a close. I was beginning to see the truth. Every article, every movie, every television show, everything about Black people I encountered gave me an upset stomach. It couldn't be done, this task I had set for myself. Already I was aware of all the lacunae in my travels. I could hear ardent voices asking: Where are the Muslims? Where is hip-hop? Where is jazz? Why didn't you go into the prisons? Why did you leave out a large chunk of the South? Where is the Negro Baseball League? What! No football, basketball, hockey, soccer players? Not enough about food! Not enough about language! What about Black insurance companies, newspapers, plumbers, undertakers, oil magnates, physicists, engineers, state department officials, singers, patent attorneys, shipbuilders, jockeys, drug addicts, trumpet players, botanists, skateboarders, marine biologists, violinists, ornithologists, midwives, candy makers, comic book authors, karate black belts, Jews, chiropodists. . . .

I looked upon what I had done, and all I could see was what I had not done.

One day, in the summer of 1996, at the Black Arts Festival in Atlanta, I had the honor and pleasure of finally meeting the award-winning writer Octavia Butler. I had interviewed her over the phone the year before I had set off on this odyssey, and I was pleased, six years later, that she remembered me. After a while, she asked what I was working on now, and, as succinctly as I could, I told her. She chuckled. "That's like saying you're writing a book on what it means to be human."

It was.

New York was going to be the *pièce de résistance* for *Walking on Water*. I had worked it all out after a lot of heady deliberation. I would interview Afrika Bambaataa, the man considered to be the father of rap music, and I would interview Mrs. Joyce Dinkins, the former First Lady of New York and descendant of an old New York family; I would interview a homeless man, and I would interview an AIDS patient at a hospice, and I would interview the writer and thinker and now Columbia University professor Manning Marable, and I would interview the kids who were selling illicit substances on my corner, and I would interview the astrophysicist Dr. Neil Tyson who had recently been made head of the Hayden Planetarium, and I would interview a friend of mine who was a gay Episcopal priest . . . and I knew there was no way in hell I would finish this book before I was ninety-seven, at the outside.

If Chicago defeated me, and California consumed me, and Louisiana kidnapped me, New York would surely kill me.

By this point everything was redundant and everything was new.

I phoned my editor and told her New York was out. I think she thought I had lost my mind. You're writing a book about African America, and you are going to leave out New York City? The place that got you involved in the first place?

Yep.

I realized later that my dream was undoable and yet done, for on my table rested not interviews and notes and thoughts, but a record of my personal history of the last six years. No longer was this about gathering facts—though I had facts aplenty. It was about feeling and interpretation and ways of seeing the world and of being in the world. The truth is there are over thirty-six million ways to be Black, from the curious guy who raises pigeons on the roof across the street from me, who wears the same jacket 365 days of the year, to the Tennessee mountain minister who teaches Greek and Latin to high school students, to the NBA player from Lake Charles, Louisiana, who loves his mother to death, to the matriarch of an apple orchard in Washington State who hates to see her children go off to school, to the crack addict in some Philadelphia alley, with a hard-on and thirty-seven cents to his name, just wanting to stay up and UP, to the congresswoman, to the cowgirl, to the fisherman to the dogcatcher to the young lovers, at this very moment, engaged in that ancient act that will undoubtedly bring, nine months hence, yet another brown-skinned girl or brown-skinned boy into this world, into this country, into this city, into this block, into this building, into this room where they shall learn their own uniqueness, and, one fine morning, say softly, I am.

To accurately accomplish what I had originally set out to do would have made it necessary to go and talk to thirty-six million people—but the truth is, even if that feat were humanly possible, the end result would be the same: inconclusive.

But to bear witness I need only one soul, and my soul is a witness.

He lived there for years, and New Yorkers even named a street in his honor. But these days would dapper Duke Ellington feel at ease taking the A train 2 1/2 miles north from midtown Manhattan to black Harlem? Not if he believed the vision this New York City community conjures up in the minds of apprehensive whites: a post-nuclear landscape of poverty and blight, where crack dealers plan gang wars in cratered tenements. To most Manhattanites from the wealthy southern part of the island, Harlem hardly exists, except as an old, obscure head wound—the beast in the attic, a maximum-security prison for the American Dream's unruly losers. Why would a white person go to this Harlem, except to buy drugs? . . .

Harlem is certainly not a harmless place for residents or itinerants, but neither is it the city's worst crime area. In any case, fear is no excuse for missing out on Harlem's cultural and historical bounty. . . .

—Richard Corliss, "Welcome to New Harlem!"
Time, April 24, 1989

I can be honest about Harlem now. Or at least I think I can. Or at least I certainly want to be. After my time on the road, I found a place right on the edge of the traditional beginnings of Harlem. One Hundred and Tenth Street, and was happy there. Over time, I came to see my original aversion as only natural, and frightening in the sense that I might never have worked out those conflicting and warring factions that threatened to split me apart. I speak of my identity as a Black person and of the representative truths that have everything and nothing to do with me. So easy it was to only associate Harlem with poverty and crime; so easy to figure that to love and to come to understand Harlem would be, in some way, tantamount to embracing those elements: to become them, that media-driven entity. But I saw through a glass darkly, and with the weight of many generations on my shoulders, the loud whispers to not become a criminal or poor or hopeless or helpless or homeless or a victim of society's blind hatred and malice. Overcome, these voices said, and, in my simple mind, Harlem had rejected the proud commandments of those dark ur-daughters and dark ur-sons not long out of the Jim Crow–haunted South; in my mind I found it necessary, physically, to separate myself, to disassociate myself from the horny possibility, from the place and image the national consciousness seemed to possess, not simply of Harlem, but of what it meant to be a Negro. I, lacking the imagination, the sense of real history, the sense of self, and the understanding to combat society's presumptions, fell victim to a silly, though prevalent, way of thinking.

Can anyone reading this, even today, Black or white, say that they are immune to these forces? Say that any of their everyday choices are free from these looming judgments?

But we must become immune. We must work at becoming. We must begin to see more deeply, reason more soundly; indeed to reason at all about these ideas of color and "race," begin to disentangle the lies from the reality.

What does it mean to be Black?

I know now, after a great deal of work and worry, that none of the obvious answers to that question hold much water. Yes, to be Black is to be composed of three essential ingredients: political, cultural, and emotional. You don't need to look long at the history, and the present, of Black America to be convinced of the ongoing political necessity for some unity among Black folks, if nothing else, to band together against discrimination, to fight for parity, to safeguard against injustice inherently aimed at a person solely because of his or her skin color.

At the same time the culture of being Black, great or small for some, but present for practically all, remains fascinating and elusive, multifaceted and ever changing, problematic and profound. Despite its Old World origins, Black American culture, the language, the art, the music, the customs, ad nauseam, is a New World creation, as varied as the geography of the Americas, and belonging to all. It is a part of America.

And most vexing to come to terms with, for me at least, on an intellectual basis, is that emotional condition called being Black. To be sure, it was created by people who wanted to create an Other, Black folk, for sinister purposes. But out of that damnable imposition sprung something I'm certain they never expected, and something which has grown into its own state of being: being Black.

It is a desire toward some spiritual connection with some larger whole. To me this yearning is at its root an existential construct: Who am I? Where do I belong? To whom do I belong? When Zora Neale Hurston cries, "My People, My People," this is the construct she addresses. This "willed affirmation" is the sense of identity that leads to people intentionally embracing the idea of "race" as a fact. And though I still do not hold with the idea of "race" as a scientific concept, I cannot easily dismiss that belief as an active force among folk, for better or for worse. Dr. Du Bois's essentialist, mystical connection to some mythical Mother Africa still holds profound emotional energy, even for me. Indeed, that mysticism bound many Black folk to decades of positive service to the race; it brought us through Middle Passage; it brought us through slavery; it brought us through Reconstruction and Redemption; it brought us through the twentieth century, and it will assuredly bring us into the future.

Yes, when I call another Black man "brother," or a Black woman "sister," I mean it. But being able to hold conflicting, complex views in my head does not cause me to short-circuit; rather, it leaves me with a rich concoction to look toward, with pride, with wonder, with awe. To paraphrase Whitman: Do I contradict myself? I contain multitudes.

Oddly enough, to finally understand—like the rest of Black folks, like the rest of America—that I am a work in progress brings me a strange peace.

> Not enough can be enough and being enough quite enough
> is enough and being enough enough is enough and being
> enough it is that. Quite all that can be what it is and all of it
> being that, quite all of it is all there is of it.
>
> —Gertrude Stein, "A Long Gay Book"

Chinquapin, New York, Chapel Hill, New York,
Rome, Oxford, Memphis, 1992–98

12

An Ahistorical
Silliness

I once heard the poet Maya Angelou declare: "I was *determined* to be brilliant." Would that it were ever so easy.

I WANTED TO write before I knew I wanted to write, and write I did, talking back, writing back, on paper, to Beatrix Potter, to Robert Louis Stevenson and Edgar Allan Poe and Tom Swift and the Hardy Boys. Bad poems about airplanes. A short-lived newspaper in the sixth grade, purple mimeographs ("The Indian Enterprise")—the lead article featuring quotes about the difficulties of changing back from daylight saving time. What the hell made Alexandre Dumas, Charles Dickens, Victor Hugo, and Jules Verne the heroes of a poor, illegitimate "love child" in the deeps of tobacco row?

I have no idea what I looked like to the no-nonsense farmer world of Chinquapin in those Nixonian days. An annoying little semi-precocious nerd wallowing in books as if they were more than a diversion. Comic books were my original vice, and still have more allure to me than sex or drugs. To spend too much time reading was a sign of laziness, plain and simple, if not worse. Decidedly evidence of bad character. Surely in my case this was true.

———————

ON SOME VERY basic level I deserved it, but in many more ways no child should be subjected to such a thing by a trusted authority figure: a teacher. And though it had been designed to crush my spirit, the opposite managed to occur, aided by some angel dust and toughening familial fire.

The teacher was named Miss Underwood. Seventh grade Social Studies. The assignment: to write a one-page personal manifesto. I think we had been studying the conquistadors or the founding of the republic. I don't know what most of my peers wrote down that day, because the next day only two of us were asked to come to the front of the room and to read our little tracts to the class. The best paper was by a white girl who, incidentally, is still a friend, a high school teacher these days, ironically, and quite a good one. The other paper was mine.

What had I been thinking? Perhaps the words I jotted down were baldly an attempt to show off how smart I was. Perhaps I was trying to impress somebody I was sweet on. Perhaps it was just dumb. I wrote a paragraph that essentially looked down its nose at what Flannery O'Connor once called Good Country People, as if I lived on *Dynasty* with Krystle and Blake, and summered in Hawaii with Magnum P.I. I wrote about how *some* people didn't care about education and art and self-improvement, and how they were—figuratively, of course—bound for the bad place, excommunicated, doomed. Unlike myself, who had seen the light: Hallelujah. It was full of broken sentences trying to break bad—I was thirteen—and Latinate words I'm not even certain I understood. I remember using the word *gauche* but spelled it "gooch"—as in "Some gooch people think that their dull lives are important." Or words to that effect.

In all honesty, with the perfect hindsight time gives, the hundred or so words were a rank horror. Or at least that is how I look upon them now. But they also revealed an insecurity and an unbridled ambition, a purpleness born from a need to impress and mystify, and, perhaps most obnoxious, a sense of self that did more than border on arrogance.

I read it with conviction, convinced that Tom Paine himself would weep with admiration. And—thanks to the astounding self-protection device that is early adolescence—instantly interpreted the class's guffaws and chiding as proof of their ignorance and as an underscoring of my crypto-Darwinian thesis on how some people just weren't good enough. It was a heartfelt though misguided declaration of self-help and self-empowerment, or some such, but it sounded more like Mussolini than Norman Vincent Peale, I'm afraid, like a little Black fascist in the making. (Where, how, why I held such a hatefully scornful, inaccurate, mean-spirited idea escapes me now; perhaps another defense measure to protect my fragile ego because I felt unathletic and unlovely in a world that highly prized athletics and beauty.) The din included Miss Underwood, whose baritone laughter mingled with theirs like a trombone accompanying a country-rock band.

Being so smart and so stupid at the same time is probably more blessing than curse. I rode away home that night full of righteous indignation. I had been wronged against and some damn body would have to pay. I did not like Miss Underwood any old how. She had always treated me mean. I think I even fantasized about her losing her job over her cruel actions.

I witnessed to my ordeal before my family, testifying as I had seen others do in prayer meetings, resolute in my holy case. I produced the very document. They read it in silence, and silence remained. I waited for the vindication, for their kindred outrage, the outrage of kin, to boil forth as had mine; for them to utter condemnation upon the Wicked Witch and to vow retribution, or some such. To say, at least, that what I had written was good. Okay?

Edythe finally spoke. Edythe always terrified me. Quite simply. She was the very model of a certain Old World steadfastness that harkened back to another century. She had a way of being polished and blunt at the same time. All through my growing up, I had heard tales of how as a little girl she had written a letter to the governor about a road situation, and how he stopped by to visit when he happened to be in the neighborhood, and how he fixed the problem; of how she graduated magna cum laude. I had the unshakeable idea that, Urge-like, she could actually create anything, make anything happen. Later, in college, when my professor described Pope Gregory XII as so iron-willed that, for him, to think of a thing was to make it so; so intense that when he walked in his garden sparks flew up from his sandals—the first image that came to my mind was of Edythe. This was not respect; this was awe.

Edythe has a way of saying my name that presages a certain level of bedrock-hard truth-telling. Equal parts maternal and prison warden. She said, "Who do you think you are?"

She reproved me for an arrogance unbecoming a thirteen year old, of being pretentious, of overweening ambition, of a lack of basic human decency toward other people. Who did I think I was?

They all nodded their heads in agreement. Looking at them looking at me, I could clearly read their thoughts: Where did we go wrong? My head was a puzzle, thinking that I had been doing them proud, had been upright and good and hardworking (mostly) and smart and . . .

What Miss Underwood had failed to achieve in public, in front of the entire class, my family had managed in their bosom.

But then the most important part of this trial by class assignment had just begun. Edythe had not finished. What kind of writing is this? What is this word? We have four dictionaries in this house. *Use them*. Boy, you know verbs have to agree with their subject. . . .

She made me rewrite the paper.

I also learned that evening—after rewriting the paper several times ("Who uses the word 'gauche'? Stop trying to impress people. What does it mean? What do you really want to say? Then say that.")—I learned that my father had killed Miss Underwood's brother.

———————

WHEN WE VISITED my father, Harry, in prison, I had no clue as to why he had been locked up. I knew he had had a serious drug problem, and I knew, in those days, that he possessed what had been euphemistically called a Bad Attitude. Perhaps I did ask, and maybe I was told "Vehicular manslaughter," or "Shut up. None of your business." The latter was probably the case.

Truth to tell, I enjoyed the few hours' trip to Whiteville more than the awkward meeting in the prison yard—all barbed wire and hurricane fences and men (mostly Black) in drab, matching duds. This did not look like the prisons I had seen on TV, and none of the men looked especially dangerous, certainly not my daddy. My granddaddy owned a massive station wagon, which to me, at the time, could have been a ship. There was a rumble seat in back; I could have spent hours back there, oblivious to what the grown folk were talking about, watching the world recede, backwards.

Harry struck me as a nice enough fellow, a big, handsome guy with a beard upon a broad and generous face, a big gap in his front teeth so that when he smiled, he made you feel good. Deep voice. He enjoyed *Gilligan's Island*, so we had something to talk about. The fact that he had a wife and a child didn't really register with me until a few years later, when I would visit them and get to know them. The connection between Harry and me I found hard to define. When my schoolmates said "my daddy," they clearly meant something different from what I meant. On the one hand, there was something almost fun about having a father who could be seen as a piratical ne'er-do-well—which was how he starred in my imagination; but on the other, I understood the notion of a certain shame, but even more a regret, a loss, something broken.

That broken feeling was even more pronounced with Clara, who birthed me. Away in Brooklyn, with a husband and two children, she would write me every so often, the letters addressed to "Master Randall Garrett Dunn" (her maiden name; mine until majority). She would visit when she came down to see her family once or twice a year. I always thought she looked like Diana Ross, only better. And she seemed to have a stronger Southern accent than anyone I knew in Duplin County.

To say that our relationship was broken would be too presumptuous. It would presuppose some foundation that was never truly constructed. The older I got, the more estrangement occurred. Missed connections. Misunderstandings. Misreadings. Misfirings. Much missed. Resentment. Indifference. Many things child psychologist Melanie Klein could have a banquet delving into.

One day you look around and the world is somehow different. You have not arrived at the place you set out to achieve, and yet you have arrived somewhere, somehow. The familiar looks foreign and the foreign looks familiar. All that went before has not passed and all that is past remains. It is sentimental to think that the bits and pieces will always align; to think there is some hidden master plan. Destiny requires much more of us than simple trust. Faith is action.

Surely we are made up of all those little battles and small victories, have them at our disposal to learn, if we so choose; and we can, if we are lucky, become better folk for the effort. Or at least that is the hope.

Years later, at the Piggly Wiggly, while home on vacation, I ran into Miss Underwood by the Cap'n Crunch. She seemed positively happy to see me. She had not changed much, and her voice was still clarion loud. She heaped praise upon my head like the cornucopia you see advertised at Thanksgiving time. Her sincerity was a palpable thing. She hugged me, wished me well, requested that I stay in touch ("Don't be a stranger"), and we parted amicably. Over the years, I had thought many hateful, scorn-ridden, nigh-murderous things about her. Now I felt lighter. The place where all that anger had taken up residence felt tingly and pulsed with possibility, like an old house newly renovated and painted and ready for move-in. Forgiveness seems trite to cite. As Marianne Moore once wrote: "Satisfaction is a lowly thing; how pure a thing is joy."

You can cry, cry, cry

I know that you know how to wail

And you can beat your head on the pavement

Until the man comes and throws you in jail.

But don't let the sun catch you cryin'

Cryin' round my front door

You done your baby so dirty

That's why she don't want you no more.

—"Don't Let the Sun Catch You Cryin',"

traditional blues song

Catch the foxes for us, the little foxes that are ruining the vineyards, While our vineyards are in blossom.

—Song of Solomon 2:15 (NAS)

LET US BE FRANK: We Americans currently live in a culture that praises, oddly enough, anti-intellectualism. Serious thinkers don't seem to exist in our popular media, and are certainly not in vogue, unless they have a gimmick, or some spectacular narrative (in which their intellect quickly takes the back seat and is belittled. Cases in point: the type of press and interest given to Stephen Hawking based on his Lou Gehrig's disease instead of the fact that he is one of the most intelligent and productive thinkers ever; the fascination over John Nash not because he is a Nobel Prize–winning mathematician who came up with groundbreaking new game theories but because he was unfortunate enough to suffer from a dramatic case of schizophrenia. Pundits abound like kudzu, and are often amusing and charming, but how often do we see award-winning anthropologists, philosophers, and astrophysicists involved in our daily discourse? The Margaret Meads and Bertrand Russells and Richard Feynmans of our era? As television critic Tom Shales once mused: "Why don't we see more smart people on TV? They would have to marry starlets and get themselves into drunken mischief to find the front page or the thirty-minute omnium-gatherum we call the nightly news."

Accordingly, so much of what passes for racial discussion these days is a perpetuation of a notion of race rooted in the idea of skin color, not culture; it is superstition, not science. Race is an antique way of looking at the world involving brain size, penis size, notions of the primitive ("Soul!"), a vision cloaked in eugenics and faulty statistics (*The Bell Curve*). Negritude doesn't even begin with the color of a Black person's skin; is not dictated by phenotype.

Racism is the handmaiden of race, but it proceeds from a different impulse, a different set of fairy tales. Whereas race is the definition of the Other ("You are different from me in some fundamental way"), racism is the narrative(s) woven around that assertion. Each growing on each, creating, in the mind of the teller and in the ear of the hearer and the reteller, a vision of Self based on the differentiation of the despised Other ("We do not do as they do")—and the Other is always hated for their differences, for not being Us, for having the gall to be alien, and therefore a threat. Threats exist to be feared. Hence what began as an excuse ("We can enslave them, for they are different from us") evolves, and right before the teller's eyes what was once a man transforms into a beast, as in the American South around the turn of the nineteenth century. After a series of rebellions and riots when Black folk let it be known that they were not interested in remaining slaves, they became in the eyes of their masters beasts, dim-witted, child-like creatures, at once sexually rapacious and lazy; a good cook, but in desperate need of Jesus—a creature to be feared.

(Miscegenation and fear. We would do well to remember that so much of the mythical, irrational justification for racism was a fear of some big, Black, exceptionally well-hung beast taking advantage of a pitiful white woman. Anyone will do. Like a boy in Mississippi was feared to have done in 1955. He was only fourteen. Miscegenation is both the cause and the camouflage of the Emmett Till case. The men who murdered him probably did not fancy him some raging rapist about to topple some white woman and pleasure himself upon her. They just didn't like him. They more than didn't like him; he was to them not a boy but an idea, a bogeyman, even at his tender age. Such a response, such a horror-film-like destruction of him, can only be seen as a devotion to a way of seeing the world, a way of seeing the Black man, no matter his age, no matter his potential danger or potential good, no matter his humanity. Fear and miscegenation.)

These dynamics are nothing new, have been the subject of literally tens of thousands of books, not to mention the hundreds of films and television shows. And yet, in the excitement of the Information Age, most of the talk, when it comes to race, seems to be profoundly ignorant of this bedrock of American history and society, and instead clings tenaciously to fairy tales and superstitions, to silliness.

I only watched a few episodes of hip-hop-star-turned-actor-turned-producer Ice Cube's *Black. White.* The six-episode series, which aired on Rupert Murdoch's FX cable network in the winter of 2005, was an update of a legendary experiment from the late 1950s, *Black like Me.*

John Howard Griffin's 1960 memoir will remain one of the most sensational, illuminating, brave and bizarre documents of the last century. A white man who darkens his skin through a medical treatment that turned him a very dark brown, Griffin "passed" for Black in the heart of the Jim Crow South—Louisiana, Mississippi, Alabama, Georgia—in 1959. The strength of the diary he kept is the continuing sense of the writer's awakening to being Black in a white supremacist society, his hypersensitivity to how he was being treated, seen, restricted. He was attendant to observations a person living a lifetime as a Black person might have become inured to.

Forty-six years later we have *Black. White.* A white family, Bruno, Carmen, and their high school daughter Rose, of Santa Monica, California, become Black (cosmetically); while a Black family from Atlanta—Brian, Renee, and their teenaged son Nick—are made up to pass for white folk. The two families share a big Los Angeles house and the emotional sparks ensue. The white father refuses to acknowledge the existence of racism; the Black father's ideas about race seem based too often on social slights; much of the show's overall emphasis is put on fashion and the most superficial aspects of social encounters (treatment in stores, impressions at a job interview, performing—not writing—slam poetry). The results were simply pitiful. It was as if no one in front of the camera, or behind it, had ever heard of A. Philip Randolph or Ida Wells Barnett, Sojourner Truth or Paul Lawrence Dunbar, Malcolm X or Mary McLeod Bethune, Phyllis Wheatley or Ralph Bunche. So many of the squabblings and misunderstandings between the two families were petty, arising from a merely surface understanding of the true cultural forces that cauterize "race in America" and were, most annoyingly, ahistoric. Though I'm sure the intentions of Ice Cube and his co-producers were righteous, this show was ultimately more about etiquette than about racial understanding.

To me this show underscores the larger problem of the dialogue between Black folks and white folks at the turn of the twenty-first century than to shed light on the true issues underlying that debate. Perhaps the fault lies in a culture that finds it difficult to have any sustained and serious discussion about anything difficult and fraught, be it death or health care or abortion. Americans love to skirt, skim the surface, raise voices and holler from a set script, for a short time, but when the topics get sticky we tend to turn the channel and leave the matter for the garbage collectors.

The entire idea of racial profiling, of snap judgments based on what the eye can see, has been (or at least should be) turned on its head in the peculiar and harsh light that shone in the hours and weeks and years since the September 11th strike on America. Can you pick out an Arab by sight? Do most Americans know the difference between a Persian and a Turk? What does a Christian Lebanese look like? There have existed Black Arabs for over a millennium. Can one visually differentiate between a Sunni and a Wahabi, a Bohra or a Druze?

These days what do we talk about, truly, when we talk about race? Silly White Person says to Silly Black Person: "You are Black because you have dark skin. Forget about your skin and you shall be as me." Silly Black Person says to Silly White Person: "My skin is my identity; the sum of my being is bound up with you, White Person, discriminating against me." These exchanges happens daily over the airwaves—without a sense of history, petty, thin, superficial—and they leave one to assume that such exchanges are occurring on the street, in the workplace, in the lobbies of movie theaters. Negritude doesn't even begin with the color of a Black person's skin, nor does it vanish when opposition fades.

Once upon a time, not too very long ago, the debate, the talk, the discussion about race was much more visceral, became physical at times, held more at stake—actually had the ability to change lives. It was not a kaffeeklatsch, not a "gotcha" game of who called whom what at some celebrity party or behind the stage last night at some awards show; it was a roiling, heartfelt, national tussle: People actually wanted to get somewhere. Somewhere new. Somewhere better.

WHO NAMED BOXING the "sweet science"?

Apparently the writer A. J. Liebling took it (he published a collection of essays called *The Sweet Science* in 1956) from an eighteenth-century text by Pierce Egan, *Boxiana*. "The Sweet Science of Bruising" is how he phrased it.

Bruising indeed. I freely admit that I have only tried it one and a half times, and I can testify that one truly does see stars when using one's head to stop an accelerating fist clothed in a leather glove. All our myths, all our dreams, all our fantasies, all our insecurities, all our narrative urges, all our wretchedness is bound up in boxing. The history of our country for the last two centuries features boxing in such a way as to appeal to our waking dreams. A phallocentric exaltation of masculinity, unapologetic and delicious in its bloody glory. Even as we feign disgust at the brutality, we seem to cherish the purity of the violent display and what lies underneath: something ancient and deeply human. We trot out stories about boxing when we are feeling pugnacious, or when we are sentimental about our will to power, our collective ability to overcome. Paintings, sculptures, movies, short stories, novels, even poems about boxing have poured forth like a mighty stream through our American musing about ourselves, our victory of the will.

All sport functions in a similar way: as ritualized battle, a way to fight and die and be reborn to fight again. We identify vicariously with one football team, one tennis player, one golfer. They become our champion. Champions have always functioned as more than mere entertainment, more than a diversion on a Sunday afternoon— too much meaning becomes attached to them. We invest them with something spiritual. Something primal. The madding soccer mobs aren't simply blowing off steam when they riot. Boxers, however, are at once more elegant and more powerful than most sports figures. Their individuality and the nature of their conflict—their physiques, their focus, their personal history—is somehow simply poetic. The stuff of epics.

Very early in the twentieth century—in fact going back to the post–Civil War years, when boxing was nothing more than brawling at the county fair—African Americans found in the sport a metaphor; something even more than a physical manifestation of power: expression, vindication, triumph, something that embodied a destiny, an existential passion play, a prophesy of their place in American society ("The champion of the world is a Black man!"). No one galvanized that narrative power more than Jack Johnson, the first Black boxing king, who won the heavyweight title in 1908 after years of being refused an opportunity to fight the white champions. Audacious even in death, he treated the onlooking world to a type of Bad Negro: arrogant, moneyed, physically unbeatable, nonchalant—even defiant—in his consorting with white women, unbowed before authority.

("That Jackson Johnson is a big, strong, burly, rough darkey, I'll admit, and being champion of the world he may feel that he has a perfect right to run over, beat up, ignore and otherwise make life miserable for others, but he should not forget that Samson ruled the world with all his strength, but his love for a woman got him killed."—Uncle Rad Kees, Indianapolis *Freeman*.)

Johnson emboldened and lifted up the public morale of the rank and file of Black America for a time, and he inspired such ire among the white populace to conjure up the idea of the Great White Hope. ("JACK JOHNSON IS CRUCIFIED FOR HIS RACE. FAMOUS FISTIC GLADIATOR SAILS FOR FRANCE AFTER BEING PERSECUTED IN THE UNITED STATES. WHAT HAS HE DONE?" —Chicago *Defender.*) The drama of his life, something akin to a Greek tragedy interspersed with comedy, is both inspiring and a cautionary tale; it reveals much about how deeply race is woven into the fabric of the American story. The way Johnson toyed with police and governments over his gambling, his choice of women, his outspokenness, rings louder than that of any sport. The life, the event, of Jack Johnson is not only a metaphor for the African in America in the early part of the twentieth century, but also the substance of things hoped for and the evidence of things yet to come.

Perhaps that explains the temptation to look upon the history of African American boxers as some sort of road map, some series of battles through which the Freedom Movement and the charts of Black folks' lives can be interpreted. These men have become symbols, and we try to make them more.

From Joe Louis, who was the antithesis of Johnson, as if he had gazed upon his titanic forebear and attempted to do everything opposite—except that he still won fights. Where Johnson was arrogant, Louis was humble; where Johnson was a spendthrift, he was frugal and enterprising; where Johnson was a philanderer and womanizer and miscegenationist, he was faithful to his Black wife; where Johnson was a gambler and good-time dandy, he was a churchgoing model of rectitude. Joe Louis held the heavyweight title for eleven years, including through World War II, and his most famous, indeed legendary, fight was against the German, Nazi-affiliated Max Schmeling, a curious Great White Hope indeed, in a pitched battle laden with propaganda and awkward, even prescient American pride, especially among the African American community.

In Floyd Patterson, in Sonny Liston, more icons emerged, but then along came Cassius Clay, a good-looking, silver-tongued, seemingly unstoppable fighter, who would dominate the sport the way none other had dominated any sport: The Greatest of All Time, as he liked to say. Moreover, the soon-renamed Muhammad Ali seemed to embody his era with almost Biblical/Koranic flair— going to jail as a conscientious objector, becoming a fixture in the civil rights movement, he bridged the gap from sit-ins and boycotts to entering the boardrooms and lecture halls and sitting anywhere on the bus Black folk damn well felt like sitting.

It is very tempting to use these icons as signposts, as talismans. For, after his successive losses and returns and ultimate retirement and descent into illness, despite the ring being crowded with fox-like, goatlike pretenders—a churlish George Foreman, an irascible Joe Frazier, a clownish Leon Spinks—Ali reigns in the hearts of Americans, of the world.

What then do we make of the less inspiring though no less supremely athletic Evander Holyfield? Of the diasporic wonder of the magnificent Lennox Lewis? And of the terror who is Mike Tyson? All these men are without a doubt phenomenal athletes and arrived at the top of the heap by dint of their will and discipline and intelligence and bodies, but none have captured the world's imagination in any way resembling the way Ali has done; none have achieved that metaphorical leap Jack Johnson or Joe Louis enjoyed, becoming indispensable parts of African American mythology. Has boxing's importance declined so sharply in so short a time? Is it the sport, the athletes, or the people? Sports figures and sports still hold a major sway over a huge swath of America, but the once symbolic power of the boxer to inspire across a number of stories seems to have dimmed. Omens of tribulations to come, perhaps? Or a sign of a certain creeping rot?

Or of the ultimate failure of the cult of personality to do more than inspire? A limit in the ability of one life's narrative to fully contain all the answers to so complex, so damnable a problem as race in America?

I think George Foreman's later public incarnation(s) simply perplexed Mr. Brown, the former boxer and boxing trainer, still in love with the sport, shouting instructions from his armchair to the fighters on TV. He would watch the former terror, now all soft and cuddly and smiling like a teddy bear as he hawked kitchen appliances. Mr. Brown was clearly bemused by Foreman's paradoxical rise and fall and rise to the overweight fortysomething making a fool of himself in the ring for money; to the preacher with five sons all named George; to the gazillionaire salesman of mufflers and an eponymous grill for fat-free cooking. When Mr. Brown's daughter gave me one of those machines for Christmas, he looked upon it as if it were radioactive. It was as if commercial success had somehow tainted another, more exalted, once-glory. Here was a man once so full of Hell that even Satan would have been afraid to go toe-to-toe with him. We remember those indelible images of him in Kinshasa just before the famous Zaire Rumble in the Jungle, under the Midas glare of the truly Satanic Mobutu Sese Seko Kuku Ngbendu Wa Za Banga, with big, tall, titanic Foreman barely verbal, full of an unspeakable and unknown bitterness and a volcanic spite I'm sure he tapped to fuel his bulging musculature.

And yet there is something quintessentially American about the many transformations of George Foreman, especially the canned exuberance he would eventually bring to his role as salesman. He dials an entirely different frequency to wild-haired, legally challenged, slantwise-wordsmith boxing promoter Don King's well-worn phrase: Only in America. Maybe, in many ways, they are the two most apt symbols to chime with the current state of Black America, making friends with the marketplace, an uneasy new comfort with a truly colorless bottom line.

O ye wicked generation, looking for a sign! To be sure, one can't help but be tempted to make hay of such an impressive list of Black heavyweight champions; to take the careers of these latter-day gladiators and read them like a soothsayer reading auguries in the entrails of a slain goat. Tempting because we have used them as symbols for so long, sometimes to great avail, sometimes to our detriment. But you can't rope-a-dope history. You can try for a spell, but sooner or later, even the best will run out of gas. Our arms are too short to box with destiny; we must learn to dance with it.

> Life is like boxing in many unsettling respects. But boxing is only like boxing.
>
> —Joyce Carol Oates

"Niggah, please!"

WHEN I WAS a boy, my two best buddies in the whole entire wide world were my cousins, the identical twins Harry and Larry. Six years my senior, they treated me like a younger brother and I was as slavishly devoted to them as a puppy. Along with them I would witness—and get involved in—boyful mischief that I was either too ignorant or too timid to attempt on my own. They took me riding on their minibikes. They took me along to dogfights. We snuck into places we had no business being in. They took me to swimming holes where they skinny-dipped and (once) fled from alligators. When I was old enough, they took me to my first juke joint. Any trouble available to rambunctious youths in Chinquapin, in our little tract of Duplin County (which, in hindsight, is a pretty small territory and about as tame as it gets) was their province. As the sons of an elementary-schoolteacher mother and a high-school-teacher and church-deacon father, they took as their mandate pulling on trouble's braids. I had a fantastic time being their mascot.

Among the tomfoolery in which they engaged was taking me to R-rated movies (I think for a brief time they, too, were underage—even more the fun). There were only two theaters in Duplin County at the time (now there are none). One was a rickety drive-in in Beulaville. The other was a proper theater in Wallace. This was in the early 1970s and the heyday of so-called blaxploitation pictures. Harry and Larry were particularly fond of Rudy Ray Moore movies—*Dolemite*, with Moore tooling around in his great big Cadillac, dressed in the most outrageous pimp style, loud and obnoxious and obscene. Not the proudest moment in African American comedy, but he probably holds a special place among the raunchiest, most off-color, and most sexually outrageous comedians of them all.

Of these days, one moment sticks in my mind—during those many viewings of *Truck Turner* and *Enter the Dragon* and *Abby* and *Blackenstein* and *Walking Tall* and *Shaft in Africa*—in 1973, while seeing *The Exorcist.* I was ten, and I know now that the experience marked me for life. (In fact, my first novel was about demonic possession, although I only made the *Exorcist* connection years after the book was published.)

Most of the time, the audience in Wallace was practically 100 percent Black. Early on in the movie, a gentleman a few rows in front of us commenced to heckle. He found the movie a bit dull. "This shit ain't scary. I thought this was supposed to be a scary pitcher. I want my money back. Who gives a shit about this little white bitch?"

The movie progressed. Clearly something was amiss with little Regan. When Linda Blair's chalky head spun around and the distinctive voice of Mercedes McCambridge croaked out, our heckling friend fled the theater. Larry (or was it Harry?) made note of the exit: "Bet that nigger's scared now!" The entire audience erupted in hoots and howls—at the scariest part of the movie.

I sing not only of horror flicks, but of Negroes' seeming affection for the word "nigger."

IN 2002, THE HARVARD LAW professor Randall Kennedy published *Nigger: The Strange Career of a Troublesome Word* (which should not be confused with Dick Gregory's classic 1964 autobiography, *Nigger.*) A short book about a heavy topic. Neither proscriptive nor condoning, Professor Kennedy's agenda is to simply put the word in context historically and legally, something rarely done when it comes to the more inflammatory racial thinking. The book created a firestorm, not least by entertaining the idea that there might a legitimate place for the word amongst those who use it most these days: Black people. Kennedy takes us back to the origin of the word, which was merely descriptive at first, and did not become derogatory until the 1830s when it became an intentional insult and much, much more. Throughout the nineteenth century, the meaning of the word "nigger" was unambiguous and accompanied by a threat and some of the worst examples of man's inhumanity to màn in recorded history.

But sometime in the early twentieth century, long before Jim Crow had been plucked and cooked, as an autonomous Black culture, both down on the farm and up in the urban rainforests, arose and took pride in itself, the use of the infamous word took on new timbres. Make no mistake: Black people were still being lynched, red-lined to their side of town, kept out of major universities, barred from voting; the meaning and sting and censoriousness of the word were still very much in effect. But "nigger" among the niggers was increasingly becoming a plastic word, something malleable, useable, manipulable; its poison could be leached out and the vessel, those six letters, used for other work. The matter was never so simple as simply turning the word on its head and making what had been bad into what was now good. Many Black people who employed the word toward other Black people meant it in as wicked a sense as did the most committed Ku Klux Klan member. Yet a multiplicity of meanings emerged, an array of uses, a variety of notes could be played with it. Among the works of the Harlem Renaissance writers are some of the most artful uses of the word—as weapon, as balm, as catnip, as Spanish fly. (Carl van Vechten, a dear white friend of both Zora Neale Hurston—who herself wielded the word like a hatchet in one hand and like a posy in the other—and Langston Hughes, wrote a novel, *Nigger Heaven*, that was much lauded by the niggerati [Hurston's coinage].)

By the 1960s and the Black Power movement, the word was a birdie on a badminton court. Black Panthers, hippies, crackers, governors, some Black Muslims, Pullman car porters, and maids used the word liberally and with moxie, both against and in the service of Black people. But never was it so acrobatically bandied about than during that earlier-mentioned, bizarre yet delicious period of celluloid during the 1970s, ushered in by Melvin Van Peebles's outrageous, obscene, militant, empowering, and industry-changing *Sweet Sweetback's Baadasssss Song.* Characters like Shaft, Black Caesar, Superfly, Cleopatra Jones, Truck Turner, Dolemite, and a peanut gallery of dark faces let fly with enough "niggers" to sink an armada. I look back on those films with mixed feelings, but largely with a sense of nostalgia and glee. Even as a child I was aware of the complexity inherent in the use of the word; I had some glimmer of understanding of the depth of its history, and also a distinct and personal identification with the word when it was used as a term of endearment or a clever tool for self-mockery.

I was a college student in 1982, the year Richard Pryor released the concert film *Live on the Sunset Strip*. This was his first film since his ill-fated freebasing accident of a few years before. Pryor had been, and still is, acknowledged as the King of Comedy, the one after whom everything changed. He had squeezed more juice out of a single word than a Minute Maid factory could from an entire Florida of orange groves, more than anyone in the long line of comics going back to the first Black minstrels, vaudeville, the chitlin circuit, and Amos 'n' Andy ever had before.

But now, in 1982, Richard told us, after a trip to Africa, after nearly meeting his maker, after seeing the beauty of the West African people (who looked so much like people back home), that he had seen the error of his ways and that he was never ever going to use the word "nigger" again. (Curiously enough, that same year, an album of his "greatest hits" hit the stands—*Supernigger.* Maybe the record company had other ideas.)

I had gone to see the movie on a Saturday night with a group of folk, including a good buddy also named Richard, and we talked about the word and Pryor's decision long into the night after the show. I had adored Richard Pryor from my time as a cub and continued to adore him, even if I disagreed with his self-censorship. At nineteen I fretted over what I saw as a largely superficial, even sentimental response to the magnitude of the African diaspora: Black folk are indeed larger than the Middle Passage, and to encounter the vastness of what slavery has wrought—from the West Indies to the Americas to the source of our legacy—is to be shocked, humbled, uplifted, chastened even. But did Pryor really just reach this insight at the age of forty-one? Should we look back upon all his riotous riffs, his cleverness, his genius with a jaundiced eye? All that wordplay? All those times he had unfurled the word "nigger" as if it were Superman's cape? Used it as a knife to white America's carotid artery? Or as a multicolored quilt, stained with blood and warmed with a mother's love to swaddle a homeboy? Can the massive frigates of history so easily be turned about? Are words so fixed in their original meanings that they cannot be reappropriated, recharged, resurrected, born again?

Some would have us believe that the word is so blood-soaked, so scornful, such a thing-maker, that to breathe it is to make a thing out of yourself, to unwittingly buy into the overarching, all-powerful worldview of white supremacy.

Nigger, please.

My friend Richard said he could see both sides. He said he was going to take the matter under advisement.

I knew even then that the use of the word "nigger" was much more complex than what Mr. Pryor had reduced it to. By denying the history the word had among Black folk—the history it had with him—he lost sight of the true genius of Black people. For me, when my lover or my brother or my mother calls me "my nigger," I know exactly what they mean, and it vibrates on levels undreamt of by people who would deny me my humanity.

Meanwhile, in the well-heeled suburbs of Scottsdale and San Diego, Shaker Heights and Scarsdale, any one of us can find a rich white boy who would take it as the highest honor on Earth for you—with great sincerity and at the top of your voice—to greet him as "Nigger."

For some these ideas are abhorrent; for them the word is fixed, eternally, in the actions and mindset of the enemy; for them language is more powerful than the user. But for me the amazing thing is that the word can still be used as a sword. At the end of the day it really is just a word, children. Like *ox* and *sin* and *fear* and *hate* and *catsup* and *peanut butter*. We use language; language does not use us. If, however, the whirligig of talk spins the other way around, you have larger, more pressing problems. Better to worry about sticks and stones, hedge funds and mortgage rates, voter-registration reform and unemployment. Those are the things that can break your bones and hurt you.

As time marched on and the entire American populace—not just the liberals—became more politically correct (i.e., polite), the word suddenly became much more dangerous than it had been even in the '50s or '60s or '70s—the huge irony being that in 1950 if you were Black and someone called you "nigger," you were probably in certain peril, one way or the other. If, in the Internet Age, you are Black and someone calls you "nigger," he or she is (a) deranged, (b) masochistic, (c) another Black person, or (d) a white person trying desperately to be hip.

At the center of this emblematic difference of viewpoint within the Black community, so many years after slavery has ended, with segregation largely squelched, and in a time when we have ourselves an Oprah Winfrey and a Condi Rice—at the center rests a disagreement about the meaning of Blackness. Though I, like my friend Richard, could always see both sides, the argument always seemed weaker than water to me.

The work needing to be done is much deeper than epithets and good manners. The roots of the problems lie in a mutual not-knowing, a mutual belief in Otherness, a reluctance to give voice to deeper mistrusts. In order to bridge that gap, bit by bit, brick by brick, we must dismantle the House of Race. It is not a word; it is a way of thinking. It is not a white thing, or a Black thing; it is an American thing.

Ethnicity, yes; race, forget about it. This shift will continue to be a tricky business, but our changing demographics make the shift not only inevitable but centrally important. It is not difficult to understand that many Americans are sentimental about race, perhaps none more so than Brother Rabbit. The great fear is that by deemphasizing race, not only will identity be lost, but some collective power; and that ancestors will be dishonored or betrayed. Regardless of those misgivings, that great work is already afoot.

Who was it who said that there is nothing more irresistible than an idea whose time has come?

I REMEMBER WITH great fondness the much-beloved and highly sentimental 1971 made-for-television movie *Brian's Song*, with its soaring music ("The Hands of Time") that can still be heard via Muzak in elevators around the world. The film is mawkish without shame: Only under the rubric of sports do you see American alpha males allow themselves to be so tender; to blubber freely and be applauded for it. Only in sports is it okay for big, strong he-men to be sentimental. Based on Gayle Sayers' best-selling memoir *I Am Third*, the movie is an account of the African American football player's friendship with his fellow Chicago Bear, Brian Piccolo, and of Piccolo's death from cancer at age twenty-seven. There is a memorable scene in which Sayers (Billy Dee Williams) and Piccolo (James Caan) are exercising and bonding. At one point, Piccolo, in a moment of mock fury, calls Sayers a nigger. They both collapse into paroxysms of laughter. It is an unforgettable scene, centuries of history and future collapsed into one indelible moment, a recognition of the folly, a leap in openness and vulnerability, an acknowledgment of these two men's fixed realities (in the 1960s) and of their love for each another. It is one of those unusual, raw, true glimpses, amidst the vast detritus of mass media, of humanity and friendship and truth. Today, despite all the *Lethal Weapons* and *Rush Hours* and *Die Hards* and all the other buddy-buddy Black-and-white, Black-and-Asian, and whatever other mixture action pictures, depictions of such genuine and telling interactions remain rare, are hardly ever captured and laid before the masses. You won't see such a thing on broadcast television today, and probably not on cable either.

MR. JOHN W. BROWN lost his eyesight just before he died. I think we refused to admit it; he admitted to some difficulty in seeing, but he managed to get around and even sat before the television, only asking now and again for us to tell him about what was going on. But once he was in the hospital, a note over his bed read *Patient is blind*. Many illusions began to fade with that, along with a certain degree of magical thinking.

He suffered from a rare vascular disorder. It had originally stricken him fourteen years before, and had actually killed him, clinically. But he had been revived and, in the fullness of time, he regained almost full health, save the loss of a thumb due to the vascular damage.

The loss of eyesight had been particularly galling, for Mr. Brown had been an avid reader. If my bookishness had struck most of the community as queer and a waste of time, I could always rely on him as a champion. Always each day began with the newspaper and a prolonged discussion about those idiots in Washington. I had delighted so much in his delight in the novel *Jaws* and sharks that in later years I would try to find more books for him featuring sharks. And books about sports figures. I remember his relish of a biography of Jackie Robinson that his daughter had given him for Christmas. The ensuing lectures about Robinson (whom he had seen from the stands), about segregation, about the dignity and symbolism and responsibility of Black athletes, could literally go on for hours.

His eyesight had been threatened once before, but in a different way.

That early spring, when the Pile* was almost worn down. By this time I knew it would soon be history. Had it been possible, I would

---

* In an earlier chapter of *The Fire This Time*, from which this essay is taken, Kenan describes how his great-aunt's daughter Edythe and her husband Mr. Brown built a house in Chinquapin, in back of which was a half acre covered with "tree stumps and immature trees and woodland refuse, high and tangled, dark and forbidding—but at the same time lush and wild. . . . To my pre-teen eyes the idea of the Pile, as we came to call it, was a permanence . . . [that] would clearly take years if not eons to remove." Yet "every day after school I would join [Mr. Brown]. As his house slowly took shape, he would be out back, every day, chopping, sawing, digging, burning, burning, burning."

have been out there that day alongside Mr. Brown, digging, chopping, burning. I loved the smell of the many fires he kept burning to get rid of the debris.

He was alone when the thorn from a bush caught his eye. The cut was deep. A true puncture. So deep in fact that the vitreous fluid quickly drained out. The eye collapsed. Edythe rushed him to the hospital in Kinston. Who knew that, if properly stitched, an eyeball will reinflate like a beach ball?

The eye patch made him look very like a pirate (my boyhood obsession), and he joked about the entire affair, but it was tinged with gravitas. No one wants to lose an eye.

Soon he was back to work.

———————

AS SIMPLE AS it seems, it's all about learning how to see.

13

Notes Toward
an Essay on
Imagining Thomas
Jefferson Watching
a Performance
of the Musical
Hamilton

At elegant gatherings and august meetings, I often scan the room and wonder aloud why I am, as people like myself are often given to ask, the Only Negro in the Room, or ONR, as Ta-Nehisi Coates and Natasha Trethewey have been known to note. Surely Black intellectuals are central to these types of inquiries, surely Black writers and artists and thinkers have something to say in the matter. And yet our involvement tends to be relegated to the margins. And our attendance tends to be poor. Our work finds its way into the discussion, 'tis true. But to quote from the landmark 1965 play by Douglas Turner Ward, *A Day of Absence*: "Where the negras at?"

I am not foreign to these gatherings; in fact, I usually have a front-row seat. This makes sense, as I have never run away from my ur-Southern rural roots or my African American heritage; in fact, for better or worse, I've run toward it, even when running away from it. I've gladly embraced it, even when it pricked me with thorns. I chose to think about and study these matters as if they matter.

No one articulated this better to me than Charles Rowell, the founder and editor of *Callaloo*, the preeminent journal of African American arts and letters. We were in Charlottesville, approaching the main and iconic building of Monticello, and we were discussing the recent hubbub surrounding the Jefferson family acknowledging their Black cousins. And Charles was talking about the very subject about which we are still concerned today: Southernness. Charles turned to me and said, "Of course we have absolutely no investment in this argument. We know the truth of the matter. We always knew the truth of the matter. We are the South."

For people steeped in the study of the African American and the African in America, anxiety about the definition of "Southern" becomes tertiary at best because it is *primary*. What has been so vividly apparent about the South was nestled close to us long before Jim Crow caused so many of us to leave the South; those great many of us who have returned over the last several decades know it intimately. We knew we were going back to what Albert Murray dubbed "South to a Very Old Place." We were returning home.

The irony of Charles Rowell educating me, hipping me to this point on the grounds of Monticello has resonated with me over the years more and more powerfully as I move away from that date in 1992. Black folk and white folk acknowledge with ease the centrality of Thomas Jefferson and his grand folly on that high hill in Virginia as being at the center of the Making of Americans, to steal from Gertrude Stein—central not only as a symbol of the industry and brilliance of the Founding Fathers but also as a material signifier of the sin and horror and mixing of blood and culture and souls. The hearth of our nation as well as its heart. So much of what makes the South "South" is embodied in that place and its history, even in its decline and resurrection, like Scarlett O'Hara and Tara. So much masking, so much denial, so much buried truth, while so much was always apparent to Black folk.

No, brothers and sisters, this anxiety over the South is not experienced by Black folk in the same way, to the same degree, because we know that Southernness is inextricably bound to Blackness. During the Great Migrations, Southernness traveled. It traveled up on the Chickenbone Special to Washington and Baltimore and, yes, Harlem, sweet, sweet Harlem. It traveled up the Mississippi to Detroit and Gary and that great hog butcher to the world, Chicago. It traveled out west from Louisiana and Texas to Los Angeles and San Francisco. I am not the first to point out that Black neighborhoods in these great metropolises are hotbeds of Southernness. Go to Crenshaw Boulevard in Los Angeles, go to the South Side of Chicago, go and see for yourself.

In 1912, the famous Swiss psychologist Carl Jung said in an interview with the *New York Times* (TRIGGER WARNING: he said some stuff that many of us today would consider racist and imperialist and just plain wicked):

> In America the Indians do not influence you now; they have fallen back before your power, and they are very few. They influenced your ancestors. You, to-day, are influenced by the negro race, which not so long ago had to call you master. In the North the negro's present influence is not great. In the South, where they are not given opportunities equal to the white race, their influence is very great. They are really in control.

I notice that your Southerners speak with the negro accent; your women are coming to walk more and more like the negro. In the South I find what they call sentiment and chivalry and romance to be the covering of cruelty. Cruelty and chivalry are another pair of opposites. The Southerners treat one another very courteously, but they treat the negro as they would treat their own unconscious mind if they know what was in it. When I see a man in a savage rage with something outside himself, I know that he is, in reality, wanting to be savage toward his own unconscious self.

Thus sayeth Carl Jung in 1912.

This is usually the point where someone wants to interrupt me and say, Mr. Brother, Professor Kenan, sir, surely you are forgetting all the poor, yeomen white men and women who toiled and bled in the South, who fought in the War of Northern Aggression, who are the proud, true, often forgotten cornerstone of the South. Not the ones who owned the plantations and the land and the cotton mills and the slaves, but the humble, the salt of the earth. Have you forgotten us?

No. I ain't forgot y'all.

I could bore you at this point with a long disquisition on Toni Morrison's 1992 book-length essay *Playing in the Dark*, where she makes a strong case for the presence of what she calls "Africanism" throughout American literature, finding it where others saw (see) no Black folk. And I could make a case for the same being true throughout Southern letters. I find it ironic that Morrison's family left Alabama, literally, in the dead of night, fleeing an unjust share-cropping situation, in fear for life and limb, and that she grew up in Lorain, Ohio, and yet her work is often cited as the epitome of Southern literature, alongside her heroes, Faulkner and Welty.

As I said, Black folk have always known these things as bedrock truths. And for us to have anxiety about a change in the power structure—something about which we've been anxious for over two hundred years—is to have anxiety about the infrastructure, not the mythology and romance that surrounds that infrastructure.

I know these assertions make a lot of folk uncomfortable—especially, primarily, a lot of white folk. "Uncomfortable" is the euphemism we use, because we all tend to be polite. But as I heard one UNC professor recently say in a meeting, "My students hate to talk about race. They just hate it." People are afraid of saying the wrong thing. People are afraid of being attacked for an innocent comment, for having an opinion. They want to say: "Hey, man, this is your thing, this ain't my thing." They want to say: "My name is Bess, and I ain't in this mess." When, in truth, this mess is our mess. Just as when you inherit a great fortune, you are the beneficiary and it becomes your joy and your responsibility, when you inherit a conundrum, it is your burden and your responsibility to manage it.

In truth, Black folk do harbor one primary anxiety about this abiding self-consciousness toward Southernness, and that worry swirls about the discussion of food. Food was the only province in which the African American contribution has not been thoroughly muted, a place where white Southerners have rushed to acknowledge the African on their plate, the okra and peanut and the rice; it's a place where a shared humanity and culture have been readily acknowledged, up to a point. Food was seen as soft, domestic, even feminine—as if that automatically made it less-than, not so very important. But now, when Whole Foods acknowledges collard greens as the "*new* Super Food" and so much "rediscovery" of Southern food actively erases Black faces, Black folk are going to have a problem with that.

So I imagine the third president of these United States, sitting in the second row of the Richard Rodgers Theatre, watching a Black man play George Washington, a Latino playing Lafayette, and a Black man playing himself, Thomas Jefferson, primary author of the Declaration of Independence. In this play, written by a Nuyorican, he comes off as a preening, brilliant, conniving, self-centered thug.

In fact, I think, oddly, that the Master of Monticello might very much sympathize with iconic African American writer Ishmael Reed's jeremiad against *Hamilton*: "It sort of distracts from the racism of the white historical characters." Reed wrote in *CounterPunch* (August 21, 2015), "The producers of this profit-hungry production are using the slave's language: Rock and Roll, Rap and Hip Hop to romanticize the careers of kidnappers and murderers." His 2018 Off-Broadway play, *The Haunting of Lin-Manuel Miranda*, lacerates the playwright for not taking the "Founding Fathers" to task for the institution of slavery, for romanticizing the largest slaveholding family in the colony of New York, the Schuylers, and for essentially Black-and-brown-washing the true, not-so-secret history of the United States.

Perhaps the second Southern president would look upon all this hubbub with bemusement and mirth. Maybe he would look upon the Black Washington and Jefferson and brown Hamilton as a sort of folly. (A folly different from Reed's, but folly nonetheless.) I think he would be confronted with what he let a-loose in the somewhat still New World. Perhaps he'd admire this portrayal as tough and clever. (I like to think the music would transport him, though.) But he'd have to acknowledge that the soul of his country is Southern; the soul of his country is Black.

The South—America—has always been multicultural, multiethnic. The myth of a monolithic South that too many hold near and dear was always just that: a myth. For the last decade, I've been preaching up the idea of pluralism. The color of our future is not white, nor is it Black and white; it is a rainbow. All those rooms full of people yet underpopulated by people of color are now under the clock—their time is running out. The eighteenth-century Enlightenment idea is simply greater than those cats who met in Philadelphia two centuries ago, greater than us, indeed. I love that the eminent historian James MacGregor Burns persisted in calling us "the American Experiment." I prefer to think of the South as a work in progress.

To paraphrase the musical *Hamilton*: "There's a million things we haven't done. Just you wait, just you wait."

14

The Many Lives of Eartha Kitt

OR, TAKING THE GIRL OUT OF THE SOUTH

I. THE LADIES WHO LUNCH

"Mr. President," I said, "what are we to do about delinquent
parents—those who have to work and are too busy to look after
their children? Don't you think it might be more appropriate
for the children to ask, 'Parents, where are you?' Because taxes
are so heavy, both parents often have to work and are forced to
leave their children alone."

"We have just passed a Social Security bill that allots millions
of dollars for day-care centers," the President replied. . . .

"But what are we going to do?" I asked.

"That's something for you women to discuss here," the
President said. Then someone took his arm and whisked him
out of the dining room.

—Eartha Kitt, *Alone with Me*

E artha Kitt made Lady Bird Johnson cry. Or so the story goes.
When? January 1968. Where? The White House. The event?
The Women Doers' Luncheon, hosted by the First Lady of the

United States. Fifty prominent women gathered together to discuss the question, "Why is there so much juvenile delinquency in the streets of America?"

Kitt writes about this life-changing event twice in great detail. She had been working with a group of young people in urban Washington, The Rebels Without a Cause, taking kids off the street, putting them to work doing community service and putting on shows. In recognition of her work, Congressmen Adam Clayton Powell Jr. and Roman Conrad Pucinski put her name forth to attend the special luncheon. Kitt says that initially she didn't want to go, but the First Lady's secretary kept insisting. Eartha relented and jetted from Beverly Hills to DC to a hotel to a limo to the White House. She came to regret that trip.

After cooling her heels with the Secret Service (something she resented, as the rest of the guests were attending a pre-luncheon reception), she finally was allowed to join the illustrious group. In Lady Bird Johnson's account, Kitt was late. She also says that Kitt smoked too much. Kitt took umbrage at both implications.

Though he was not on the schedule, it was a foregone conclusion that Lyndon Baines Johnson would make an appearance. "It was Hollywood time in Washington," Kitt writes. Very early into the luncheon he popped in, and, in Kitt's account, launched into platitudinous comments, ("I want you to go back to your communities and tell them what a great family you have in the White House"). He lauded his own efforts with Social Security reforms. Kitt found his words banal. She raised her hand. She dared ask the President of the United States what he was going to do for working people. By all accounts the president was taken aback and not pleased with the unscripted questioning.

She added lemon to the wound, later, during the actual luncheon. Kitt doesn't remember the menu, but she remembers how much the talk annoyed her, increasingly. She wanted to discuss the

THE MANY LIVES OF EARTHA KITT   163

working poor, the problem of educating children, the Vietnam War, but more and more the ladies who lunched wanted to praise Lady Bird's American Beautification Project. Eartha kept raising her hand, hoping to steer the conversation back to delinquency. The First Lady asked that Miss Kitt wait her turn. Finally it was Eartha's chance to speak. "I think we have missed out on something here today," she said:

> I thought the question was why there is so much juvenile delinquency on the streets of America . . . Not how to beautify America, but how to prevent the kids from getting into trouble when they don't understand why one or other of us parents are not there to console them in the time of need.

She went on to talk about the dilemma of America's involvement in the Southeast Asian conflict, about how young men felt the country's overseas war was "unAmerican." "This is one of the reasons the boys smoke pot, too, to sleep away their frustrations. Vietnam is the main reason we are having trouble with the youth of America." Kitt remembers that many of the women bowed their heads in embarrassment.

After Kitt yielded the floor, Lady Bird Johnson rather famously said: "Just because there is a war going on, I see no reason to be uncivilized." Kitt remembers no tears.

Upon returning to her hotel, hearing on the radio how she had offended the First Lady, her LA friends and family insisted she leave Washington immediately. A Black Panther escorted her to the airport and handed her a pair of black eyeshades.

IN THE MEANTIME, President Johnson was making it obvious to all the media that I was out of favour. He didn't want to see my face anywhere—ever. Out of sight, out of mind, out of work. Here started the erasing of Eartha Kitt. . . . I had in my hand contracts for Los Angeles, Las Vegas, Detroit, Chicago, but it made no difference—all were cancelled.

—Eartha Kitt, *I'm Still Here*

II. EARTHA KITT: SUPERHERO

The first time I saw Eartha Kitt (on television), the first time I became aware of her as a Force of Nature—and, let's face it, that is exactly how she hits the brain—of course I did not think of her as "Southern." In fact Southernness was the farthest thing from my mind. Nothing about her was what I associated with my preteen understanding of the Black South: the accent, the rural nature, the agriculture and livestock, the Protestant, Hallelujah churches, the women in big hats, men in coveralls riding tractors, ham hocks and collard greens, and the ominous and ever-present racial firestorms that still flared up in the 1970s of my youth. No. Here was this feline entity, this world-weary sophisticate; from her ravishing mouth emerged this elegant, clipped, oh-so-precise diction that would make even the Queen of England sound rude, and with a bearing even more regal in her Hermès and Oscar de la Renta and Carolina Herrera. And that purr, her sonic secret weapon; disarming, yes, but something more, a warning, an embrace of her female power; yes, she was catlike, but more lioness than house cat. Her acting, her singing, her persona. Yes, she played with the gold-digger image, the sexually promiscuous and free "vamp," but like Mae West and Shirley MacLaine and Josephine Baker before her, she deconstructed the gold-digger archetype, remade it as a self-starting, self-stopping, self-justifying powerhouse. In fact I would go so far as to say she became a feminist icon long before *Feminist Mystique* rhetoric; surely she led her life that way. No, there was nothing overtly Southern about Eartha Kitt as I saw her on the talk shows and variety hours, singing her seductive songs around a potentially sexy Santa Claus. But the South was not only the crucible that formed her, but the sinew in her style.

She began as a dancer in the 1940s, already singular in looks and style, with a jaded affect, an air of entitlement, deliciously louche at the ripe old age of twenty-two. She would go on to become one of the twentieth century's great triple threats—singer, dancer, actor—and a lot more. Broadway, movies, television, and a recording career that lasted more than five decades. She was one of the first African Americans internationally recognized as a sex symbol and pinup girl (after Lena Horne during WWII). Her stage style clearly set the template for later American chanteuses the likes of Diana Ross, Janet Jackson, Madonna—"I was the original Material Girl," Kitt once quipped. "C'est si bon," "Love for Sale," and "Santa Baby," early hits, remain popular emblems of the American popular music lexicon. The wife to three wealthy (white) men, including a banking heir and a cosmetics magnate, and once involved in a rather complicated relationship with Orson Welles (who famously bit her lip, drawing blood, during an on-stage kiss, because, he said, he was overwhelmed by her sexual energy), she was no stranger to luxury, and wore her fame like a mink stole. Welles once called her "the most exciting woman alive." Nonetheless she seemed to enjoy making fun of her over-the-top image even from the beginning, finally embracing, like the great Mae West, a campy persona and overheated predator stature. And yet she could still say with a straight face, and somewhat convincingly: "I'm a dirt person. I trust the dirt. I don't trust diamonds and gold."

She spoke four languages and sang in seven. She was the first Black Catwoman, thirty-eight years before Halle Berry. She was nominated for three Tonys and won a Grammy in 1994. She wrote three autobiographies, *Thursday's Child* (1956), *Alone with Me*

(1976), *I'm Still Here: Confessions of a Sex Kitten* (1989), and, in her mid-seventies, a self-help book about beauty, *Rejuvenate! It's Never Too Late* (2001). Kitt marched and worked throughout the 1960s on the front lines of the civil rights movement, at times alongside Dr. Martin Luther King Jr. And she embraced her gay followers as she grew older, speaking no-nonsense advocacy for gay rights and same-sex marriage. She would also dedicate time to UNICEF on behalf of homeless children.

I can hear a chorus of dyed-in-the-wool feminist voices singing that Kitt's brand of feminine wile is not power at all, but merely the capitulation to and manipulation of male power. But I would caution them to think on the time, and to think on the subversive nature of this sort of power; it is un-ironic, ironic, practical, effective. Moreover, as I see it, in most ways, the lady won, in the end. The price was mighty high, but nobody gets to ride for free.

Years later I would come to appreciate that this woman became what she was primarily because she was a Southerner, not despite her Southern origins. Kitt harked back to another vision of the South that was outward-looking, not in love with its own provincialism, a type of Southerner who neither apologizes for her origins nor allows those roots to hold her back. Kitt never seemed to misrepresent where she came from, or shun it, but rather her humble Southern beginnings became a significant part of her myth: She wanted people to know she started dirt poor in the Jim Crow South. As with Booker T. Washington, the rise was the best part of the story. Like Leontyne Price (Mississippi) or Jessye Norman (Georgia) or Ella Fitzgerald (Virginia) or Odetta (Alabama) or Tina Turner (Tennessee), Kitt in fact was representative of a long line of Southern artistes who, in the face of white supremacy, used intellect, style, and enterprise to achieve, to overcome. *Ain't nobody gonna hold her body down.*

It is rather easy for us now to look back upon her, now with our Audra McDonalds and Beyoncés and Viola Davises, and to forget the atmosphere in which this brown-skinned woman rose to the very high rungs of international entertainment. How she not only defied the odds but persevered, decade after decade, in the face of not only segregation and overt racism but also in the face of pissing off some extremely powerful people, one being, oddly and paradoxically, one of our great civil rights reforming presidents. Later in life when Kitt sang Sondheim's *Follies* number, "I'm Still Here," the tune carried a deeper resonance than for most.

For me there was a lesson in Miss Kitt and how she negotiated the shoals of race and region and gender and the existential problem of being. Her way was full of electricity and light and excitement. And style. And humor. Always humor: the great antidote to the blues of being a human being.

III. "YELLA GAL"

Her life story alone belongs to another era, pre-industrial revolution, more fitting to a Dickens novel, very like the unsinkable Becky Sharp from William Makepeace Thackeray's *Vanity Fair*; Eartha Kitt out—Moll Flanders Daniel Defoe's *Moll Flanders*.

Consider: Born in the isolated hamlet of North, South Carolina, in 1927. Orangeburg County. A cotton plantation. Eartha Mae Keith came to consciousness as the daughter of Anna Mae Riley, whom she thought to be her mother. Of course. She worked in cotton fields, she would: "[c]lean the house, feed the pigs, let the cow out of pasture, let the chickens out of their coops, feed them." She writes of that time:

This being a full-time job, I had very little if any time to play until Sundays, which I spent hiding under the house because most of the time visitors came over on the Sabbath and, in order for them not to make fun of me, I thought it better to stay out of everyone's sight.

When Eartha was eight, Anna Mae fell in with a man who wanted to make her his wife, but he wanted nothing to do with a "yella" skinned child. So Eartha Mae lived with another family, ("the stern woman"), a semi-orphan, until her Anna Mae died not long after in childbirth.

Directly Eartha was sent to New York to live with a woman she initially thought to be her aunt Mamie Kitt, who was part Black and part Cherokee like her "mother." By and by, Eartha would discover, rather dramatically, that Mamie was in fact her mother. Eartha had been the child of trauma: Her mother had been raped by a white man. His identity was never known to Kitt. Her relationship with Mamie did not go well. Mamie abused and beat young Eartha. At one point Mamie stopped feeding Eartha altogether. (Mamie: "You're nothing but a no-good. I knew I shouldn't have brought you up here. I should have left you down South to pick cotton like the rest of them, for the rest of your life. . . . I'm tired of having to look out for you. You don't know how much agony you've caused me, having to feed you and clothe you. . . .") Eartha ran away often, literally depending on the kindness of strangers, and took odd jobs and sometimes slept on roofs and subways. Mamie terrified her. *Thursday's Child*, the first account of this Cinderella childhood, which is written in spare, precise, direct style, reads like a Grimms' fairy story. *Thursday's child has far to go.*

WHERE DOES ONE go from such an origin? Surely to become a superhero.

IV. "I LOOOOOOVE TO READ!"

I had gotten in trouble with my friend Sheila Anderson when, back in 1989, in New York City, all full of excitement and self-important retro-cool, I insisted we go see Miss Peggy Lee perform. Sheila first said, "Is she still living?" But she reluctantly agreed to accompany me. It would be a lark, she said. Alas, at the last minute, I had to cancel on her—why, I don't remember—but she wound up taking a friend. To this day Sheila stills rib me about the event, and the wonderful, still (barely) living Peggy Lee's performance. Sheila enjoyed it, in the end, but blamed me on her being the youngest woman in the audience at the Rainbow Room that night. And the only Black woman.

About a year later, when I saw that Eartha Kitt was performing at a new cabaret in Chelsea, and was having an early Sunday show, I knew I had to go. For years, she had appeared at the Carlyle, one of those Upper East Side New York landmarks that has appeared in Woody Allen movies more often than the Carnegie Deli, known for its long association with performers such as Bobby Short and Rosemary Clooney and Barbara Cook. For some reason, I had never ventured yonder to see her, perhaps intimidated by the posh reputation.

But this time I called up a bunch of friends—Sheila first, of course. I have no idea how I convinced them; perhaps I didn't need to do much selling, but the next Sunday afternoon our small troupe marched to the matinee: me, Sheila, and four other friends.

We arrived at the newly styled Ballroom, with rows and rows of tables, a stage with black-velvet teasers and tormentors, a bar manned by a tuxedo-wearing bartender. Though we were not that early, we six were the only folk there other than the band, which was already tuning and warming up. When two o'clock rolled around, we were the entire audience. But the show went on. The band struck up a driving tune. Eartha Mae Kitt emerged, begowned, glittering, her smile great big and inviting.

Whether or not she was disappointed to be playing to a room of six (how could she not be?), she certainly never let on. After all, the woman was a consummate professional. She sang as if she were singing to a packed house, full of electricity and humor and sexual brio, gyrating and thrusting and gesturing in a manner that conjured up Paris and Berlin and Rome and Istanbul. She sang many of her old hits, a number of standards reinterpreted with her signature growl and purr and the imprint of her singular diction. Her humor was a seductive thing, and before long she was literally talking to us between songs, her patter inclusive and seductive and funny. She did two sets and an encore. All six of us were on our feet and ecstatic and utterly charmed at the end.

After she left the stage, and we were preparing to go, a gentleman approached.

"Miss Kitt would like to know if you would like to join her in her dressing room."

I had visited Lena Horne once backstage after a performance in London. She was regal. She smiled when I told her I was from North Carolina. "Like my friend Ava," Miss Horne said to me.

But with Eartha it was like visiting an aunt, homey and downhome. She had somehow retained that Southern sense of how to make strangers feel instantly at home. I think she even offered us something to drink. We politely declined. The cliché is "Southern hospitality," but there is something more to the art. To be sure, Southerners have no monopoly on hospitality, but there is a familial tone, a self-effacing spirit of graciousness that I mark as being particularly Southern. Her head was wrapped, she was dressed casually and comfortably in tan. She asked many questions about us and our jobs. She thanked us for coming to see her. She talked about how she loved being back in Connecticut and in the country, and how much she enjoyed walking.

When Sheila told Miss Kitt that I was a writer (I was much too bashful to admit to any such activity), Eartha Mae Kitt cooed and clasped my hand. "I loooooove to read," she purred.

V. WHERE DID YOU COME FROM?

Eartha Kitt was not sui generis. With such women it is quite easy—and lazy—to explain her away as a sport of nature. Of course there is the raw material, the physical beauty, the voice, the intelligence, the ambition. But at sixteen, Eartha met one of her most important mentors: Katherine Dunham.

Dunham (1909–2006) was an anthropologist, dancer, choreographer, songwriter, activist, and one of the most beautiful prose stylists of the twentieth century. Her 1959 third-person memoir, *A Touch of Innocence*, is a much-neglected classic. But certainly best remembered for her world-renowned and supremely influential dance company, Dunham was known as the Matriarch and Queen Mother of Black Dance, or simply Katherine the Great. James Dean, Shelley Winters, Sidney Poitier, Warren Beatty, Marlon Brando, Charles Mingus all studied with her at various points in their development. Eartha Mae Kitt joined the Dunham Dance Company in 1943 and danced with the company until 1948. "Katherine Dunham had created a better world for many of us, at the same time making the path easier for those who had guts enough to follow."

But make no mistake: Dunham was no fairy godmother: She was as tough as nails:

> I wanted to talk to her many times—ask questions, say what
> I felt to her, but I was afraid to get too close. She was not
> the kind of person one walks right up to and buttonholes. I

couldn't really reach her, but I got sensitivity from her. A spiritual kind of feeling, like a wave being received, but uneven. Our communication was always rough.

Kitt remained grateful to Dunham, but was never sentimental about the difficult woman who never let her forget what Eartha owed her.

There is something definitely fairy-tale-like about Kitt's rise after her stay with Dunham, meteoric to be true, but also irresistible and seemingly inevitable. Stepping out on her own to become a cabaret singer in Paris. Quickly perfecting her own style: a little Piaf, a little Dietrich, a little Baker, and, if you listen closely, subtly, nuanced, alongside the purr, woven into the interstices of her crisp pronunciation ("vaguely foreign" the *New York Times* once wrote), you will find something of South Carolina: an aural warmth, a field hand's grit, a sense of self-invention known most keenly by those with little to lose and much to gain. Her first recordings, in English, in French, in Turkish, laid the foundation of this created self, something of which Benjamin Franklin and Walt Whitman and Gertrude Stein would have approved; something quintessentially American. Her messy relationship with Orson Welles began in 1950 when he launched her on stage as Helen of Troy in his *Faust*, first in France and later in Germany. The Germans went nuts over Eartha.

Back in New York, she became a member of another illustrious troupe of now-and-future stars—including Carol Lawrence, Alice Ghostley, Paul Lynde, and Mel Brooks. *New Faces of 1952* ran on Broadway for 365 performances and was followed by a 1954 movie, *New Faces*, in which Eartha Kitt performed. "Monotonous." "Uska Dara." "C'est si bon." She was now truly famous. Her monster hit "Santa Baby" was released in 1953. During the 1950s, she would appear in films alongside Sidney Poitier and Sammy Davis Jr. and Nat King Cole. She won her first Emmy for a guest spot on *I Spy* in

1965. And the next year she took the role that meant so very much to me as a little boy.

> "Well, you see officer, I'm Eartha Kitt, and I have to drive a manual by eight o'clock this morning because I'm playing Cat-woman in the Batman series and this was the only time I had to learn. You should see the car they are making me drive. It's absolutely crazy! The car has cat ears and cat eyes for the front lights and a wishbone for a steering wheel, and even whiskers . . ." I went on like a nervous cat in heat.
>
> "Okay, okay, okay. Catwoman, eh? . . . All right, Miss Kitt, you can go. My eight-year-old son would never forgive me if I told him I gave Catwoman a ticket."
>
> —Eartha Kitt, *I'm Still Here*

VI. CATWOMAN

I am not proud to admit that Batman takes up a great deal of the real estate of my mind. Which is not to say that Faulkner and Morrison and Mishima and Kurosawa don't take up a lot of space, but Bob Kane's 1939 creation has always had an enormous emotional purchase on me. For better or worse. Call it idealism. Call it latent altruism. Call it the spirit of a boy who refuses to grow up and who still believes a man in a cape can always save the day.

As a child of the '60s and '70s, of course my initial introduction to the Caped Crusader was the campy CBS confection that originally aired between 1966 and 1968, starring Adam West and Burt Ward (I would spend most of the rest of my life saying evil things about this incarnation, once I came upon the "hip" Detective Comics as I grew older and found a Batman more skulking and self-involved and morose than Spider-Man on a bad day.) This is where I first met Miss Kitt.

She was the third Catwoman, after Julie Newmar and Lee Meriwether. Even now I find it difficult to believe that she only appeared in three episodes. O but what a joy it was to see this weird, wild, powerful, sexy Black woman, albeit a villain, in my favorite of programs. There was nothing subtle about my fascination and adulation—there were so few Black people on TV! Certainly none on television for kids. And not only was she Black, but she was totally, awesomely, amazingly, *cool!* Moreover, let's face it, the supervillains on Batman were never really evil. They weren't even that bad. Misguided misfits looking for attention. But Catwoman had a little something extra: a little something-something going with Batman, *often saving his life.* As far as I was concerned, she was a superhero too.

(I find it greatly amusing now, to look back at a TV guest spot Kitt did in 1962. She looks to be no older than twelve years old, and is being shot from below, in a close frame, like a girl at play, confidential. The song, "I Want to be Evil" [Judson/Taylor] would be more precisely titled "I Want to Be Mischievous," for the lyrics don't strike one as more than that of a playful, strong spirit wanting to break free of convention—"I wanna sing songs like the guy who cries / I wanna be horrid, I wanna drink booze." You can never imagine such a cherubic creature to be evil. But a trickster? You bet. A supreme trickster, which is exactly what Eartha Kitt was.)

VII. COME OUT OF THE WILDERNESS

Eartha wandered in the wilderness of de facto exile for close to a decade after the infamous Johnson luncheon. That she was blacklisted was not a matter of imagination or paranoia. LBJ really did see to it that she didn't get work. Johnson was feared and powerful, and few were willing to cross him merely to put a great talent to work. She fell back on her cabaret act, singing in night clubs throughout Europe and Africa and Asia. I remember a photo essay about her in *Ebony* magazine, back in the 1970s, touring apartheid-shackled South Africa. She was elegantly dressed and riding in limousines, grim-visaged and talking on telephones in the back seat, greeting crowds who came out to see her, a sharp contrast with the shanty-towns and ill-clad Africans whose plight she had come to expose. This was the first glimmer I had of Catwoman's social activism.

Those were hard and lonely years, though she seemed to endure in style and with a flourish.

Two things heralded her comeback: In 1978 she was invited to the Carter White House, and she returned to Broadway in an all-Black remake of the musical *Kismet*, redubbed *Timbuktu!* Kitt received a Tony nomination. It was as if to say, I'm Still Here.

THERE SHE WAS again in 1984. I was graduating from college, going to gay bars for the first time. Videos smiled down on the sweaty, grinding young men. Disco was supposedly dead, but it danced after dark in such quarters. There came the telltale growl through the speakers, accompanied by the bump-bump beat, and there, on the giant screen, stood a vintage Eartha Kitt, cigarette-holder in hand, on the balcony of some Monaco palace, some Swiss chalet bedroom, the foyer of some Nice villa, now full-on camp, her world-weariness no longer an act, but no less tongue in cheek. "Where Is My Man" was a funky and curious hit; a wry and wicked send-up of her Material Girl image ("Where is my baby? When will he start / to use his Visa / Right to my heart . . ."). I never found her adamant play with the gender intersections of money, materialism, sex, lust, desire, and power to be frivolous, but always a biting critique. In fact there was something refresh-ing about her honesty, if, in fact, she bought into this persona. And whether or not she did, the persona itself spoke to elements in the society most often left acknowledged but unexamined.

Call me naive, but I believe she knew exactly what she was doing. (I shan't discuss her unfortunate foray with the Pet Shop Boys and "Cha Cha Heels," which is a bit painful to hear. The Pet Shop Boys were out of their depth when they sought to produce Miss Kitt; their style itself is a form of flat-footed irony—it gave EK nowhere to go.)

———————

SURELY BEING EARTHA KITT had to be a lonely gig sometimes. Surely she had to sometimes dream of escape. But that is my fantasy, my empathy. Her last marriage ended in divorce in 1965, but she had her daughter, Kitty, and later grandchildren, all of whom she seemed to adore, to lavish with the love and care she failed to receive as a child. And there were the fans and the social work in which she seemed to be constantly engaged. Perhaps she had more than enough. Or, as the comedian Steven Wright once said: "You can't have everything. Where would you put it?"

———————

WAS EARTHA KITT a great singer? I think so. Her instrument was not as elaborate and powerful and multicolored as so many of her contemporaries, but she mastered what she had, or, to paraphrase the late Thurgood Marshall by way of homily: "She did the best she could with what she had." Her top range was sweet and girlish and could be sharp like lime juice, but she did have an aggressive bottom register and more often than not her phrasing could match the masters of the form. As she grew older the bottom register dominated but remained agile, and she compensated mightily with a seeming innate sense of phrasing that can only be considered natural—perhaps even a birthright of Southern culture. She was, at base, a chanteuse, an almost lost art form in the age of YouTube and the Dumbledores of the engineering studios, with their electronic bits and bytes and digital wizardry. Seeing Kitt and hearing Kitt and being in the presence of her own South Carolina-influenced witchcraft was a singular and enchanting thing.

"I SHOW MY LEGS. I love to tease men with my legs," she said in a 2007 *Jet* magazine interview. "I love men and I like to get their attention. Every time I see a man, I want to tease him."

VIII. MIMI LE DUCK

I was living in North Carolina when I read, in 2006, in *New York* magazine, I think it was, that Eartha Kitt was appearing in a new Off-Broadway show, *Mimi le Duck*. Sheila laughed when I called her and asked if she'd join me: "I wouldn't miss it for the world." I bought the tickets and booked my flight. It never occurred to me to justify the expense.

Sheila and I had a lovely supper on Restaurant Row and walked over to the theater on West Fiftieth Street. The musical had its small charms—about a Midwest housefrau who's had enough and improbably runs off to Paris to discover herself. She encounters amusing stock characters, her spirit guides, and ultimately love. Kitt's role was surprisingly slim: she played Madame Vallet, a faded Parisian torch singer (and another incarnation of the Magical Negro) who sings truth to the white suburban in search of herself, and only appeared in a few scenes, mainly to sing. Kitt was seventy-nine and appeared in a dress that showed all her curves. She was not merely brave but defiant. "Here it is, y'all," she was saying, "and damnit, I still look good." She lavished upon the few songs perhaps more care and dignity and nuance than they deserved, but she brought down the house. The standing ovations were more than merely goodwill.

After the show, Sheila asked me if I wanted to try to make it backstage. I considered it, but thought, after our 1990 encounter, this time was bound to be anticlimactic. I was jealous of our first encounter with the legend and felt it would be greedy to try again. We had no way of knowing that Kitt had already been diagnosed with colon cancer, but she continued to work.

I missed the tribute for her the next year to mark her eightieth birthday, held at Carnegie Hall, joined by the likes of Janet Jackson and Ben Vereen and Diahann Carroll. She was the singer chosen to rechristen the opening of the renovated Café Carlyle that same year.

The week *Mimi le Duck* opened, she showed up on NBC's *Today Show*, bright and early one morning in Rockefeller Center. She performed outside, near the skating rink by the bronze gilded statue of Prometheus stealing fire. Before she performs in the early morning sun, she is interviewed by the tall, dashing, handsome, distinguished Lester Holt. Kitt looks wonderful, not like a woman in her late seventies trying to look young, but full grown, mature, elegant, beautiful. She was a completed woman, at ease and in charge of her powers. Holt is rather quickly reduced to a giggling schoolboy, and Kitt appears not only fully in control but also enjoying the newsman's tongue-tied befuddlement. At some point in the interview, you realize: He is not faking it: he's truly smitten.

I MET THE LATE, wonderful novelist Don Belton at the MacDowell Colony in the summer of 1990. We struck up a decades-long friendship, two gay Black men in love with pop culture. Somewhere down the line he claimed his personal avatar as being the Detroit-born superstar Diana Ross, about whom he was writing a novel. Who was my Black diva avatar? It didn't take me much thinking: Why, Miss Eartha Kitt, of course. Don laughed in the New Hampshire eve, not long after our witnessing a rare showing of the northern lights, all green and massive and alien and otherworldly. "Of course," he said,

"I can see it." Surely that was one of the greatest compliments any-one has ever paid me.

A few years later, when Don visited me in New York, he gave me a box set, *Eartha-Quake*. Five discs. All the great hits and so much more. One hundred and thirty-two songs. It was one of the very rare times I felt somebody actually knew me.

WHEN WE THINK of "Southern," too often we think of the provin-cial, the local, the quaint, of hearth and home and a particular type of representation. To be sure, Southern culture is made up of the bits and pieces of daily life, the food, the language, the rituals, the stories. But the Southern spirit can also be the spirit of the ambas-sador, the one who takes home along with them, despite what Zora Neale Hurston, in the language of country folk, once called "form and fashion and outside show to the world." That very sense of self, of course, is what it means to be a performer. But we all strut across stages, in our day-to-day, and we carry with us, to varying degrees, the essence of our origins, whether we like it or not. Miss Eartha Kitt's Southernness was not overt, but it was real and it was abiding, and it made her an icon.

15

The Good Ship
Jesus

BALDWIN, BERGMAN,
AND THE PROTESTANT IMAGINATION

I have once or twice in my life toyed with the idea of committing suicide.

—Ingmar Bergman, *The Magic Lantern* (1988)

This fight begins, however, in the heart and it now had been laid to my charge to keep my own heart free of hatred and despair.

—James Baldwin, "Notes of a Native Son" (1955)

In 1959, James Baldwin traveled to the studios of AB Svensk Filmindustri (or Svensk Filmindustri), outside Stockholm, Sweden, to interview the acclaimed filmmaker Ingmar Bergman for *Esquire*. The fruit of that visit was published as "The Precarious Vogue of Ingmar Bergman" in April 1960. The profile was reprinted in 1961 in his collection of essays, *Nobody Knows My Name*, as "The Northern Protestant."

Baldwin—by then no stranger to Europe—was deeply impressed by the legacy of the Svensk Film Industry, as he calls the company in the piece, which he notes as one of the oldest in the world. In particular he was impressed by how the Scandinavian setup afforded Bergman so much liberty. "[Bergman] is one of the very few genuine artists now working in films. He is also, beyond doubt, the freest." Unlike American directors, and unlike Baldwin, so much was already made available for Bergman; no one second-guessed the auteur's casting; the money was there, even though "most of his twenty-odd movies were not successful when they were made." Other directors brought in the money, while Bergman brought in the prizes and the prestige. Hence the "Vogue" of Baldwin's original title.

At the time, Ingmar Bergman was forty-one, James Baldwin thirty-five. The two artists seemed to get along well, and although Baldwin suffered from a cold and Bergman therefore acted solicitously toward him ("Can I do anything? . . . I know what it is like to be ill and alone in a strange city"), with the economy of a good fiction writer Baldwin makes it abundantly clear that there was something a bit aloof and distant and locked inside about the grand master, something for which he had acquired a reputation. Indeed, his temper was as internationally famous as was he. Later in life, Bergman himself would joke about his notorious ill-temper, making fun of and acknowledging his nature. Baldwin refers to this characteristic as "the evangelical distance of someone possessed by a vision."

They discussed Bergman's films. Although Baldwin admits to not having seen them all, he had his favorites. He wrote of *The Seventh Seal*, however, that it "impressed me less than some of the others." Bergman admitted that *Summer Interlude* was his favorite. "I don't mean," he added, "that it's my best. I don't know which is my best." Baldwin agreed with him. For Baldwin, motion pictures such as *The Waiting Women/Secrets of Women I*, *Smiles of a Summer Night* (and later, perhaps, he might have added *Persona*, *Autumn Sonata*, *Cries and Whispers*, and *Scenes from a Marriage*)—those that centered on women—impressed him the most. He most admired, that is, those movies in which women were the source of intelligence, of passion, ingenuity, relationships; and men were, more often than not, "helpless before the female force." Baldwin saw the pictures with men at their center as "shadowy." Even a film like *Wild Strawberries* (1957)—which annoyed Baldwin—turns on the protagonist's realization that he has been awful to the women in his life.

Baldwin outlines what he feels are Bergman's key obsessions: "his preoccupations with time and the inevitability of death, the comedy of human entanglements, the nature of illusion, the nature of egotism, the price of art." In the profile, Baldwin gives a fairly compact assessment of Bergman's origins, of how he started so young, and how he had always been inflexible, and how his intractability was a cover for his youth and his insecurity, the tantrums, the bad behavior: refusing to speak to coworkers for long spells. How theater had always been the wellspring to which Bergman returned, from film to film. How Hollywood would never be for him: "I am home here. . . . It took me a long time, but now I have all my instruments—everything—where I want them."

Together they tease out how Bergman came to write *The Seventh Seal*—which remains, probably, his most famous and influential film—how it was inspired by a Victor Sjöström movie, which itself was based on a novel and on folktales with deep Scandinavian roots. It is the story of a sinner's outwitting Death by the use of his very humanity—he uses his own weakness as his weapon. Hence the famous image of playing chess with black-hooded Death.

Baldwin takes his leave. The profile is not terribly long, occupying roughly eighteen pages in *Nobody Knows My Name*. Bergman would go on to direct a production of Baldwin's play, *Blues for Mister Charlie*, in Stockholm in 1965, with Swedish actors and with no mention of skin color.

Three other touchstones stand out in Baldwin's essay:

1. Baldwin had an uncanny ability to make anything and everything about America's ongoing struggle with race. Whether or not his special superpower was a blessing or a curse, it was his reality. Race-talk was expected of him; it was expected that he, usurper of Richard Wright and Ralph Ellison as *the* Black American Writer of his Time, *the* literary voice of the civil rights movement, would tell his readers what Time it Was with regard to race. That is why magazines hired him. That is the primary reason he was read, for better or for worse. It was a fate he could not escape, certainly not in 1960. *Esquire* knew what it would get when they assigned the piece to Baldwin, and to be honest, his musings comparing the young men of Sweden to the "American Negro," his fears over the "Americanization" of Stockholm, and how these young street folk all wanted to look like James Dean in *Rebel without a Cause*—and the ubiquity and difficulty of truly importing/exporting authentic jazz—altogether a loving tablespoonful among the eighteen pages, don't feel gratuitous and yet they are. For, in truth, Baldwin when writing on race was never writing only about race, as some would say in attempting to reduce him to a one-issue writer. When James Baldwin wrote about race, he was actually writing about something much more cosmic and philosophical—theological even—than the quaint, reductive, supernatural nineteenth-century concept that ruled the American psyche and American politics.

2. Baldwin identified with Bergman over their severe and religious fathers. Although Baldwin does not spend a great deal of space on this point, he acknowledges the profound resonance with his own paternal struggles, and it moves him: in fact, he uses that touchstone to pull the entire piece together. The Master American essayist—so effortlessly, so light-handedly, almost as if done with the pinky finger of his left hand—pulling together filmmaking, religion, father-son relationships, "the blue-jeaned

boys" of Stockholm, and forgiveness and reconciliation. "I told him I envied him," writes Baldwin.

3. At the penultimate moment in this piece of writing—a profile that is, rightly or wrongly, not discussed as a powerfully important part of his œuvre, in truth a pop-culture profile for a popular culture magazine, *Esquire*, a "men's magazine" with its frequent nods to High Culture and luxe living, and publishing high-class fiction, at a time when "popular" did not exactly mean fluff but encompassed the larger *vox populi*, high and low, in which movie actors, jazz musicians, painters, and authors, as well as MLK Jr. and JFK and Malcolm X, were all considered celebrities, and when Baldwin's true vocation was writing the Great American Novel—just before he closes the piece like a sermon, he devotes roughly a page and a half to a film fantasy of his: "I amused myself, on the ride back to town, by projecting a movie, which, if I were a movie-maker, would occupy, among my own productions, the place *The Seventh Seal* holds among Bergman's."

Ah, the fascinating unmade Baldwin film. The great unwritten Baldwin novel.

FANNY, ALEXANDER, AND INGMAR

The first Ingmar Bergman movie I ever saw was *Fanny and Alexander*, and the experience of seeing this film can only be discussed with great reverence and moment: *'Twas this film that changed my life. Forever.* I do not mean to be that melodramatic, but the movie excited me in a new way. I had been aware of Bergman's reputation, and had been prepared for some dire, black-and-white passion play full of grim—but fetching—blonde folk, and accompanied by lots of difficult metaphors, maybe even a glimpse of the Grim Reaper. For although this was in the years before videos made movies as easy to come by as apples, and at a time when seeing foreign films still very much belonged to the big-city elite, Bergman, as a name, as an idea, as a commodity ripe for parody, was well known. In 1973, you need not have seen *The Seventh Seal* to get the *New Yorker* jokes, or the sendups on television's *The Smothers Brothers*. I knew who Ingmar Bergman was and what he was supposed to be all about.

By this point in my passage, I was deeply in love with the Latin Boom writers, although the tail of that bright comet was already in retreat. Gabriel García Márquez. Carlos Fuentes. Mario Vargas Llosa. Manuel Puig. Jorge Luis Borges. You could not tell me that these cats weren't writing about me and my world—for me—despite writing in Spanish, in and about a Latin America with a very different history and makeup from my South, but it was still an American South, with a powerfully similar mix of European, American Indian, and African creolization and folk life—Jesus and The Great Spirit, jaguar ghosts and talking alligators, grandmothers who saw the future, slave grit, mulatto blues, rapacious greed from on high looking low. Much to my delight and surprise, Bergman's 1982 movie—which in many ways was a departure from his earlier work, and at the time was what he considered to be his final film—fell right in with that very American folk world with which I had become so enamored. The picture was *Fanny and Alexander*. Here was the looming Church, here were matriarchs of sly might, and candles lit by farts, toys moving by themselves, ghosts both sinister and loving, merchants who sold magic.

The story is set in 1907. Young Alexander and young Fanny belong to a well-off theater family—the Ekdahls—who all seem rowdy and raucous, robust and smart, amusing and full of sunshine. But then their father suffers a fatal stroke, and their charming mother is wed to a local Lutheran bishop. This is the stuff of fairy tales, for the handsome clergyman is in truth a monster, a Christian sadist, and a punishing lout. He virtually imprisons his new wife and stepchildren in his sepulchral manse, and engages in a battle with Alexander, trying to break his will. But the indomitable Ekdahls come to the rescue and literally, by hook, by crook, and by magic, kidnap the children to freedom. The mother's liberty comes by her own hand and by poison and fire. But as with any fairy tale the end is festival and celebration . . . except for the penultimate scene, wherein the ghost of the bishop appears before Alexander, reminding the boy he will be haunted forever.

To be sure, more than anything, as the old truism had always held, this filmic adventure proved to me that world culture was indeed more alike than alien, but was even more the blending of folk culture with so-called high culture, the withering critique of Christendom, the fairy-tale elements, and the irresistible yet unsentimental sweetness of the young actors, Bertil Guve as Alexander, and Pernilla Allwin as Fanny—all combined to make a powerful impression on me that only a handful of works of arts from my college days had managed. Here was a film by an acknowledged High Priest of Western culture; its pedigree was beyond question, its acceptance among the intelligentsia beyond reproach (it won the Academy Award for Best Foreign Language Film in 1983). As Vincent Canby wrote in the *New York Times*, "*Fanny and Alexander* . . . has that quality of enchantment that usually attaches only to the best movies in retrospect, long after you've seen them, when they've been absorbed into the memory to seem sweeter, wiser, more magical than anything ever does in its own time. This immediate resonance is the distinguishing feature of this superb film, which is both quintessential Bergman and unlike anything else he has ever done before." Thus the movie made a greater impact on me than any social realism I could remember: it revealed to me what I had always wanted to do, yet the resistance from my academic overlords up to that point had been intensely negative. "Write social realism, son," they said. "Nobody wants to read about ghosts!" In short,

Bergman's masterwork validated my way of looking at the world. And I would be forever grateful.

TALKING AT THE GATES/HOUSE NIGGER

This is the movie Baldwin describes near the end of the Bergman profile:

> I did not have, to hold my films together, the Northern sagas; but I had the Southern music. From the African tom-toms, to Congo Square, to New Orleans, to Harlem—and, finally, all the way to Stockholm, and the European sectors of African towns. My film would begin with slaves, boarding the good ship *Jesus*: a white ship, on a dark sea, with masters as white as the sails of their ships, and slaves as black as the ocean. There would be one intransient slave, an eternal figure, destined to appear, and to be put to death in every generation. In the hold of the slave ship, he would be a witch-doctor or a chief or a prince or a singer; and he would die, be hurled into the ocean, for protecting a black woman. Who would bear his child, however, and this child would lead a slave insurrection; and be hanged. During the Reconstruction, he would be murdered upon leaving Congress. He would be a returning soldier during the first World War, and be buried alive; and then, during the Depression, he would become a jazz musician, and go mad. Which would bring him up to our own day—what would his fate be now? What would I entitle this grim and vengeful fantasy? What would be happening, during all this time, to the descendants of the masters?

This passage is the most involved description of the movie by Baldwin that remains extant (at least published). Intriguingly, it was also the plot of a novel he had planned at least five years earlier. Baldwin biographer David Leeming mentions it as "Talking at the Gates," outlined in his 1955 application for a Ford Foundation grant. According to William J. Weatherby's biography, he was still talking about a book in 1965, now called *House Nigger*, which would be a sprawling novel about slavery. According to his biographer, James T. Campbell, "Talking at the Gates"—or "Talking at the Big Gate," as per the Ford Foundation application—"would be less concerned with race than with the relationships which have obtained in a 'very complex society,' and with what happens to those relationships once the basis for the particular society crumbles." Baldwin writes that he wants to "explore his belief that black and white in America were bound by strong ties, including blood ties, and that it was the pathological denial of these bonds, as opposed to actual differences, that fueled the racial nightmare." Campbell notes that Baldwin was frank about his lack of knowledge about slave culture and the material antebellum world, and he suggests that Baldwin did not complete the book, as "it was not his style to embark on detailed research for a book."

Interestingly, a key part of the movie description in the Bergman essay prefigures the character Rufus Scott, a jazz drummer in *Another Country* (1962), whose madness, despair, and suicide were all based on Baldwin's relationship with the real, tragic Eugene Worth, who had killed himself in the same fashion, hurtling himself from a bridge.

Part of me still wishes, perhaps wistfully, after this great unwritten novel. Perhaps the concept intrigues me because it is so foreign to his œuvre, as Campbell suggests—almost all of Baldwin's fiction is, if not highly autobiographical, based largely on his personal experiences. Even the historical passages in the middle of *Go Tell It on the Mountain* are surely inspired by stories told to him as a boy by his nonagenarian Louisiana grandmother. More striking to me is how this historical idea has resonated with other African American authors. Certainly Margaret Walker (Alexander)'s 1966 historical marvel, *Jubilee*, is mined from this same vein of precious metal. Decades later, the impact of Alex Haley's 1976 Pulitzer Prize–winning *Roots: The Saga of an American Family* is still being felt (even with the appropriate nods to Harold Courlander and his woefully, Haley-cribbed 1967 novel, *The African*). And in large measure and small, the tales of African slaves and the Middle Passage have been the subject of African American novels, from Toni Morrison's *Beloved* to Charles Johnson's *Middle Passage*, from Sherley Anne Williams's *Dessa Rose* to multiple retellings of the mutiny on the slave ship *Amistad*, and so many others.

Perhaps the most resonant with Baldwin's vision is in fact a Brazilian novel by the estimable João Ubaldo Ribeiro. Originally written in Portuguese and translated into English by the author, *An Invincible Memory* (*Hail the Brazilian People*, in the Portuguese version) is indeed a sprawling epic that tells the history of Brazil through the lives of two families—one rich and European, the other Black and Indian and struggling to get by. It goes back four hundred years to the original days of colonization. A reincarnated soul accompanies us from the first page to the last, very like Baldwin's unusual concept.

But even more than the lamentation over the novel by James Baldwin I am highly likely not to read, when I read and reread this passage from *Nobody Knows My Name*, this description of an epic movie, the blockbuster novel of Middle Passage from my youth, I am struck again and again by Baldwin's sadness, his bitterness. He says:

> It did not seem likely, after all, that I would ever be able to make of my past, on film, what Bergman had been able to make of his. . . . Perhaps what divided the black Protestant

from the white one was the nature of my still unwieldy, unac-
cepted bitterness . . . and it then occurred to me that my bitterness might be turned to good account if I should dare to
envision the tragic hero for whom I was searching—as myself."

THE GOOD SHIP *JESUS*

I find it deeply interesting that Baldwin invokes the mythological
slave ship *Jesus* in his description. The irony of kidnapped Africans
being carried across the Atlantic for a life of bondage in a vessel
named after the Christian savior is mighty rich.

Despite my above statements regarding the quality and quantity
of novels, short stories, plays, television shows, and movies about the
Middle Passage, I believe not enough literary attention has been
given to this most harrowing of American misadventures. Consider
the amount of work produced about World War II, about the Civil
War, about the Great Depression, about Vietnam. When compared
with the mountains of work historians have produced over the
decades, the creative work focused on slavery is overshadowed as
if by Everest; the facts, figures, details, and accounts lie there like
an Undiscovered Country. But to the great masses, knowledge of
the institution of slavery is astoundingly lacking, and among Black
folk—especially among the young—that absence is profound and
sad. Despite the lauded work of some of our finest artists, I believe
we have barely scratched the surface in doing to that material what
artists do—make it live, lay it bare, come closer to understanding it
and how the experience has formed us all.

But for Americans—and in a peculiar way, particularly for Black
folk—the subject of the Middle Passage, of the intimate horrors of
slavery, and of all the history and its concomitant emotions, it feels
to many on the one hand dull, and on the other, still much too raw.
But the command of history is ever upon us. There actually was a

slave ship named *Jesus*. Often known as "the Good Ship *Jesus*," the *Jesus of Lübeck* was built in Lübeck, Germany. It was purchased by England's Henry VIII as a warship in 1544; in 1568, it was sunk somewhere in the Gulf of Mexico by the Spanish Armada. Henry's daughter, Queen Elizabeth I, "rented" it to Captain John Hawkins. Part merchant, part pirate, a "self-made man," Hawkins, sometime in the early 1560s, made a voyage from the east coast of Africa to South Carolina with over three hundred prisoners. This was not his first such voyage (it was probably his second), nor was it the first journey of its type, as some have erroneously affirmed. For if it had been, it would make Hawkins the Captain Zero of the Middle Passage, as his adventure would have a particular poignancy. The captured would have been the first of all slave cargoes to American shores to be aboard a ship named *Jesus*.

"BEHOLD, I SEND TO YOU PROPHETS, WISE MEN, AND SCRIBES." —MATT. 23:34

My first recollections of James Baldwin come not from having read him, but from having seen him in the pages of *Ebony* and *Jet*. This speaks to how popular—indeed, famous—James Baldwin was as late as the mid-1970s. For a young Black boy in a barbershop in the backwoods of eastern North Carolina, to be thumbing through colorful images, and black-and-white images, of Ella Fitzgerald and Muhammad Ali and Pam Grier and Senator Edward Brooke and the Jackson Five, and to come upon this "frog-eyed," slight-framed man, elegantly dressed (sometimes in an ascot!), his hands raised up, minister-like, his face radiating some prophetic ardor, or simply looking sage—yes, I knew who James Baldwin was long before I read his words.

Ironically, the first time I actually read a Baldwin sentence was for an odd and completely prurient reason: I overhead some of my cousins, schoolteachers, deaconesses of the church, talking about this new book by James Baldwin, *Just Above My Head*. The year would have been 1977. They spoke in hushed tones, which of course made me heed them with greater intensity.

> "Child, I read it, and I couldn't believe. . . . Well, you know, there is some of that funny business in there."
>
> "What do you mean, Mildred? *'Funny business?'* "
>
> "Girl, you know. That man-on-man stuff. Disgusting. I don't know why he put that in there."
>
> The women shook their heads and gave out grunts and tsks of disapproval.

Man-on-man stuff? Of course I had to find out for myself. So I somehow found a copy—it was almost as popular to own in those days as were *Roots* and *Black Like Me*—and I scoured the pages for "man-on-man stuff." What I found tickled me. Perhaps this was my first reading of queer sex, and certainly it was the first of queer love. It initially took me a while to accept the Words of Baldwin—not so much accept them, as to appreciate them, come to love them. Despite what may seem obvious similarities, parallels, connections, to this dark-skinned teenager from the rural South, the commonalities felt slim at best. His Blackness and his queerness were simply too elementary for me. I was interested in science and science fiction. I was not only a country boy, I was lovingly surrounded by an extended family that felt like a nation. His urban poverty and desperation were moving and Dickensian, but remote to me. And despite the ambiance and knowledge brought down by my cousins from Newark, the Bronx, New York, and Philadelphia during the summers and around Christmastime, his Harlem might as well have been on Neptune. His hurt, his angst, his churchliness, and later his European exoticism, all felt alien to me. Moreover, by the time I was old enough to understand who he was and to taste a few of his sentences, he had already belonged to the black-and-white era of segregated drinking fountains, fire hoses, police dogs, marches on Selma, and assassinations. I was an affirmative action baby. I intended to be a science officer on a starship headed for places where race meant something else entirely.

James Baldwin is not the sort of writer one embraces with the ease of the latest horror writer or thriller hack. I became interested in letters as a side effect of my interest in becoming a science fiction writer. My wisest teachers insisted I read Baldwin. I groaned to myself, and thought, Gee whiz, do you have any *original* thoughts? Reading *Go Tell It on the Mountain* was not exactly a chore, but I did wonder why he fancied such elaborate prose. Had he not read Hemingway or Isaac Asimov? But the biblical language of the King James Version caught my attention. The culture of the church was immanent in his writing, and the crush John has on Elisha, was expressed sotto voce although supernaturally known, boy to boy. In the end, it occurred to me that the obvious connections were the least of what bound us.

By the time I met Baldwin in the fall of 1984, I had "discovered" his essays in the way Columbus discovered North America. I was already in awe of him. By then I had allowed my deep love of science fiction to linger on some special shelf of receding boyhood. I now thirsted after a different type of storytelling, something that made sense of the seen world. There he stood before us, as wondrously strange as I had imagined, with electricity and a command of language breathtaking and arch and overwhelming. He was a presence, at once sweet and authoritative, about which so many have written and borne witness. I wanted to know how he did that, not just the writing, but also the *being*. For it occurred to me that the commonalities I had been too young and dumb to grasp had made his path that much more daunting and unlikely. The young man had so much more to discover. I remember that I had recently received a copy of a radio interview Baldwin had done with Studs Terkel in 1961 upon the publication of *Nobody Knows My Name*. I had listened to the interview countless times, practically memorizing it. As he stood before us in class in 1984, small, dark and mystically elegant, during questions I quoted an answer he gave to Terkel about the responsibility of the Black writer. Did he still feel the same way now?

Baldwin squinted at me: "Do you honestly think I remember something I said in an interview twenty-three years ago?"

BLACK PROTESTANT MEETS WHITE PROTESTANT

I arrived in New York at a time when the movie repertory houses were in their last blaze of glory. The VHS tape was on the scene but had not yet sent the many theaters the way of the passenger pigeon. It now looks like a mania, as if I were trying to capture something I had lost, something unavailable to me in my brief two decades. Yet the pull, the reason I became such a habitué of these funky, often run-down, just-about-to-close establishments, had more to do with vision: seeing the world in a multiplicity of ways, to be a witness. It was all a new food for me, and I glutted on it. I would go to these movies almost every night (provided I had the cash). Uptown, downtown, the Village, Harlem, Midtown, even Queens and Brooklyn. Month-long film festivals, revivals of silent classics, classics from the 1930s and '40s, 1970s blaxploitation films, independent films, documentaries, and many, many foreign films—the great German directors of the post–World War II era, Tarkovsky, Kurosawa, Fellini, and yes, Ingmar Bergman.

There is something deeply sobering about going from the enchantment of *Fanny and Alexander* to the black-and-white medievalism of *The Seventh Seal*, the harsh glare of *Persona*, the bitterness of *Autumn Sonata*, and the gothic dread and physical pain of *Cries and Whispers* (a true masterpiece). Bergman's darkness, in the vast middle of the body of his work, is all-encompassing. It is stark and forbidding, like the midnight-sun landscape that engendered it; the fruits of sin are dire to the soul, and the happenstance of life is perilous; it is both the vagary of an indifferent God and the visitation of a punishing deity—aesthetic, educating, entreating. This medicine is particularly strong for one in his early twenties. It galvanizes a certain bleak view of life, corroborates one's worst fears about the world around and the doom that surrounds all human relationships. But I did not feel cheated, merely wiser, for I still held that first Bergman experience close to the center of a growing aesthetic of my own *as* my own. Moreover, I was not a Swede.

Of the many things I learned from and about Bergman was the fixation on a particular brand of Protestantism, and a particular Calvinist vision of the world. This had been one of my connections to the 1982 film, and over time I appreciated how dark and sinister that view of the world could be. Indeed, the Calvinism of the Baptist Church echoed with the Swedish Lutheranism in the least of Bergman's films. Man is fallen and only God can save us. We must behave as if we are saints, although the saved have already been preordained. Eternal life comes only through God's grace. One must repent and believe. In short, the world without God is a hell. (Bergman: "Most of our upbringing was based on such concepts as sin, confession, punishment, forgiveness and grace, concrete factors between children and parents and God. . . . We had never heard of freedom and knew even less what it tasted like. In a hierarchical system, all doors are closed.")

Aside from Jesus and Protestantism, the consonant constant between Baldwin and Bergman is the Dark Father, the Bishop in the adjacent bedroom with a strap in his hand, the Torquemada who is kin, the Dark Clad minister ascending the pulpit. Baldwin

wrote almost obsessively about his stepfather, David, and the physical and psychological torment to which the Pentecostal minister
subjected him. Bergman, too, suffered the same humiliation at the
hands of a highly religious father. He writes in his autobiography:

> So punishments were something self-evident, never ques-
> tioned. They could be swift and simple, a slap over the face or
> a smack on the bottom. . . . If I wet myself, which often hap-
> pened, and all too easily, I was made to wear a red knee-length
> skirt for the rest of the day.

At one point, he writes of watching his mother bathe his brother's back after a beating "where the carpet beater had loosened the
skin and streaked his back with bloody weals." He describes how
the psychological abuse was even more lasting than the physical,
how he would be "frozen out" or interrogated in front of visitors
after dinner parties as if the evening's entertainment. But Bergman became a defiant rebel early on. He would come to fight back;
he would run away. He would adopt ways and thoughts contrary
to his early teachings. He became an artist. He differs from Baldwin in two significant ways on this front: first, he had the means
to escape into a well-established arts community, first the theater
and then the world of film; second, he came to reconcile with his
parents—especially his father—via both empathy and his art.

When Bergman writes of his father's death in 1970, it is at odds
with Baldwin's account of his father's death in "Notes of a Native
Son." Bergman has been at his father's deathbed for many days:

> 29 April 1970: Father is dead. He passed away on Sunday at
> twenty past four in the afternoon. His death was peaceful. I
> find it difficult to explain what I felt about seeing him. He was
> totally unrecognizable, his face most of all reminding me of

pictures of the dead in the concentration camps. It was a face of death. I think of him from a despairing distance, but with tenderness. Things are bad for Bergman this day, despite the friendly light over the sea. The yearning for something at last to touch me, to give me grace. Things are bad this day. Not that I feel ill—on the contrary—but my soul.

Bergman was always Bergman, of course. Which is to say that he remained difficult, temperamental, difficult to please, always searching for that elusive, existential grace that most of us are apt never to find. Yet his relationship with his father had grown mellow and understanding over time as he watched the pastor slide into decline. In fact, early in his biography Bergman states: "Nowadays, I understand my parents' desperation. A pastor's family lives as if on a tray, unprotected from other eyes. The parsonage must always be open to criticism and comments from the congregation. Both Father and Mother were perfectionists who sagged beneath this unreasonable pressure." His emotional life was never easy or uncomplicated. Thus his overwhelming dark vision is touched, now and again, by the saving graces of the maternal instinct (which sometimes fails miserably), and by some special moment that gives us a glimmer at the promised salvation.

After Baldwin describes the movie/novel near the end of his Bergman piece, he says, "It did not seem likely, after all, that I would ever be able to make of my past, on film, what Bergman has been able to make of his." His past was easier to access, Baldwin reckons, "more remote and more present." "Perhaps what divided the black Protestant from the white one was the nature of my still unwieldy, unacceptable bitterness." He realizes that his tragic hero, the embodiment of the travails of all Black folk, our stand-in, would be coming to a dead-in. This outcome was, to him, the only end he could conceive in 1959, at that moment in time. Whereas for Bergman, his "authority seemed, then, to come from the fact that he was reconciled to this arduous, delicate, and disciplined self-exposure."

Indeed when Baldwin wrote those resounding lines of clarity regarding his father and to humankind when nearing the end of "Notes of a Native Son," he had just begun this journey, and true reconciliation would be decades away. His father, David Baldwin, the root of his personal bitterness, had become a sort of synecdoche for Baldwin's larger source of rage: the Racial Nightmare of America. In fact, Baldwin's bitterness would be exacerbated by the civil rights movement, with which he'd only begun to work, and by the rash of assassinations of men he knew and admired. When he made Europe his last home in the late 1960s, his interviews and open letters and essays reveal a man who had not, in fact, unburdened his heart of bitterness.

From the start of his writing career, this frankness, this willingness to acknowledge the broken wing of the African American soul, is largely what separates James Baldwin from the rest of the pack, and what makes him so very valuable. With a few notable exceptions (perhaps Richard Wright, perhaps Toni Morrison, perhaps Amiri Baraka), the great corpus of the writing of Americans of African descent tends to stress not the bitterness and hatred engendered by over 250 years of slavery, and another one hundred of Redemption and segregation, but instead the strength, the perseverance, the dignity, the moral force, the indomitable spirit of Black folk. From the early slave narratives, from Frederick Douglass, from Booker T. Washington—think Zora Neale Hurston, think Alice Walker, think Langston Hughes—African American literature has largely been the literature of uplift and inspiration. And let us praise it.

Baldwin's work resonates with those sermons of uplift—preacher and Bible scholar that he was—but his prophetic nature, lamenting the plight of his people, also gave his homilies an edge of darkness: he did not run away from the bitterness. To be sure, Baldwin acknowledges the power and beauty of the sons and daughters of the slaves (*What will happen to all this beauty?*—the resonant line from *The Fire Next Time*). But on balance, his work is an admission of bitterness, in the main, and personal. In the profile he says: "All art is a kind of confession, more or less oblique. All artists, if they are to survive, are forced, at last, to tell the whole story, to vomit the anguish up."

THE BITTERNESS OF BLACKFOLK

If I could, I surely would,

Stand on the rock where Moses stood.

Pharaoh's army got drownded,

Oh Mary don't you weep.

—"Mary Don't You Weep," traditional

An interesting personal moment: I am watching Chris Rock's 1999 HBO special, *Bigger and Blacker*, which spawned his first Grammy-winning album. In one of his comedic runs, he talks about the hatred Black men of a certain age bear toward white people. Not only how this rage has been (and for some still is) expertly disguised in the presence of white folk, but also how, behind their backs, the bile comes forth like molten lava. ("When it comes to racism, do you know who is the most racist?—old Black men! You find a Black man over sixty. . . . Willie hates your guts!") It is a riveting, hilarious piece worthy of his predecessor, Richard Pryor. But the stunning element for me was that thing we prize most in our comics: I had never heard anyone articulate this truth so cogently and accurately and baldly. It struck me with great force the understanding that this subterfuge had long been a part of our culture, the emotional internalization and how that amplified the resentment of that anger. Of course I had been aware of this phenomenon all my life. In many ways it was not even an open secret but a simple reality: Black men who lived through those times had every right to hate white folk with the mania of a serial killer.

But Chris Rock, my contemporary, was experiencing the anger of these men from the outside. He was not including himself in this activity. He saw himself in a different light. The act these beautiful men had to put on for the world was now a thing of the past, history. Rock's treatment of the matter seemed to signal for me that the country had indeed turned a significant corner. But it is important to remember a great many of these men are still alive, in this newfangled, confusing, chaotic Obama-nation. Where did they put their bitterness? James Baldwin belongs to those earlier generations.

It is the bitterness that fascinates me. Baldwin was never shy about admitting his personal bitterness, which for his generation of African Americans was a given. To be Black in the pre-1970s was to live with an ineffable bitterness, the taste of which cannot be exorcised by salves and potions and televangelists.

BALDWIN THEN AND Baldwin even later. For so many of James Baldwin's contemporaries, those who lived through the heights of the civil rights movement, those who read of his exploits, and who read his writings, those, indeed, who first read *The Fire Next Time* and *Another Country*, those who recognized him as a burning bush in the rhetoric of the freedom movement—for them, by the late 1970s and early '80s, James Baldwin had become a rather exotic figure. His lust for the abroad, for France and Turkey, and ultimately again France, overshadowed his continual participation, from a distance and at home, in the discussion of the African American situation on the American scene.

Had Baldwin, unwittingly, succumbed to the bitterness he had avowed to eschew in 1955? It would be simpleminded to suggest that this type of overcoming could ever be a onetime event. No human being progresses along a linear path. There are mountains, there are valleys, and there are trenches. Baldwin clearly acknowledges his pain and his grief over the many murders of men he knew by the end of the 1960s. He addresses this perhaps most vividly in the memoir *No Name in the Street* (1972), perhaps his crescendo aria on the movement revisited. He said of that book in a 1972 interview:

HERBERT R. LOTTMAN: May I ask what you think is going to happen back home?

BALDWIN: I've already said that I see a holocaust coming. That is the subject of my new book, *No Name in the Street*, which appeared in the United States this spring. It is the story of the civil rights movement up to the death of Martin Luther King, but it's not a documentary. It's a personal book—my own testimony.

Everyone overlooks the impact on the black population of our country of the present Administration, and that is very sinister. It's an insult to every black American that the President of the United States should be in competition with the governor of Alabama for votes. The civil rights laws? Bullshit. . . . Americans who have managed to learn nothing are now about to learn a great deal.

To be sure, Baldwin always had the fiery condemnatory tone of the truth-telling Prophet at the Gates, but in light of his history and his very recent past, and being spoken from his bucolic Saint-Paul de Vence estate in southern France, these 1970s interviews sometimes ring a rather shrill note.

In 1970, he told Ida Lewis in an interview for *Essence*: "I kept leaving for a short time—to do this, to do that—but to save myself I finally had to leave for good. . . . One makes decisions in funny ways; you make a decision without knowing you've made it. I suppose my decision was made when Malcolm X was killed." And he lists King and all the others who were killed. "I'm the last witness—everybody else is dead. I couldn't stay in America, I had to leave. . . . With those great men, the possibility of a certain kind of dialogue in America has ended." When asked by Lottman if his attitude has changed, Baldwin responds: "I'm much sadder now, which doesn't mean that I'm discouraged." Read closely, the prevailing tone of these many interviews, appearing in glossy magazines and intellectual journals, is a healthy mix of clear-eyed assessments of the political scene, intense memories, and some regrets. A man in his fifties has much more material to sift through than a man in his twenties.

And then there is his final book, *The Evidence of Things Not Seen* (1985). His visitation to Atlanta to investigate the mysterious disappearances and murders of African American children was a fraught exercise both in reporting and in writing. Baldwin's strong suit was not as a reporter but as an observer, or as he would say, a witness. The book did not represent his greatest work, and it in fact foundered for a spell in finding a publisher. But to his credit, the most remarkable element in the book is his seeing through Wayne Williams, the convicted murderer (of two children out of twenty-three, later growing to more than thirty-one). That part of the book stands out as fascinating and compelling and insightful. Here is Baldwin at his best, with his sharpest indictment of the racist American system. In the 1995 reissue of the book, legal scholar Derrick Bell writes: "There is in this work—as there is in so much of Baldwin's literary legacy—a finely balanced *cry of despair* and a quiet prayer of wonderment" (emphasis added). In a final set of interviews published in 1988, with the poet Quincy Troupe, Baldwin's tone strikes the reader as particularly severe. He speaks of his disappointments in relationships with certain fellow Black writers, and of his disenchantment with the American system. At one point he says:

> You know, I was trying to tell the truth and it takes a long time to realize that you can't—that there's no point in going to the mat, so to speak, no point in going to Texas again. There's no point in saying this again. It's been said, and it's been said, and it's been said. It's been heard and not heard. You are a broken motor. . . . You're a running motor and you're repeating, you're repeating and it causes a breakdown, lessening of will power. And sooner or later your will gives out—it has to.

And later: "And further, I don't see anything in American life—for myself—to aspire to. Nothing at all. It's all so very false, so shallow, so plastic, so morally and ethically corrupt." In all fairness, these shards are surrounded by certain hopes for future writers, for future generations. The question is a vexing one, indeed, metaphysical. Does one find a lack of bitterness on the path to a state of nirvana? The prospect seems highly unlikely. Perhaps the true unfairness in comparing Bergman's latter-day clemency with that of Baldwin's is that Bergman's source of angst was his father; Baldwin's was an entire nation—in fact, a world. And although the state of Baldwin's soul on December 1, 1987, cannot be known, it may be safe to say he was disappointed with the halting nature of American progress, but that such fatherly regret did not taint the roots of his faith. Faith was the ultimate touchstone.

It is important to remember, at this passage, that the best-known and most favored Christian hymn in the world, "Amazing Grace," was written by John Newton, a tormented man who spent many years as a slave ship captain. Indeed, Newton would go on to become one of the greatest voices of abolitionism, and an Anglican priest. Many like to believe he wrote the song—by his own account, while at sail on a stormy sea—after his famous spiritual revelation. But he himself admits that after his conversion to Christianity, sometime in the late 1740s, he continued in the slave trade for at least four more years. Redemption is a complicated matter indeed.

UP FROM BITTERNESS

When I was ten years old, my older sister moved back to North Carolina from New York, with her elegant Harlemite husband and newborn daughter in tow. They lived at home with us for a year while they were building their own house. And every Sunday, without fail, she would put one album on to play as we ate breakfast and prepared ourselves for church. *Every Sunday*. The year was 1973, and Aretha Franklin's album *Amazing Grace*, the best-selling gospel album of all time, was less than a year old.

I remember in particular how I became instantly bewitched by her version of "Mary Don't You Weep," a song older than the Civil War, what historians call a "slave song," what W. E. B. Du Bois called a "Sorrow Song." It has seen a great many incarnations, and having been a perennial at civil rights marches, had to have been in the recent memory of Ms. Franklin. But her version includes something any young boy would find captivating: The resurrection of a dead man, Lazarus. Why she chose to insert this half-spoken/half-sung fable about the power of faith is a mystery (although likely inspired by yet another spiritual), but the force of it, backed by the chanting and syncopated clapping of the choir, rising as the story progresses—as Jesus questions the faith of Mary and Martha over whether or not he can bring back their dead brother, and calls forth the dead man: "For the benefit of you who don't believe"—is a visceral, graphic demonstration of what the sons and daughters of the

Middle Passage were being asked, what their faith had to be. In the original version of the song, we are asked to have faith that the Egyptian army attacking the fleeing Israelites will be "smote," and indeed they get "drownded in the Red Sea." Franklin, in an act of jazz-like musical quotation, overlays that call to faith with an even more bedrock faith that questions Death itself. Aretha Franklin doubles down on the matter of faith.

––––––––––

THE THEOLOGIAN DIETRICH BONHOEFFER also knew bitterness. Fairly or unfairly, he will go down in history as a man who returned from the United States to Germany in 1940 and involved himself in a plot to overthrow Adolf Hitler, even if by means of assassination. Bonhoeffer had taught Sunday school in the 1930s at the Abyssinian Baptist Church in Harlem, around the time James Baldwin would have been a boy. For obvious reasons, these dramatic events and his execution at the hands of the Nazis have overshadowed his theology.

One of his most enduring concepts was that of cheap grace versus costly grace. Bonhoeffer believed strongly in the imitation of Christ and in what he called "religionless Christianity." He wrote and preached against the easy way out, against easy piety, easy forgiveness, easy consolation. Cheap grace, he writes, is "grace without price; grace without cost!" "Costly grace," Bonhoeffer says, "is the gospel which must be sought again and again, the gift which must be asked for, the door at which a man must knock." *Again and again.* In nonreligious terms, I like to view this concept as parallel to the psychic health of modern man, and of the artist. Forgiveness, both in personal and societal terms, does not come cheaply. Lip service, a smile, and good etiquette may convince many, but the truth of deep forgiveness comes at a price. This, as Baldwin often wrote, is the true Price of the Ticket.

As a person who aspires to the artistic to "tell the whole story," to "vomit up the anguish," as Baldwin admonishes, I struggle with that cost. I wonder after the means by which, as a society and personally, we truly exorcise the bitterness. Bergman's œuvre points out that the journey does not deliver us, one fine morning, into some shining green field where the lion lies down with the lamb, and milk and honey flow everlasting. The darkness remains in our inherited, Calvinist vision of the world. Yet there is indeed, a promised salvation, but it cannot be claimed cavalierly. In order to stand on the rock like Moses, with unshakable conviction and faith, to believe the dead can walk again, you must look unflinchingly at the world the way it is. The world is dark. The world is ugly. The world seems unyielding. That work can be hard on the back and limbs, but it's worth the effort.

I do not know how much Baldwin had read of Bonhoeffer, or what he might have thought of him, but one sees, in the great overview of his work, the transformation from a self-recognition toward a desire for self-exorcism. The wandering, dark years, the many interviews he gave from sun-dappled Saint-Paul de Vence, his output after 1968, and his so-called self-exile, add up to a man in a very biblical self-struggle, very like Jonah, very like Moses; indeed, very like Jesus. It is an archetypal struggle, and as Bonhoeffer tells us, the path is not easy. This grace—the freedom from bitterness—is a costly and earned prize. Whether or not Baldwin achieved this desired state is a mystery, very like his unwritten novel, his unproduced movie. I hope and pray he found it.

> God gave Noah the rainbow sign,
> No more water, but fire next time. Pharaoh's army got drownded,
> Oh Mary don't you weep.
>
> —"Mary Don't You Weep," traditional

16

There's a Hellhound on Your Trail

HOW TO SEE LIKE GORDON PARKS

I got to keep movin', I've got to keep movin'
Blues fallin' down like hail, blues fallin' down like hail
Umm mmm mmm mmm
Blues fallin' down like hail, blues fallin' down like hail
And the days keeps on worryin' me,
There's a hellhound on my trail,
Hellhound on my trail, hellhound on my trail
If today was Christmas eve, if today was Christmas eve,
And tomorrow was Christmas day
If today was Christmas eve,
And tomorrow was Christmas day
All I would need my little sweet rider
Just to pass the time away, huh huh, to pass the time away
You sprinkled hot foot powder, mmm mmm
Around my door, all around my door
You sprinkled hot foot powder, mmm,
All around your daddy's door, hmm hmm hmm
It keep me with ramblin' mind, rider
Every old place I go, every old place I go
I can tell, the wind is risin',
The leaves tremblin' on the tree,
Tremblin' on the tree

I can tell, the wind is risin',
Leaves tremblin' on the tree
Hmm hmm mmm mmm
All I need's my little sweet woman,
And to keep my company, hmmm hmm, hey, hey, hey
My company
I got to keep movin', I've got to keep movin'
Blues fallin' down like hail, blues fallin' down like hail
And the days keeps on worryin' me,
There's a hellhound on my trail,
Hellhound on my trail, hellhound on my trail

Good morning, graduates: Aaron, Matthew, Tracy, Anna, Aaron, Haodong, Ava, Jonna, Nicholas, Windrose, Libi, Alina, and Grant, I just came to tell you, there's a hellhound on your trail.

I know this is a happy occasion, a happy day, and this type of address should be full of congratulatory good wishes and smiley faces and time-worn platitudes and advice on how to court success and good fortune. But what I have to tell you is the Gospel Truth, but not necessarily the Good News. Unless you consider the blues good news.

Being an inveterate news junky, I kept thinking about the drought in California, the North Carolina legislature and coal ash, about the furor over same-sex marriage and the recent Baltimore uprisings; about all the implications for our collective future, where we are headed, what to expect. As if I really had a clue . . .

So I keep coming back to Gordon Parks and the blues.

Gordon Parks was a true renaissance man, one of my own early personal heroes, and a hero to a great many more. A photographer, a musician, a writer of fiction and nonfiction, a poet, a movie maker—in fact he was the first African American to direct a major motion picture for Hollywood.

While MLK Jr. was the voice and face and moral conscience of the later years we think of as the American civil rights movement, and while James Baldwin was its major literary and intellectual chronicler, and while Malcolm X its articulate firebrand, Gordon Parks was its great image capturer. I can say without hesitation, and many have testified to this before me, that during that era and long after that era, his images published and republished in major venues like *Life* and *Look* magazines and the great news services, helped define how people at the time thought about the life and times of Black folk, and continue to do so.

Perhaps his most famous image, created in 1942, *American Gothic, Washington, D.C.*, is a photograph of Ella Watson, a cleaning woman positioned in front of an American flag, holding a mop and a broom. Meant to echo the famous Grant Wood painting, *American Gothic.* This photograph told and tells a story, one that made folk uncomfortable, but it told the truth, simply and directly—which was a hallmark of Parks's style and sensibility, uncomfortable truths, a complete complex story in a single composition, lines as messages, hues and tones as feeling, shadows as sermons.

It is no small thing to say that when any American thinks of the freedom movement of the 1950s and 1960s, most of the images already swimming in our heads are images made by Mr. Gordon Parks.

IT SHOULD COME as little surprise that Parks, born in 1912, got his professional start working for the Farm Security Administration in 1941, chronicling the lives of Black farmers and workers. Following in the tradition of those photographers who essentially invented photographic Americana—Walker Evans, Dorothea Lange, Margaret Bourke-White—the FSA focused on poor small-farm owners, sharecroppers, migrant farmworkers—their mission to chronicle and document these American lives.

Photography as we know it was still a relatively new thing, getting its start in the 1830s. So only about one hundred years to get its act together. But of course these pioneers had centuries of paintings and drawings and sculptures to draw upon and to teach them how to see and what to look for. They did not create this art form whole cloth. Plus they had the stories and the great novels to teach them a vision of what was most important in capturing the human being.

ALONG WITH PARKS was his oft-neglected photographic contemporary living in the heart of the South. When I lived in the Delta, I got to meet Mr. Ernest C. Withers, who would give us the definitive images of Memphis, Tennessee, in our collective hours of tumult and heartbreak. Even when you visit the Lorain Motel in person today, it is Ernest Withers's images that haunt your retinas, and the visions of striking Black garbage workers carrying signs that Mr. Withers captured.

(I think specifically this very day of a twenty-six-year-old man, Devin Allen, in Baltimore, whose photography has seized our nation's attention with such ardor. This is the man whose photograph of the young man running in front of an advancing line of police was put on the cover of *Time* magazine a few weeks back. So much has been said and written about how Allen is self-taught, but even he acknowledges the influence of Gordon Parks. It is almost as if Gordon Parks's photography taught this young brother how to see. I never really understood the value of Instagram, other than as a medium for vanity and self-indulgence, until I started following Mr. Allen and waking up each morning to these fascinating images. There is so much NEWS in each picture. So much story. Each saturated in history and meaning. So much feeling. Allen has come under a lot of fire for his captions, and for being an unapologetic advocate. Gordon Parks himself writes about the idea of objectivity versus subjectivity in one of his memoirs. On visiting Birmingham in the wake of the 1963 church bombing he writes: "No one can decipher the trials of oppressed people with more fire and passion than a black preacher, and I tried to touch that power with my camera.")

———————

WHAT IS THIS so-called capturing? Why is it so important? What is its value? Why are some images more important than others? What are they saying to us?

———————

I PROBABLY SPEND too much time thinking about the differences between fiction and nonfiction, what one requires that the other one does not, and how they are ultimately more alike than different. How we look for the same thing in both. What do we wish to capture in the end? How do we do it? But more, I want to muddy the water and get at the shared tactics and strategies that writers of fiction and nonfiction must use to achieve a similar goal—to create a person on the page with dark squiggles on white paper. In many ways this is a perverse goal. This is something only a writer can become obsessed with. In the non-writing world, it is insane to suggest a real person has any parity with a made-up one. But we word-pushers know differently. We know what those unsuspecting word- and image-consumers don't. We know that in their minds, Madame Bovary, Captain Ahab, Little Orphan Annie, and Atticus Finch and Sherlock Holmes, Bigger Thomas, John Henry, and Anna Karenina are as real as Edward Snowden and Mother Teresa and Lindsay Lohan and Hillary Clinton and Johnny Depp and Kim Kardashian and Dean Smith and Bill O'Reilly—assuming Bill O'Reilly is an actual human being. And let's not yet touch upon the subject of all those historical figures—George Washington, Hannibal of Carthage, Henry VIII, Elizabeth I, Queen Hatshepsut, Julius

Caesar, Benjamin Franklin, Abe Lincoln, Caligula, Jesus—all of whom have been re-invented in works of fiction (and nonfiction), and all of whom our non-scribbling brethren and sistren consider they've come to know as flesh and blood, but to whom they have come to feel personally close via the pens of David McCullough or Robert Graves or Doris Kearns Goodwin or Joseph Ellis or Norman Mailer or the cameras of Ken Burns or Roma Downey and Mark Burnett.

I am talking about creation and re-creation, if not recreation. I am talking about capturing the truth, that elusive ghost, which leads us back to the blues:

———————

WHAT THE HELL is the blues?

———————

WE ALL KNOW it as a type of song, a genre. Associated with the American South and its African American inventors. We think of a specific lyric form, and all those fancy anthropological terms like retentions from West African music and syncretism with forms of European music; we think of instrumentation, specifically the guitar and other string instruments, and we think of call-and-response. And we think of the content: loss, downheartedness, depression. We think of W. C. Handy and Charley Patton and Blind Lemon Jefferson and Son House and Elizabeth Cotten and Moses Rascoe and Bessie Smith and Ma Rainey and Robert Johnson.

Robert Johnson.

Robert Johnson—probably more than any of the aforementioned artists, despite their formidable contributions—remains our High Priest of the Blues, the one we look to as definer and guru, the legend, the vortex of myths. Not only in terms of the crossroads and getting his gift from the devil, but in dying so young and in showing so many the way, decades after his death.

> You better come on in my kitchen
>
> It's goin' to be rainin' outdoors
>
> When a woman gets in trouble
>
> Everybody throws her down
>
> Lookin' for your good friend
>
> None can be found
>
> You better come on in my kitchen
>
> It's goin' to be rainin' outdoors
>
> The woman I love, took from my best friend
>
> Some joker got lucky, stole her back again
>
> She better come on in my kitchen
>
> Baby, it's goin' to be rainin' outdoors
>
> Mama, can't you hear that wind howl?
>
> Oh how the wind do howl
>
> You better come on in my kitchen
>
> Baby, it's goin' to be rainin' outdoors
>
> The woman that I love, I crave to see
>
> She's up the country, won't write to me
>
> Then, you better come on in my kitchen
>
> Goin' to be rainin' outdoors
>
> I went to the mountain, far as my eyes could see
>
> Some other man got my woman,
>
> Lonesome blues got me
>
> But she better come on in my kitchen
>
> 'Cause it's goin' to be rainin' outdoors
>
> My mama dead, papa well's to be
>
> Ain't got nobody to love and care for me
>
> She better come on in this kitchen
>
> 'Cause it's goin' to be rainin' outdoors

But for some of us, the blues is much more than the sum of its parts. It is a philosophy, it is a theology, it is a blueprint. A road map.

The blues is personified by the great Billie Holiday, who could take a sad song and make it happy, and who could take a happy song and make it sad. An inheritance she collected from Louis Armstrong.

The blues is a trickster. You can't really trust it, but you ain't got no choice.

Some of us look to the blues as an art form the disenfranchised, marginalized, embittered, and shackled people used to express their own humanity and to steal back the power of truth. We can talk about technique and strategies until we are hoarse, but in the end, the truth of the truth, our ultimate goal is to create, or re-create a feeling, and that feeling in and of itself is truth.

Feeling is the ultimate goal, the thing that unites the forms—writing, photography, videos, movies, installation art, sound. Documentation in a vacuum is specious: facts, figures, measurements, recordings only. Like blues songs, your calling, my young friends, is to take us higher, to hunt for a meaning, to make us uncomfortable, to make us feel the truth.

IN 1903, W. E. B. DU BOIS wrote in his seminal essay: "On the Sorrow Songs":

> They that walked in darkness sang songs in the olden days—
> Sorrow Songs—for they were weary at heart. . . . Ever since I
> was a child these songs have stirred me strangely. They came
> out of the South unknown to me, one by one, and yet at once
> I knew them as of me and of mine. Then in after years when
> I came to Nashville I saw the great temple builded of these
> songs towering over the pale city. To me Jubilee Hall seemed
> ever made of the songs themselves, and its bricks were red
> with the blood and dust of toil. Out of them rose for me
> morning, noon, and night, bursts of wonderful melody, full

of the voices of my brothers and sisters, full of the voices of the past.

Little of beauty has America given the world save the rude grandeur God himself stamped on her bosom; the human spirit in this new world has expressed itself in vigor and ingenuity rather than in beauty. And so by fateful chance the Negro folk-song—the rhythmic cry of the slave—stands to-day not simply as the sole American music, but as the most beautiful expression of human experience born this side the seas. It has been neglected, it has been, and is, half despised, and above all it has been persistently mistaken and misunderstood; but notwithstanding, it still remains as the singular spiritual heritage of the nation and the greatest gift of the Negro people.

THE LEARNING TREE

Gordon Parks's 1963 novel, *The Learning Tree*, could have been one of those photographs he took while working for the Farm Security Administration come to life. To be sure, it was his life, based largely on his experiences growing up on a small farm in rural Kansas in the 1920s and 1930s. It is a story of a young teenager and racism and poverty, and to some degree sexuality and growing up.

He was born Gordon Roger Alexander Buchanan Parks on November 30, 1912, in Fort Scott, Kansas, the youngest of fifteen children. His mother died when he was sixteen. For a brief while, he lived with an older sister in St. Paul, Minnesota, but things did not work out so he struck out on his own. He quit school and took on a number of jobs, including working as a (self-taught) pianist with an all-white band and with the Civilian Conservation Corps.

Gordon Parks had a lot to sing the blues about. To borrow from some of our leading literary scholars, like Houston Baker and Albert Murray, it is safe to say, Parks is an archetypical blues hero.

(As Melvin Van Peebles writes in the introduction to Parks's 1990 autobiography, *Voices in the Mirror*, "Gordon Parks was my first idol in the flesh." The other two being Jesus and Joe Louis.)

There was a time in this country when *The Learning Tree*, along with *I Know Why the Caged Bird Sings* and *To Kill a Mockingbird*, was found on a great many high school syllabuses throughout the United States.

———

THE TRUTH IS not sentimental. The truth is dangerous. The truth will get you in trouble. In his 1979 memoir, *To Smile in Autumn*, Parks talks about how telling the truth in his images made many of his editors at *Life* and *Time* uncomfortable, and the nimble thinking and acting he had to do in the segregated South to walk into heated situations as the "Negro with a camera around his neck." What was he doing there? He was in the Jim Crow South capturing the truth, a truth frankly many white folk did not want exposed. Imagine the reactions he got.

———

THE SCARY TRUTH about fiction and nonfiction is that when it comes to writing, to capturing—the difference is that there is no difference. Anyone who believes there is a difference in how we approach the actual craft of fiction-making and the craft of creating nonfiction narrative is suffering under a cloud of delusion. And I have discovered of late, that many people suffer from this misconception.

———

I TAKE TWO of my favorites as examples: Joseph Mitchell's masterpiece, *Joe Gould's Secret*, and Robert Penn Warren's *All the King's Men*.

Joe Mitchell was a country boy from my homeland, down east North Carolina, from Fairmont, to be exact. After matriculating at the University of North Carolina at Chapel Hill, he went to find his fortune in New York City, where he wrote for many of the major newspapers before signing on as a staff writer for the *New Yorker* magazine. If you don't know the work of Joseph Mitchell, it is important to know that he was the prose counterpart to those photographers I mentioned earlier. He was writing in the same era with those same concerns, those same sensibilities, often the same subject matter. Or in his words: "Down among the cranks and the misfits and the one-lungers and the has-beens and the might've-beens and the would-bes and the never-wills and the God-knows-whats." *Talk about the blues!* He loved hanging out with fishermen and bartenders and circus performers, and policemen and conmen, and ticket-takers and oddballs of every sort. His crowning achievement was based on what we today would identify as a homeless person. In those days known abrasively as a bum.

In Mitchell's *Joe Gould's Secret* he writes:

> Joe Gould was an odd and penniless and unemployable little man who came to the city in 1916 and ducked and dodged and held on as hard as he could for over thirty-five years. He was a member of one of the oldest families in New England ("The Goulds were the Goulds," he used to say, "when the Cabots and the Lowells were clamdiggers"), he was brought up in a town near Boston in which his father was a leading citizen, and he went to Harvard, as did his father and grandfather before him, but he claimed that until he arrived in New York City he had always felt out of place . . .
>
> Gould looked like a bum and lived like a bum. He wore castoff clothes, and he slept in flophouses or in the cheapest rooms in cheap hotels. Sometimes he slept in doorways.

Later: a description of the first time he saw Joe Gould:

He was around five feet four or five, and quite thin; he could
hardly have weighed more than ninety pounds. He was bareheaded, and he carried his head cocked on one side, like an
English sparrow. His hair was long, and he had a bushy beard.
There were streaks of dirt on his forehead, obviously from rubbing it with dirty fingers. He was wearing an overcoat that was
several sizes too larger for him; it reached almost to the floor.
He held his hands clasped together for warmth–it was a bitter-
cold day—and the sleeves forming a sort of muff. Despite his
beard, the man, in the oversized overcoat, bareheaded and
dirty-faced, had something childlike and lost about him: a
child who had been up in the attic with other children trying on grownups' clothes and had become tired of the game
and wandered off. He stood still for a few moments, getting
his bearings, and then he came over to Panagakos [the diner
owner] and said, "Can I have something to eat now, Harry? I
can't wait until tonight."

Here is the thing about Joseph Mitchell's work that I personally
adore. The aforementioned photographs, the ones made famous
during that era of Hard Times, were all about capturing the
humanity of those people. The subject of the gaze is not merely
an object, simply a poor individual defined by their sad plight, but
an actual human being, with a story, worthy of dignity. There is
an impulse behind this type of work that urges you to identify, to
see the commonality, to make you feel, not pity, but a kinship and
a decency. When you look at a photograph by Dorothea Lange or
Gordon Parks, you don't think, "Brother, can you spare a dime?"
but you think, this is somebody, somebody like me, somebody real.
You see truth.

As a fiction writer, I am particularly interested in how we achieve this type of portraiture in prose fiction. So I turn to Robert Penn Warren, who once wrote, "Verisimilitude is everything," and to his Pulitzer Prize–winning 1947 novel, *All the King's Men*. In many ways this is a fictional equivalent to the school of photography I have been referencing and to the contemporary work of Joseph Mitchell. It is easy to read *All the King's Men* as a fictionalized biography—as many do—of the life of Huey Long, the autocratic governor of Louisiana, from 1928 to 1932, and US Senator from 1932 until his assassination in 1935. Famously Huey Long championed the poor, made a free college education possible in his home state, and health care accessible to the masses. He was also one of the most corrupt motherfuckers to hold elected office in this country. I would go so far as to nominate this epic tragedy a blues novel, and its hero, Willie Stark, as a quintessential blues hero. (No, you don't have to be Black to be a blues hero.) It is not by coincidence that I select here a novel that deals with the same era and same people as the school of photography that gave us Gordon Parks and the reportage of Joseph Mitchell. I want to know: How did Warren do it?

Our first encounter with Willie Stark is a bit artful. We see all the people around him—the driver, his son; we see the people's reaction when he comes to a small Louisiana town:

"It's Willie!"

The Boss kept walking straight ahead, his head bowed a little, the way a man bows his head when he is out walking by himself and has something on his mind. His hair fell down over his forehead, for he was carrying his hat in his hand. I knew his hair was down over his forehead, for I saw him give his head a quick jerk once or twice, the way he always did when he was walking alone and it fell down toward his eyes, the kind of motion a horse gives just after the bit is in and he's full of beans.

He walked straight across the street and across the patch of grass roots and up the steps of the courthouse. Nobody else followed him up the steps. At the top he turned around, slow, to face the crowd. He simply looked at them, blinking his big eyes a little, just as though he had just stepped out of the open doors and the dark hall of the courthouse behind him and was blinking to get his eyes adjusted to the light. He stood up there blinking, the hair down on his forehead, and the dark sweat patch showing under each arm of his Palm Beach coat. Then he gave his head a twitch, and his eyes bulged wide suddenly, even if the light was hitting him full in the face, and you cold see the glitter in them.

It's *coming*, I thought.

IF WE HAD world enough and time I could talk at length about how Mitchell and Warren use so many of the same devices and techniques, how very like Joseph Mitchell Jack Burden, the novel's narrator, is; how the tone of these narrators affects the reader's view of the character; how dialogue—the chief weapon of characterization—is deployed over and over again, slyly and with force; how action—think of Long/Stark's theater of stump-speaking, or the minutiae of Gould asking for a cup of tomato soup—is both deliberately chosen and illuminating of character.

Moreover, both Mitchell and Warren are first and last *storytellers*. They never forget the main thrust of their story (what does your character want?—in the case of Joe Gould, it is to obscure the fact that his great idea, *The Oral History*, was never completed, and in the case of Willie Stark, he simply wishes to become President of the United States and push the world into his radical populist vision); Mitchell and Warren use how other characters view their main subject; they flirt and subvert stereotype, that mental baggage we all bring along with us; they exploit the unpredictable; ultimately they give us that Aristotelian moment of discovery—learning, changing (and they are also aware of the fact that some people do not change!) These writers and photographers use place ruthlessly and with great art—in the case of Mitchell it is New York, always a character in his writing; and in the case of Warren it is the entire state of Louisiana, a love letter to a landscape.

———————

THIS, OF COURSE, you realize, is all witchcraft. Hocus pocus. And witchcraft can be black or white.

The same can be said of the blues.

"I am not the potter, or the potter's wheel." Both fiction and nonfiction are made things. Writers, creators, above all, must always be mindful of this bedrock truth. We are making stuff.

Gordon Parks said: "I saw that the camera could be a weapon against poverty, against racism, against all sorts of social wrongs. I knew at that point I had to have a camera."

———————

IN 1969, GORDON PARKS wrote the screenplay based on his 1963 novel, *The Learning Tree*, and directed the film released by Warner Brothers. He also collaborated on the film's score. As I said earlier, it was the first major motion picture directed by an African American, and would go on to be included in the National Film Registry in 1989. Then in 1971 would come *Shaft*. *Shaft* capitalized on Melvin Van Peebles's runaway success with his film *Sweet Sweetback's Baadasssss Song*, (which, until *The Blair Witch Project*, was the highest-grossing independent movie of all time). Whereas Van Peebles's notorious movie is a somewhat romanticized version of urban Black life and a vision of the Black outlaw as hero, John Shaft is a police detective and an unblemished hero, *Shaft* nonetheless set the stage for almost a decade of blaxploitation films, glorifying Black criminality as Black cool, some of these flicks made by Parks himself.

Isaac Hayes won an Academy Award and a Grammy for the musical score and for best song:

> . . . *You know that cat Shaft was a bad mother* . . .

Parks would go on to make a film for PBS in 1984, *Solomon North-up's Odyssey*, based on the important 1853 slave narrative *12 Years a Slave*—twenty-nine years before Steve McQueen and John Ridley got there. He would also make a biopic for television, *Leadbelly*, based on the life of blues legend Huddie Leadbelly, a true blues hero if ever there was one. I wonder, did Parks identify? I'm sure he did.

———

PARKS HAD WRITTEN an orchestral work back in the 1950s, a concerto for piano and orchestra, and *The Tree Symphony* in 1967. He wrote a hit song called "No Love," and composed and directed a ballet based on the life of Martin Luther King Jr., in 1990.

"I didn't set out to do all that I did," Parks once told an interviewer. "I think there was always fear—fear of not being educated. All the things I did were done because of the fear of failure."

———

CONSIDER THREE POWERFUL stories from our cultural history: *Robinson Crusoe, Moby-Dick, Mutiny on the Bounty.*

In the case of Alexander Selkirk, he did exist. He was the man, he was there, he suffered. He was a Scots man who was castaway on a deserted island in the Pacific in 1703 and who was finally rescued in 1709. Years later, several accounts, including accounts written by Selkirk himself, were published. But we remember Daniel Defoe's 1719 novel, *The Life and Adventures of Robinson Crusoe*, best. In fact, many people believe he was an actual fellow. Why?

Herman Melville spent many years at sea as a whaler, so it made sense that he would undertake to transmute *The Narrative of the Most Extraordinary and Distressing Shipwreck of the Whale-Ship Essex*, written in 1821, into his 1851 masterwork, *Moby-Dick, or The Whale*.

THERE'S A HELLHOUND ON YOUR TRAIL   223

Owen Chase was the first mate and one of eight survivors, and his book was out of print at the time and essentially forgotten. But why do we remember Moby Dick and Ahab and Ishmael, and not—until recently, with the publication of a powerful new work of nonfiction—the *Essex*?

And lastly, *Mutiny on the Bounty*. The books, the movies—three so far and counting. As a boy, when I first saw the Charles Laughton version, I had no idea there actually was a Captain Bligh and a Fletcher Christian, and that there was actually a ship called *Bounty*, and that Captain Bligh actually did live through one of the most amazing stories of survival at sea—forty-seven days—to live and write about it, and to be written about. It is through fiction that we remember his tale most vividly.

_____

WHY DO WE recognize the fictionalized versions of these stories more than we recognize the originals, many of which had gone begging and out of print in the lifetime of the chroniclers? Where did Defoe, Melville, Charles Laughton, and even Robert Penn Warren and Joseph Mitchell go right? Why is telling the facts alone not enough?

_____

I SUBMIT TO YOU that storytelling is older than Samuel Richardson and Lady Murasaki's *Tale of Genji*; I submit to you that the atoms of storytelling are essentially the same, and that ultimately, if well done, the story itself, even greater than the original flesh and blood, will live on—if it's told right; if it is captured right; if it holds some nugget of truth.

We are talking here about the stuff of alchemy, truly arcane stuff, the stuff of dreams, changing, transforming, transmuting elements. Taking the dull, uninteresting lead of life and making it shine, making it mean, making it sing.

We are speaking of an act of imagination and an act of faith. As I intimated earlier: witchcraft. Are you a black witch or are you a white witch?

———————

GORDON PARKS DIED in 2006 at the age of ninety-three. He was the author of books of poetry, three memoirs, three novels, manuals on photography and filmmaking; he had directed over eleven films; he had been a founder of *Essence* magazine; and his photographs became the subject of innumerable exhibitions, continuing to this day. He donated 227 original prints to the permanent collection of the Corcoran Gallery of Art in Washington in 1998. His motto: "Not allowing anyone to set boundaries, cutting loose the imagination and then making the new horizons."

———————

SO HERE IS the question, my friends: Will you be willing to tell the truth? To sing the blues? To work to create in your brothers and sisters that feeling of eye-witness, to let us all know what it was like to be there? Will you, like James Agee and Walker Evans, go into the wilds of the world and fearlessly capture and stick your finger into the eyes of the Henry Luces of the world? Will you like Gordon Parks go into that same corporate entity and that same Southern wild, and bring back witness that will teach us how to see and feel? Will you be capable of singing the blues even when you are sitting on a pile of gold? Do you have what it takes to become your own blues heroes?

Will you have the guts to stare down that hellhound and say, *Git! Git on away from me! I got work to do.*

I hope and pray that you may.

If you do, I assure you, the sun is gonna shine in your back door one day.

PART III
THAT
ETERNAL
BURNING

17

Finding the
Forgotten

For some odd reason, I keep thinking of William Faulkner's *Intruder in the Dust*. The classic novel is best remembered for the scene in which a Black man and a white man dig up a body in order to clear another man jailed for murder. And though race, the dead, the South, and crime are all involved in the story of Richmond's historic Evergreen Cemetery, the scene this morning is in many ways the complete opposite of Faulkner's whodunit. Now the dead remain underground, and Black and white folk are collaborating in the sunshine to clear and honor their resting places. A century ago, Evergreen was the premier burial place for African Americans in Richmond. But the sixty-acre site has been severely neglected for decades. Attempts to reclaim it from the forest have started and stopped for more than thirty years. Today is the first concerted effort in three years, and it is remarkable to see how swiftly a forest can retake a graveyard.

It's Saturday, bright and early. A line of cars leads the way, and at the entrance to Evergreen, a silver-haired woman stands behind a folding table, taking names. Three men hang up a long banner—

MAGGIE L. WALKER HIGH SCHOOL CLASS OF 1967 (an all-Black school at the time)—and smile for pictures. Marvin Harris, a member of that class and the lead volunteer cleanup coordinator for this formidable project, greets me. He is a powerfully built man with hands as strong as wire cables. In the distance: chain saws, lawn mowers, the sounds of chopping, cutting. People calling out to one another. About forty people have gathered, and all are at work.

A Richmond native, Harris is the owner and CEO of Harris Group Promotions and Supply, an industrial supply company in the city. Eight years ago, he read an article in the local paper about Evergreen and other African American cemeteries in Richmond. He called a friend who had a relative buried here and scheduled twelve people to come help. Only four showed up. "It was quite a situation," Harris says. This initial effort led to more and more investment of time, and sweat, and outreach for help. "Somebody had to step up to the plate," he continues. "If we handle this as a community, we can get it back to the glory days."

The forest is dense and thick and reminds me of the woods I roamed as a boy. But this density was once a place for families to come honor their dead in pastoral reverence and green splendor. In the late nineteenth and early twentieth centuries, having picnics in cemeteries was not uncommon for most Americans. Save for the marble markers now poking up periodically—choked by weeds, surrounded by tall grass, or swallowed by ivy—one might never realize we're in the midst of a graveyard.

II.

This part of the city east of I-95 is distinctly suburban, the towers of Richmond receding in the distance. A multitude of cemeteries dot the landscape, decorously. Most are well manicured and unassuming. Hollywood—near the center of town, on the banks of the James

River—is where the high and mighty ultimately come to rest. Presidents Monroe and Tyler and Confederate president Jefferson Davis are buried there. Following Reconstruction, four African American cemeteries were established in this eastern section of town, in light of Jim Crow segregation: East End, Colored Pauper's Cemetery, Woodland Cemetery, and the largest, Evergreen. Established in 1891, Evergreen was meant to be the dark mirror of Hollywood.

Of all the bustling cities of the American South during the Jim Crow era, Richmond laid claim to one of the nation's largest Black middle classes. As a result, they had the means to memorialize their dead grandly.

The most commanding grave marker stands in the central section of Evergreen, a marble cross about ten feet tall. It rests over Maggie L. Walker, the first woman (of any color) to establish and become president of a bank in the United States. In 1903, she successfully chartered the St. Luke Penny Savings Bank. This led to a merger with two other banks to form the Consolidated Bank and Trust Company, which became a significant institution for African Americans in Richmond. Walker was also a teacher and a leader in education and women's rights. Many organizations throughout Richmond and the rest of Virginia have been named after her, and her home has become a National Historic Site. Until this morning, her grave and monument had been engulfed in impassable brush, hard to find, even harder to reach. But already volunteers have cleared the immediate area surrounding it, the grave and marker now free and clear, along with dozens of others.

Not too far from Walker are the graves of John Mitchell Jr. and his mother. Mitchell was a bank president, and the editor and publisher of the *Richmond Planet*, a leading voice against lynching at the turn of the twentieth century. He unsuccessfully ran for governor of Virginia in 1921.

For more than thirty years, African Americans were interred

here, the prominent—eminent ministers, doctors, lawyers, successful businessmen, and their families—and the not-so-prominent.
But something went sadly wrong. Neglect set in sometime after
the crash of 1929 and the onset of the Great Depression. Buri-
als continued for a while, but the graveyard slowly disappeared
into the forest. Nobody knows exactly how many people are buried here. Some estimates run as high as sixty thousand graves in
Evergreen alone.

III.

John Shuck is originally from Iowa. A farm boy, He has lived in Virginia since 2001 and over the years has taken the lead in many ways
in reclaiming much of the smaller, neighboring East End Cemetery.
(He estimates East End, at sixteen acres, is now approximately 25
percent cleared.) Now he coordinates volunteer work for the reclamation of both Evergreen and East End, and most Saturday morn-
ings you can find him cutting brush, raking, pointing out resting
places of note.

Shuck is tall and professorial, with the mien of a museum docent,
and a touch of Indiana Jones with his wide-brimmed floppy explor-
er's hat. No cemetery records for Evergreen exist prior to 1929, he
tells me. "So there are no existing records of who is buried here, or
where." He had been a graveyard hobbyist, photographing tombstones and researching genealogies, when he first heard about
the cemeteries and came out to photograph in June 2008. He had
never seen a cemetery that looked like this. "I thought it might be
interesting to clear a plot or two, and that was eight years ago," he
says. "Investigating the history of these people helped me learn the
history of Richmond." Shuck and his team of volunteers recently
uncovered their two-thousandth grave marker at East End. He posts
photos of the markers online so that family members can find them.

Shuck leads me to a particularly heartbreaking monument in Evergreen. It lies away from the central area the workers have been clearing this morning. Trees and overgrown ivy surround the monument, and it's difficult to negotiate. We climb over felled trunks and limbs; the final step includes a big jump down over a ledge. Not much is known of the Braxton family, though some of their descendants still live in Richmond. The narrow mausoleum was probably erected in the mid-1920s. Five coffins rest within. At some point, probably in the 1950s, the steel door was ripped off, and the caskets removed and desecrated. Someone ran an illegal still inside the mausoleum, Shuck tells me. You can still see smoke stains on the ceiling.

The graveyard has a tendency to attract paranormal seekers. Shuck remembers finding odd string structures hung above and among the graves, telltale signs of hoodoo rituals. Vandals intruded for decades. Marijuana was grown on the property. It became, perversely, a destination for prostitution. Condom wrappers were a common find.

IV.

The volunteers are mighty busy. Within hours, an area at the center of the graveyard, radiating out from the Walker marker, looks as if it has always been well kept.

"God called us to help fix it," Marvin Harris tells me. "If the owners allow us to help fix it, it will get fixed." The land is privately owned, and work came to a halt three years ago because of a dispute about using volunteers on private land. But that conflict was recently resolved. "For the average person with any type of heart," Harris says, "I can't see how they could not get involved."

I speak with some of the volunteers. Bud Funk is a seventy-one-year-old trial attorney. He joined in after hearing Harris speak to

a local group. "Marvin gets inside your heart," Funk says. The first
time Funk saw the site years ago it was "daunting." Now he not only
volunteers his back and limbs, but also does legal work in partner-
ship with Enrichmond, a nonprofit that supports the effort. Other
members of the Maggie L. Walker High School class of 1967 here
this day include civil servants, an executive chef, and family members of those buried here. "My grandfather," one man tells me. "I
would come by here before, looking, and all I could see was trash."

"No cemetery should fall into this type of landscape," says John
Baliles, a Richmond city councilman representing the 1st District.
When I first spot him, he is doing battle with a long vine snaking
its way about a large tombstone. "This will take a strong volunteer
effort. But it is easier to preserve if you maintain it."

There's a stark contrast between the acreage cleared this morning
and the work yet to be done. Just within a copse of trees, a dozen or
more gravestones poke up from the grass and undergrowth. Clearing the area will require heavier equipment and skill. Shuck and
Harris have been discussing bringing in a herd of goats to help and
inviting a different corporate sponsor each month to pay for them.

V.

A Virginia historian and business owner, Veronica Davis literally
wrote the book about Richmond's African American cemeteries,
Here I Lay My Burdens Down, in 2003. Davis says the reclamation
efforts began with a former National Park Service superintendent,
Dwight Storke. Heartsick at these languishing sites of African
American history, he spearheaded an attempt in the 1980s to have
them cleared and restored. One part elbow grease, another part
education, it started with a gathering of volunteers in celebration
of Maggie Walker's birthday. The initial volunteers removed fifteen
truckloads of debris.

Over the decades, a series of Parks officials and local organizations arranged cleanups, and in the late 1990s, Davis herself created a group, Virginia Roots, to continue the efforts, but it has been slow going. Family members and volunteers move away or die off, and the cemeteries have gone through a number of private owners through the years. Without a system of perpetual care or funding, the work is difficult to maintain. Nor is the situation at Evergreen unique. Migration of families to the North during Jim Crow, scanty records, and a lack of public and private funds for upkeep have all led to the neglect of other historic African American cemeteries across the region.

"I thank God for this work every day," Davis says. "We have to show our ancestors respect for what they have done. We're talking about choices here, and we need to remember that one of the choices that the dead made was to fight for our freedom. Now we have another choice to make."

VI.

Midday: The Tony Award–winning actress L. Scott Caldwell arrives, dressed to work. Caldwell plays a formerly enslaved woman named Belinda on the PBS historical drama *Mercy Street*, which is shot on location in Richmond and nearby Petersburg. The actress is known for taking her research seriously, and visits not only the local museums and historical societies but also places and sites central to African American history. She had heard about the project on the morning news. "It was a question of doing what I can to become a part of the community," she says. "Where we are, there I am." She was haunted by the story of Julia Hoggett, who was born into slavery. Hoggett's gravestone is tucked under a mighty oak, and kudzu threatens to overgrow it. Caldwell had read about this marker during her research and was keen to see it in person. It reads:

IN MEMORY OF MY MAMMY,

JULIA HOGGETT

1849–1930

She was born a slave and a slave she chose to remain.

Slave to duty, a slave to love.

Few people of any race or condition of life have lived so unselfishly,

which is the same as saying so nobly.

—LAMOTTE BLAKELY

Who was LaMotte Blakely? Was he a white child Julia Hoggett raised? "This spoke to me in a literal way," Caldwell says. She is referring partly to her character, who in her freedom chooses to be the good and faithful servant of a well-to-do white family. But it's more than that—there is a humanity here, a complexity, a dignity. She's less interested in the big names and monuments, she tells me, than in those workers with unsung lives whose secrets are interred with their bones. "I'm more intrigued by the unknown than the known," she says. "This is history."

18

Chitlins and Chimichangas: A Southern Tale in Black and Latin

A PROPOSAL FOR A DOCUMENTARY

Synopsis: Rural Duplin County, North Carolina, the archetypical Southern home of tobacco and hog farms—the real "Mayberry," has, seemingly overnight, become the home of a large number of Mexican migrants. This is the story of how the African American and Mexican populations are grappling with change and each other. (Fifty words—needs to be twenty-five! This is the basic information, but it needs to be pithier and more precise.)

———————

TOBACCO ROAD. DOG PATCH. Hog Heaven. Land of Cotton. All these terms have been used to describe this part of rural North Carolina. Though much has changed in the last twenty years, in many ways the landscape and livelihoods have not strayed far from that agrarian past. Now, at the turn of the twenty-first century, a shift has occurred that augurs a heretofore unimagined future. *Chitlins and Chimichangas* will examine this shift from being a humble community of white and Black yeomen farmers to becoming an increasingly volatile mix of white, Black, and Mexican. This documentary delves into that change, shows the Duplin County landscape, the people involved, and their hopes and their dreams and delusions. [–new hog farms (more hogs than people in Duplin Co. and North Carolina)] [–Discrimination against Mexicans by Black folk; Mexicans' feelings toward Black folk. The idea of xenophobia and how African Americans are responding to the "other."]

The overall narrative structure of the documentary will follow that of the personal essay. I grew up in the hamlet of Chinquapin (pop. 250) and lived there until I went off to college. As a person who intimately knows the people who live there, my observations will be a key to telling this story. The changes in culture and makeup, twenty years after I left, are staggering to me. Woven throughout the film will be my personal observations and questions regarding how this shift in demography will ultimately affect the region. I will offer musings on possible futures and possible conflicts and possible benefits not only to Duplin County but also to North Carolina and to the United States.

At present we are considering structuring the narrative into five sections: 1) a brief look at the current state of Duplin County; 2) a step back in time, looking at Duplin County's past through the eyes of its African American citizens; 3) a look at how the Mexican population began and how it grew; 4) the clashes, attitudes, and present realities of these two groups; 5) a glimpse into the future.

INTRODUCTION:

This brief section will give a visual taste of the new Mexican North Carolina. A drive-through of the sleepy Southern town of Chinquapin, now home to a number of thriving Mexican bodegas and iglesias, or churches. Young men clustered outside the post office. Children at play. There will be scenes of the landscape as it exists today, the hog farms, Mexicans at work in the fields, the mixed nature of the shopping environments, multitudes of signs in Spanish.

THE STATUS QUO:

Perhaps to an outsider these changes might not seem so dramatic. This section will help lay the groundwork for understanding how remarkable this shift has been. For that reason this section will also be the most personal and the most historical. It will contain interviews with Black residents about the past of Chinquapin and Duplin County. I will interview relatives and teachers, farmers and ministers, and other memorable members of the community. A brief history of the area will be woven into the discussion. [Folk culture.]

EXPLOSION:

Here we will quickly examine how and why the Mexican population grew so quickly; how an exploited migrant population laid down roots and sprang into a viable and integral segment of the area. For this section I will interview some of the longer-term residents and explore their reasons for remaining in North Carolina. We will end with the current statistics, and scenes of the small Duplin County towns of Magnolia and Faison and Calypso and Rose Hill, which now have significant Mexican populations.

STEW:

This, the longest section, will focus on the current situation and will consist primarily of interviews with people—both Mexican and Black—giving anecdotes, observations, and reflections. We will talk to them about clashes and incidents, large and small.

We will examine how these two populations are colliding, the problems and feelings involved; how some Black folk are using methods and attitudes that whites once used against them; how Mexicans feel about the Black residents and how they feel about their segregated position. And perhaps most poignantly—to me— the sense of isolation among young Latinos in such a rural area, and their experiences in school.

EPILOGUE: SPANISH HIP-HOP AND
COLLARD GREEN TORTILLAS:

Finally, as an epilogue or coda, we will look toward the future. What are the implications of this new population? What problems are on the horizon? What ways will they learn to work together? What are the possibilities of their alliance? Situations that inspire hope about a productive future together. De rigueur to this vision of the future will be a scene from Walmart on the weekend, a postmodern snapshot of the current state of affairs. This concluding section will be peppered with bits of conversation from people speculating about the future.

Musically speaking, this documentary offers exciting possibilities. Both these cultures have made significant contributions in terms of their musical idioms. Most familiar to practically everyone would be the Mexican mariachi tradition and the more recent Tejano music from the border. North Carolina's African Americans have long been famous for their contributions to the spiritual and gospel forms, as well as their own brand of the blues and even jazz.

But beyond the obvious choices [. . . Hip-hop . . . ideas regarding the score . . .]

During the last twenty-five years, outside of programming regarding the civil rights movement and music, public television has not paid much attention to rural Black people in the Southeast. This project will be primarily about the African American and Mexican communities. [Being an African American from the area gives me a singular insight into this milieu.—already stated? Overstatement?]

Stories like this one are essential for a deeper understanding of the totality of the United States and the changes that are underway. In many ways this unfolding drama is a synecdoche for the current transformation of North America and its institutions, as well as a living model of how America has always gone about absorbing new cultures. These are the sorts of stories that public television can tell best.

INFORMATION AND SCENES to Work into the Body:
- Interview with Cousin Seymour (Black farmer) and his work experience with Mexicans. He has an atypical view of these men and has established good working relationships.
- church scenes; family reunion
- scenes of farm workers

19

Letter from
North Carolina

LEARNING FROM GHOSTS OF THE CIVIL WAR

The war has only just begun.

Dear ones,
'Tis the season for toppling Confederate monuments.

And this particular location feels as if it were the epicenter, the beginning, when students tore down the "iconic" statue at the front gates of the University of North Carolina on the evening of August 20, 2018, leading to the confrontation between Klansmen and right-wing activists and fresh-faced students, and the firing of our chancellor. Looking at the videos of cops manhandling and clashing with young people—Black, white, and Asian—feels prescient. But I can't help thinking of the lithe Bree Newsome who climbed the flagpole in Columbia, South Carolina, in 2015 and ripped down the Confederate flag as a galvanizing and generative moment. Yes, Black Lives Matter was a full-fledged movement by that point, but a certain focus had already begun to take over the young folk, and the memorialization of the Confederacy felt absolutely galling.

It was galling before, but the idea that something could be done about the celebration of the "Lost Cause" had become imaginable. But it wasn't only about the Civil War. It was about Jim Crow. It was about UpSouth Chicago and Detroit. It was about gentrification.

I was an undergraduate here at UNC in the 1980s and walked past Silent Sam every day. It is not that I didn't see it or know its history—on the day of its dedication, a local millionaire, Julian Carr, who paid for it, bragged about whipping a Black "wench" until he shredded her clothes. Every Black student I knew knew that story, and it cut us to our core, yet imagining it actually coming down was not considered a possibility; the fact that it would stand so arrogantly, well into the twenty-second century, seemed an inevitability. That such righteous destruction would one day happen in Charlotte, Durham, Fayetteville, New Orleans, and ultimately Richmond, the capital of the Confederacy, would have struck me as science fiction in 1984. That the names of racist generals would be stripped from one-hundred-year-old buildings, the least possible. (Our current chancellor has announced most of these buildings will now be renamed.)

Still, what I most would have struggled to imagine, is that certain people would be up in arms were it to ever happen. That they would quite literally take over a state capitol building, bearing arms in anger to keep monuments up. That we might have another civil war over the matter.

Can we seize the moment? We all must now readjust our thinking.

For me—a poor Black boy from the swamps of eastern North Carolina—the Civil War was far from a lost cause, let alone a done war. I had underestimated how unfinished. Most Southern states are host to many Civil War reenactors, many of them quite literate, supposedly sticklers for historical accuracy who can argue about geography all night, but the fantasies these monuments and symbols represent don't embarrass them. I find this mystifying. They still defend these murderous, enslaving individuals, these traitors. Even though—being such students of "the War of Northern Aggression"—they know full well these monuments were erected decades after the War had been won—not a lost cause at all—to bolster the Big Brother eyes of Jim Crow, to reinforce the notion of racial superiority. These statues are monuments to that war, not the war of Lee and Sherman and Grant.

The coming war will not be about the monuments, but the mentalities. Let's be clear on what that future war will be about: Why hold on to these antiquated notions of skin color signifying some type of superiority? Why cling to a past of loss and degradation? (Those who fought for the Confederacy were clearly back-broken in the end.) Why was holding other human beings in bondage a cause worth fighting for, other than money? When most of the white men who died for the Confederacy were as poor as church mice?

Yes, it is hard to imagine we have come to this moment in the early years of the twenty-first century. As a life-long fan of *Star Trek*, who lived to see the first Black Vulcan elected to the presidency of the United States, this entire situation feels very like something out of the back of Gene Roddenberry's mind. (I love that MLK exhorted Nichelle Nichols to keep her job as Lieutenant Uhura because she was the only Black woman on television who represented Black women in a position that was not a maid. It is fun and amazing to think: what would MLK think of Kamala Harris?

Roddenberry might could have imagined such a 2020, but I never might have imagined it. Today is impossible. The convergence of Donald J. Trump, the coronavirus pandemic, the unrest over police abuse, and the tumbling of Confederate monuments were all unimaginable decades back. Can we seize the moment? We all must now readjust our thinking. The war has only just begun.

Chapel Hill is a truly spooky place right now. It feels like a ghost town where fifty thousand young folk used to play. Now only one or two students amble about the halls. The large, long campus is populated by a small percentage of their once-robust population, where thousands thronged among the century-old Federal-style buildings. There is nothing but grass where the silent statue once stood. The public-safety officers who once wrangled teenagers to the ground like military police in a war zone are now herding them apart when they gather in crowds. The not-knowing keeps everyone on edge. But the country's oldest public university is truly haunted by its mythical Confederate past. Even ghosts can teach us a thing or two.

20

That Eternal
Burning

A boy watches fire: What does he see? In its hot tongues, in its impossible redness—what does he see? What does he hear? Does he see history, atrocious and bloody? Hear the cries of his mothers giving birth, the muffled clops of mules in the fields, the screams of his fathers being lynched? Does the fire speak as a voice did to Moses, saying: I am? Or does it hum and spank out some sweet bluesology:

Got to get on back to my getting back
Got to get on back to my getting back
Got to get on outta here

Mothers of the church, revival preachers, barbers, beauticians, truck drivers, cooks, guitar pickers, farmers, all meet in him, in this boy of ours.

(He, no more than thirteen? Twelve? Eleven? He with his head full of hip-hop and basketball and comic books and mischief; he, so American, so Mark Twain-young, a Huckleberry, a Sawyer, a fan of Michael Jordan, perhaps, and the X-Men, he . . .)

They, we, pray for his soul; they, we, plead for his attention, praying:

O Lord, creator of the Universe, in him is so much history, so much past, so much future, watch over him, Father-God. Lord, our hearts bleed, and our minds ache with worry over him. His brothers and sisters see so much trouble. His people done come a mighty long way. Reach out to him, Father-God, and don't let his feet stray. Keep him on the narrow path, Sweet Jesus. Lord, don't move his mountain, but give him the strength to climb, and don't take away his stumbling block, but lead him the way around. He is our future, Father-God, and if your eyes are on the sparrow . . . Amen and Amen.

We pray this prayer like an ancient song, its riffs and melody and notes so familiar and threadbare, but we believe that they have power, and, for the sake of one so young, we have faith that they do. For this boy watching this fire.

(Look, his eyes: Bright they are, wide and glowing, like the fire. Such open, inquisitive eyes, eyes that are older and younger, eyes of a sprite, eyes of kindness, tender eyes, merciful eyes, eyes that do not know how to hate, eyes that barely know the tangle and demands, the heat and damnation of love, eyes so new they make old men smile and old women tear with joy. A boy's own eyes)

What does the fire say to him? Does it speak in English or Hebrew or Ibo or Yoruba or Hausa or Arabic, Greek, Chinese? Does the fire tell him stories? Does the fire tell the boy something about himself? Or something about the world? Or by telling him something about the world, does the fire tell the boy something about himself? For the world our boy inhabits is richer than he may know. Someone saw it once. Tried to capture its fleeting essence. Did that someone succeed? The angels know. The angels, we are certain, hover and glide about this land, earthy in their concern; divine in their envy of humanity's pain and longing.

(You can feel it in the very land. Look: the fields: a sea of black earth, fecund and ripe and birth-giving. Pierced and yielding, furrowed and adorned, large:—What is that carcass? Who left it there to plow around?

Grace enchants this land. Surely the angels attend these people, this land: Land of sorrow, land of sweat, land of memory, land of midnight trains, land of the screech owl and the bear and the katydid and the coon and the timber rattler and the panther, land of tractors, land of foreclosures, land of once-slave and now-freedom, land of money, land of hogs and cows and chickens and turkeys and farm cats and dogs, land of corn and soybean, land of cotton, land of fear, land of hate, land of painful memories, land of God, land of Satan, land of pine and sycamore and spruce and maple and magnolia, land of love, land of heartbreak, land of misery, land of hope . . . Land of grace. Yet, grace)

Ah! See that ole cotton gin, gone to wreck and ruin. World don't need it no more, don't want it no more. Sad ole gin. Rods of light tickle through and alight the pity of the past, walls done buckled round and down, rafters, beams, contorted, twisted, all about is the presence of a goneness. That time's done and gone. Goodbye. But what now?

Now, there is still working in the fields. See the cotton fields: the fluffy-whiteness—deceptive soft, but a pain in plucking

(Picking up paw-paws
Putting em in a basket)

Such history in cotton. Cotton can tell a tale. Such money, now as it ever was. The bud, the boll, the flower. Alas, the trickle of its wealth never washes over the pickers, just a cool drop to drink, their fin-

gers to bleed, to callus, to harden, to ache. Better to be driving that
tractor, there you can gather wool and think: Of tonight? Of next
year? Of last year? Of that gal? So sweet . . . What did she call me . . .
Did she mean it? Perhaps remember the nape of her neck, the curve
of her buttock . . . Think of . . . anything except ole cotton.

But after work is done:

Hear who's coming to town? Powerhouse!

Let's go see: Let's go home and get clean smelling and comb our
hair and rush out. Let's join the crowd. Let's be caught up in the
singer's charisma. O look at them pretty girls! Lord, that boy can
sing and play! Let us dance: Dance to the rhythm and the blues,
dance—asses waving, arms flinging in the air,

to the rhythm
to the rhythm
to the rhythm
to the beat

a force, a feeling like the very sweat, the very funk, the very laughter
like brown sugar to the ear. (Yeah, boy, you got it now! Come on,
girl, show me what you got! Anybody want to party?) Feel the letting
go of the world, the forgetting and worries gone (for now: no bills,
no work, no rent due, no woman left you, no man took all your
money and gone, no mama sick, no daddy mean) and more forgetting: remembering, perhaps some promise engendered in the loins,
some promise of release, but distant, but vague, but seen only in a
hip, in a grind, in the sweet lips of one so near, yet ever far. Yes . . .

Or, to a juke joint

("We Welcome You" "Live Shows" "Cold Beer" "Big Record Spin"
"We Party" "No Drugs")

Gather round with friends, have a smoke, have a cold one, pull
up a chair—got a fresh new deck. Re-learn laughter again, and

make merry, under the Christmas lights in July. ("Gonna pitch a Wangdangdoodle!") See that woman over there shooting pool (hear the click of those cool smooth balls, the pop of the black 8-ball going in; the rattle of a score) Ain't she something else? Like her style. Like her form. Like her spirit. Like her. Like our boy in a way: Somebody's daughter, somebody's love—perhaps out to find love, she is, out to find fun. All gussied up like she is. You look good, girl.

But we, they, us, must go at some point, must sleep away the dreams of dreams, the day dreams and the dreams of day: Where? Home. A house. Is it a lonesome dwelling? Humble and alone? But that don't matter now cause we'll make the bed warm with our warm hopes and the promise of sleep: sleep: and be happy to lay the head down, lay the body down: sleep: and in sleep the bright (ssssshhh—*dimmed*, not to wake them, sleeping O so soundly) angels brush them, each and one, with their wings, with abiding—though briefly felt—comfort: sleep.

(But somebody's a-tossing, somebody's a-stirring, somebody's (two bodies) a-loving, somebody can't forget trying to forget, some mother's praying over her boy on that chain gang, like our boy once, our boy attending the wonder of fire.)

Until dawn comes and, soon in the morning, the fog rolls out, over the land, over the town. Listen: Hear the footsteps of a solitary figure striding brisk in the blue morning air, again to work, again to the fields, among, through, past, around these few buildings, buildings slowly leaning into themselves, into the dust of the streets: The earth. Before the trucks start rolling, tractors start humming, the cash registers start chinging and toil begins again, and sleep becomes a memory—gone.

But by afternoon—it's a Saturday!—there are scores of brown faces, here and there, a baby on a hip, a girl looking for her boy, a boy looking for his girl, a mama telling her child, Don't! Men sitting on

the stoops catching up—Did you hear? No. Well, let me tell you . . .
Come to find out . . . You gone away from here! If I'm lying I'm flying.—Old girl with that pretty dress on, where you going so fast?

Each with a face—though they don't know it, don't realize it—
quite unique, touching, if you look, open, full, in time transfixed
and fixed: Walking on a Saturday afternoon, carrying with them
the same promise, the same memories, the same past, the same
future, though different very alike, like our boy—Where are they
coming from? Where are they going?

Gone get something to eat! Mama's cooking's good, but every
now and again got to get out, got to go down to Elma's or to

("OLD FASHION COOKING BREAKFAST LUNCH DINNER
CHITTERLINGS BEANS HAMBURGERS FISH HOT DOGS
CHICKEN FRENCH FRIES GREENS" "SOUL FOOD")

Get some of them ribs, lick that good sauce off your fingers, get
messy with it cause that's when you known it's good. Some hog meat
is good eating. Get you some greens and some potato salad and,
boy, you know where God lives—or at least how he's eating.

(Hmm . . . we wonder what our boy likes: Hamburger and fries?
Hot dogs? Apple pie?)

After eating is done, after our mouths are made happy and our
bellies get full, after we've cleaned the plate and can't eat no more,
and we lean back and begin feeling that momentary feeling of
our body's own goodness, a calm descends, a blessing—(from the
angels?)—and our souls slowly get restless. Perhaps our souls want
to keep this peace forever, and know the feeling won't tarry—Is it
melancholy? What do we do?

We need music.

Yes. Music.

(Look: A man alone in a room, peaceful, looking out the window, the tune the tune of a time not here and yet always here. Hear? Man sits strumming at the guitar—picks, and frets, and a bottle on the finger—What's that sound? Why does it make the very gut twinge inside? What does it do to you? Does it stir the soul to be strong? To take wings? Like the angels? Does it roil lust? Does it quicken dread? Does it set you on fire?)

The fife's trill. The drum's giving beat.—Play that thang, boy!

Loved a girl on down the road
Loved a girl on down the road
Loved her so
And now she's gone

But this sound, like the song the fire may be singing to our boy, like the music of the angels, is fleeting, and comes in many forms, many guises. Some folks don't reckon that to be true: But it is.

Look: A woman is crying

(She got a letter this morning . . . How do you reckon it read? . . . Said hurry, on account of the man you love is dead . . . She grabbed up her suitcase and took out down the road . . . When she got there he was laying on the cooling board . . .)

See the people there? They come to bury their dead: As the casket goes down, they stand around feeling something, something like bewilderment, something like awe, something like, very like, a new-found absence. Yes. That's what it is.

(She didn't know she loved him till they lay him down . . .)

They come here to this graveyard, full of tombstones and crosses—See that cross under a tree? Like a promise from another world. Full of peace. Full of the inevitable. Quiet earth. Quiet death. Quiet. Surely the angels are here too—Ah, yes, see them. We, they, us, all come to here. In the end. Better get ready.

So Sunday morning that's where you'll find us—well, many of

us in church clapping, singing, shouting. We want to get ready. Put on our traveling shoes. Hear the Good News—Preach it! And here comes that sound again, in the piano, in the organ, in the throat like a mighty rumble that steals the heart, but this time it don't chase nothing, no—it brings: Bring me my salvation, cause I need to be redeemed! Sanctified. Gonna give up my soul in this rocky place, yes Lord, let the Angels carry me over there.

Over there.
Over there.
Over there.

("Take me to the waaaatterrr! To Be Baptized!")

The water is cool, if not cold; towels and robes dripping, little boys, little girls in white—think of innocence (think of our boy)— older men and women in white as well, all, all dunked down and raised as if a-new: this is their belief: this is what their religion teaches: to be baptized. So they come to the river.

Same river, the same water, that flows in those swamps up a ways, the cypress trees full of snakes and chiggers and possums and squirrels, catfish in the water, frogs and muskrat, briefly interrupted by the angelic heron (Even the angels pause with attention and envy and awe) in this land.

Land of vistas of fields, fields of vistas, the plain and the forest, the swamp and the street—this is the Mississippi landscape and lone and inspiring, vast in its still contemplations (Does the land imagine? Does the land dream?) Vast in its good bounty and troublesome history, vast in time and vast in space: Hear the melody of the earth, singing:

All God's Chillun Got Wings
All God's Chillun

All God's

All

Like our boy. Watching a fire.

We must wonder: Is the fire's voice kind and gentle, instructive; or does the fire boom and crash with Yahweh's might—What does God sound like?—frightening, subduing our boy, chastising him for being the seed of Adam, for sins he has not yet committed. Is the fire omniscient, giving the boy prophesy of the end, the ruination of man, or her salvation? Or, yet again, is the fire, like the boy, a new thing? Curious, wanting, sweet in its probing, new to language, new to this earth, vulnerable, unaware even that its touch can burn, awaiting the day when that realization will cause it confusion and pain, the beginning of sorrow? Does the fire realize, sense, that it is alone, that it will soon and very soon, grow old and die, leaving behind only its ember and ash, a testament to its having been, once, on this plain, conversing with a boy, whose eyes glow and whose face, inscrutable, youth-wise . . . ?

(That face, the open visage, it is at once as mysterious and infinite as it is simple and good.)

A boy watches fire: What does he see? What does he hear?

We cannot tell, we cannot know, we do not know, we will not know. This image—just as the cotton field, the baptism, the hallelujah prayer meetings and the pool hall and the juke joint, yes, even the mothers, the grandmothers, the fathers, the grandfathers, the sons, the daughters, good and bad, (How do we know? Could we ever know?) are all unknowable, and wondrously so, bewitching, strange, mutable, yet—made in a brief moment in time—are now always. Just like the fire. The fire our elfin lad tends with such passionate impassivity. This brief burning that lives in the soul of us all.

21

Love and Labor

And whatsoever mine eyes desired I kept not from them, I with-
held not my heart from any joy; for my heart rejoiced in all my
labour: and this was my portion of all my labour.

—Ecclesiastes 2:10

Whatsoever thy hand findeth to do, do it with thy might; for
there is no work, nor device, nor knowledge, nor wisdom, in
the grave, whither thou goest.

—Ecclesiastes 9:10

He that laboureth, laboureth for himself; for his mouth craveth
it of him.

—Proverbs 16:26

In the end it's all about play, isn't it?

———————

OF COURSE those of us who are supposed to take ourselves seriously—
take what we do seriously—must cower in fear of being found out—
found out by the bankers, the grocers, the lawyers, who frown with
secret contempt anyway at the idea of a writer. What is that? You
bake no bread, you mend no bones, you birth no babies, you tend
no busted carburetors, you build no houses—what is it exactly that
you do but sit around and make up things in your head? You, grown
man, grown woman, you do nothing but play all day.

Suppose you've published something. Suppose you're one of the luckier ones who's been hired to presume to teach the craft. Suppose a bit of ink has been spilt in your name and in your favor. Just suppose.

(Oh, and dear possums, forget it if you're the genius-in-hiding, working at the video store, or the brilliant lass who waits tables by day, both of you dedicated Flauberts and Hurstons by night, hunched over laptop or IBM Selectric or Underwood— Because, honey, you've got a whole lot of proving to do; first of all to yourself; second of all to the world. But of course you do work, I mean real work, and there are W-2 forms and Social Security taxes to prove that hallowed point. Convince anyone that those stacks of paper, both the ones on the desk and the ones wadded up in the garbage can are more than play, and I'm certain Hillary Clinton has a job waiting for you in public relations. Just forget trying to be taken seriously. It ain't apt to happen. But take yourself seriously. Take what you do even more seriously. That's what matters. That's what's important. That's what gets you through the nights of editing, re-writing, re-casting, reading, pulling your hair out, cussing at the blank page, and the full page, and dumping your girl/boyfriend who never even heard of James Agee.)

But suppose these fleeting, wonderful, at-times-agonizing, at-times-joyful, but always productive days, weeks, months, years—and yes, for some of us, alas, decades—are come to an end: _Granta_ has bought two of your stories, your poem will be included in an anthology of young poets, a bright young editor at Simon and Schuster has paid you more than five nickels for your racy and well-written bildungsroman, which Michiko Kakutani of the _New York Times_ will call a dazzling debut; you're invited to the Miami Book Fair along with 150 other authors—yeah, you're an author now, and someone actually gives a flapdoodle about what you're tapping away at on your laptop, your IBM Selectric, your Underwood. Yes, Jean, you've been taken seriously, as an artist, as a craftsperson, as a writer. Let us just suppose.

Say your name is Toni Morrison, or Cynthia Shearer, or David Mamet, or Richard Howard, or Larry Brown, or Arundhati Roy, or this one or that one. Oh, yes, all those brilliant little day-dreamed eggs have finally hatched and they're sprouting glorious feathers. Let's just suppose.

Now what?

At some point, sooner or later, a writer must confront this frightening question, a question that goes well beyond the goodies and bangles of material success. This crossroads, as I see it, is the crux at the center of writing. Almost Zen in its simplicity/complexity, yet so many people—including myself—so often peer around it, over it, beyond it, but never really at this most simple of truths: a) writing is a tremendous amount of work; b) writing is a tremendous amount of play. The best writing comes after a great deal of labor; the labor a writer puts into her or his work must come from a type of love: a writer must love what he writes, what she actually does, or the work is not even born a still-born thing; rather, it is an embryo that never develops legs, let alone wings.

Or, as someone once wrote, A man labors for that which he loves, and loves that for which he labors.

A question I ask my students, my fellow writers, and myself most often:

> Take away the Nobel Prize, and the Pulitzer too; take away massive advances, movie rights, foreign rights, and bestseller lists; take away the *New Yorker* and the *Paris Review* and *The Yalobusha Review*; take away excellent book jackets and beautiful type; take away readings, Broadway, radio interviews, and all the vanity associated with authordom—take it all away. Now ask yourself: Would you still write?

Why do you write? Why does anyone?

I think of Michel de Montaigne. A French nobleman of the late sixteenth century, he wrote out of a need to understand, to express himself, to grapple with his mind and its relation to the world . . . or so he writes.

Here is Montaigne on death:

> Wherever your life ends, it is all there. The advantage of living is not measured by length, but by use; some men have lived long, and lived little; attend to it while you are in it. It lies in your will, not in the number of years, for you to have lived enough. Did you think you would never arrive where you never ceased going? Yet there is no road but has its end. And if company can comfort you, does not the world keep pace with you?

I enjoy reading Montaigne, for I feel I can see his mind at work. There is a grace, there is a bold honesty, there is a special brand of wisdom. Four hundred years later, his words seem uncannily fresh and relevant. Mind you, fellow traveler, Montaigne could not count on Oprah's Book Club to rescue his works from so-called obscurity. He surely didn't sit by the phone, either, waiting for James Cameron to call about a movie deal. To be sure, Montaigne was a man of material means—not a fact to let slip by easily—yet the fact remains: He wrote. Why?

I think of Jane Austen. A few years ago, at the Academy Awards, the British actor, Emma Thompson, upon accepting an award for her work on a movie adaptation of a Jane Austen novel, said something to the effect: "I don't know if she knows it, but Jane Austen is big in Paraguay right now."

Indeed, 181 years after her death, the novels of Jane Austen are "big." Her readership could populate entire countries. Today. But we often forget that during her lifetime, the number of people who read her books numbered fewer than the readership of one well-received first novel published today; that is to say, only a few thousand. Why on earth did Jane Austen write?

Folk write for various and sundry reasons, obviously. Some write for fame and fortune, and some happily achieve these elusive and powerful goals. Some write to exorcise (or exercise) their personal demons, and some succeed in that exercise. Some write to calm or even hear a calm voice within, or to realize some pageant, some drama taking place in their brain, to find meaning in the beautiful chaos of life. Some succeed. Many do not. But those who fail and those who succeed all engage in the same activity: Writing: Why?

Nowadays, to speak of what is "good" can get a person frowned upon, or worse. For better or for worse, "good" has been re-defined, democratized. For example: my earlier use of Montaigne and Austen could be viewed as the most reprehensible form of Eurocentric, essentially paternalistic, canonical propaganda. There can be some merit to that nonexclusive point of view. Granted, so-called genre work—police procedurals, Westerns, romances, humorous sketches, fantasy, science fiction, popular song lyrics, comic books—can all be done excellently, and even in the least rigorously realized stuff (i.e., trash—and yes, that is a value judgment) some work went into creating it, some something can be taken out of it, either learned, felt, or understood.

But there again is my rub: whatever the form, whatever one's objective goal, whatever levels of accomplishment one uses as a measure—there is a degree of work involved. Saul Bellow may have worked a little harder and a little longer on *The Adventures of Augie March* than did Neil Gaiman on his latest issue of the *Sandman* comic, but they both did some work, a certain type of work, a mental work which ultimately came together in the form of squiggles and dots on a page. Let us lay aside, for the moment, issues of quality, for I am about something more fundamental, something about the nature of putting pen to paper.

What is this thing we do when we write? I do not presume to have any special authority to speak knowingly on the actual mechanism within our brains that makes and forms sentences, characters, scenarios, ideas. I have no Oliver Sacks–like learning on the mind, nor any Howard Gardner–like hypotheses on how the brain works. Rather I can speak on the value of that work, of that mysterious labor which, as aforementioned, is marked by no physical change in the wide world. Often quiet, often un-known, un-seen, un-felt.

A writer must, at some point, admit to the self that there may be no payoff at the end of the Yellow Brick Road; that more trouble might be invited into the life than abated or banished; that the words set down might not quite work, ever; that the fickle, questionable—and purely subjective—Muse of Talent may never ever visit their none-the-less deserving cranium or soul. However, at some level, at some propitious time, the writer must make a faithful decision: to honor the work. To take seriously that peculiar labor of talking to one's own self on the page. To honor the actual labor involved in composition of whatever and however. To love the labor of the work of writing. I speak not of the artifacts of the trade—the pens, the pencil sharpener, the fresh ream of Hammermill paper, the 24 megs of RAM and the 18" pixelated screen attached to the 5 gigs of memory and the Pentium chip and WordPerfect, Word, Write—right; no, I speak of what goes on in the brain. Folk who've done this type of work know that the process of writing is work. Real work.

We live in a society, just at this moment of the world, where we are taught to put a great deal of value on Product. On visible Service. We are taught also to disparage the value of the process. In fact we spend time and energy and money trying to find ways to reduce the process, make it more efficient, speed it up, cut to the chase.

Question: How, exactly, do you speed up the imagination?

Vladimir Nabokov once gave a lecture at Cornell University on what he called "uncommon sense." Common Sense, according to

Nabokov, was not what a writer needed, or wanted; common sense surrounds and abounds at car dealerships, beauty salons, on military bases, at Walmarts, and at casinos. Common sense, quite literally, rules the world. Uncommon sense, however, is rare and powerful. Think of the uncommon sense of *Crime and Punishment*, of *Beloved*, of *All the King's Men*, of *The Color Purple*, of *Pilgrim at Tinker Creek*, of *West with the Night*. And please, let's not leave out *Batman*, *Spider-Man*, *Roseanne*, Richard Pryor's comedy, and the stories of the late, beloved Isaac Asimov. Strange, curious works, from strange, beautiful imaginations, full of uncommon sense.

And, as I mentioned earlier, though I have no special dispensation to make this case stick, I do feel in my bones that only in the imagination—outside and away from the paper-minded men and women with their credit-card eyes—can uncommon worlds be achieved, realized, thought up. Only in the imagination can such ideas be played with. Ah, play!—such fun. But such serious fun. The writer labors within that fun of the imagined. She labors to put down what she has witnessed in the realm of her imagination: of how a little girl got lost in the woods and encountered a snark or a bear, and did battle for her life; of how a poor fellow of honest heart fell in love with a princess of surpassing beauty and intelligence and proved himself worthy of her hand; of how three sisters turned on their youngest sibling and had her cast from the family; of visions of castles and wars and magical goings-on down by the river; dramas of betrayal, malice, hubris, sickness, love—sweet, sweet love— bittersweet success, happy failure; of memories most precious, like jewels; of other ways of living life, coping, learning, being. . . . But without first having played there in the fields of her mind, she has little of value to say.

But here is the dilemma: For grown folk to admit such a thing is to be visited by guilt—a guilt imposed, directly and indirectly, by society.

For we must be held accountable for the time spent, the electricity burned, the money gone. Are you writing a bestseller? Some undying prose to win grand awards? Some poesy for your beau? Some ephemeral gobbledygook? What exactly are you doing, Mary? Is it of value?

Value? In the real world, it is simply not possible to keep questions of quality and worth at bay for too long. We structure our lives based on a system of priorities: What's more important? What's better? How much does it cost? I have no intention of wasting anybody's time trying to debate whether *Moby-Dick* is more or less valuable than Action Comics, or whether Paul Simon's song lyrics should stand beside Gwendolyn Brooks's poems—that's another game. The truth is I'm glad we have them all.

But I do contend that the act of writing—more often than not, a labor of love, mysterious, uncommon, painful, rewarding, on the page, with each unfolding, new, revealing, exciting, dangerous sentence—is, in and of itself, of more worth than most living and breathing Americans are willing to accord it, let alone say out loud. The process, more than the product. The actual imagination, more than its remnants. True, the remnants are precious, but we must never forget these words are treasures brought back from Otherworlds. We must never forget to honor the traveler's moxie for taking that brave journey.

By the same token, the writer has no right to whine—No one appreciates how hard I work! No one gives me my just due!—Nope. And why should anyone? As the novelist Mordecai Richler once observed: Nobody asked you to do it anyway. You volunteered. (He that laboureth, laboureth for himself.) So forget about the banker's sneer and the grocer's quibble and the lawyer's scoff, for, when done right, the writer's work is rewarded by its own fealty. External validation is tertiary at best. For the weary sojourner of the mind has discovered: we truly do contain multitudes.

If you don't believe me, the proof is there on the page . . .

In the end, for writer, reader, mom, dad, lover, employer, idle looker-on, fellow citizen, the decision of which I speak—to honor the process and keep it Holy—in this workaday, give-and-take, get-what-you-can-while-you-can, hurry-up-and-wait world, is actually more easily said than done.

The avowal, too, takes work, but it is work well worth the effort.

22

Letter to Self

D^{ear} Garrett,

Buy Apple stock.

Seriously. Buy lots of it.

Don't be blue. Despite how you feel sometimes, you really don't have a lot to be blue about. True, you're a poor country boy from the swamps of North Carolina. But in time, that will be one of your mightiest assets. I know, I know, difficult to swallow, huh? But, as improbable as it may seem, where you come from will become one of your greatest assets as a human being.

Look at everything. Remember everything. Nothing is too small or insignificant. Observe everything, from what it's like to be in a tobacco field in the July heat to what the old women at First Baptist wear and the rhythm of the deacons' prayers. Remember what it feels like to walk up on a rattlesnake. Remember the argument you had with Mrs. Johnson about your article in the school paper. Remember the funerals and the band practices and the nights you spent with the EMTs at the fire and rescue squad. Everything is important. Now and later. Remember.

Keep reading the dictionary for fun. When people make fun of you, just keep on doing what you're doing. You've got the right idea. That is as important as buying Apple stock. However, dropping $150 words in casual conversation is not always a great idea. It makes you look like a smart-ass know-it-all. You are a smart-ass know-it-all, but you don't have to let everybody know it but your family and closest friends. Remember they love you despite your faults. This fact will be important. Physics, science fiction, classical music—if you're interested, keep on studying it. Don't let anybody tell you it's a waste of time or not something a Black kid should be interested in. Don't ever worry about being "Black enough" for anybody. You are not merely an "honorary Negro." Your ancestors paid that bill for you a long time ago.

That crush you have on T. S.? Don't let it trouble you too much. I am sorry: He is not going to return your affection. But his indifference is not the end of the world. In fact he will not be the last man with whom you become infatuated who won't give you the time of day. Yeah, it hurts, buddy. That pain is real. But, as kooky as it may sound, unrequited love/lust is not necessarily a bad thing. You must learn how to take those feelings you have and put them into making stuff. Whatever you can create, make. Creation is the great healing thing. And when you look back, you'll have that wonderful thing, no matter what it is, to remind you of your heart storm; moreover this creation, *this creating*, makes you a better and larger person. It's kinda like magic actually. It's kinda cool. It's kinda like being a shaman.

You grew up in the Church and right now the Church is strong with you. You worry about your so-called "unnatural affections" and the Scriptures and what Jesus thinks. Despite what people say, to quote one of your favorite songs in a few years, "The Lord don't mind." It's foolish to think that any type of loving is wrong. That cat, Jesus, was all about love. So please don't waste time focusing on the species of love but the quality of the love. Keep studying theology; it will come in handy later in a strange and wonderful way. (Please note: I said theology, not religion.)

You were born rich in identity—Black, Southern, Queer. Don't ever let anybody tell you any bit of it is a burden. The sooner you start seeing your background, your reality, as a diamond mine, the sooner you will see yourself as a force to be reckoned with. In fact, though you don't know it, you are a force already—just don't mention it in casual conversation. That would be a little obnoxious. Just *be* a force. "O to be a dragon"!

The world is going to change in many ways for the better for Black folk and for queer folk. However, ways of looking at Black men, despite our achievements and accomplishments in the great world, will remain a vexed thing. So much of how the culture at large looks at Black man and its view of what a "man" should be is pure fantasy. A lot of this claptrap is designed to hurt you and to cut you down. To keep you in a box. To tell you what you should and should not do. Later for all that noise, brother.

And how this country looks at queer Black men, in particular— well, I hate to tell you but you'll still be a strange and exotic creature in the eyes of a great many Americans. Big deal. Do not waste a minute fretting over how they look upon you. You have the power to define yourself—remember that power; take that control. It's like a superpower, really, to be whom you want to be, to do what you want to do, to fly where you want to fly. Your life will get more complicated, but think of it as a great adventure, every damn day. You're going to have fun.

Fun is waiting for you to have it.

Oh, and get this book and read it: *The Art of Worldly Wisdom* by Baltasar Gracián. I didn't discover it until I was thirty-one, and I wish I'd read it when I was your age. It can help you through some dark moments.

Don't smoke. Pay your taxes. Be wise in matters of sex and your body—a plague is coming: you can and will survive it, though the casualties will break your heart. Just keep making.

And please buy lots of Apple stock. You'll thank me. And I don't mean the Beatles' music company, either. Leave that to Michael Jackson. Trust me.

> For I remain,
> Your loving self

ACKNOWLEDGMENTS

It seems presumptuous to write acknowledgments in place of the author, and yet, downright negligent not to have done so sooner given the love and care that went into this book from so many. First, celebrated author Daniel Wallace, Randall Kenan's dear friend, neighbor, confidant, health care proxy, and sometime "boss" as director of the creative writing program at the University of North Carolina–Chapel Hill. Daniel took on the physical, bureaucratic, and emotional labor of sorting all of Kenan's papers, thousands of books, and other belongings, searching his files for unpublished and uncollected work, and serving as the linchpin between Kenan's professional life and his family. He remains informal literary advisor to the Kenan estate. Nakia Brown, Randall's cousin and executor, gave her blessing to this project. Jin Auh of the Wylie Agency was the dedicated goad that a good agent should be; without her prodding, we might not have *If I Had Two Wings*, Kenan's last work of fiction, and without her confidence and her efforts—and those of Maggie Aschmeyer and Abram Scharf in clearing permissions— we would not have *Black Folk Could Fly*. My colleagues around the editorial board table at W. W. Norton & Company, especially sales director Stephen Pace, supported this project unanimously and with enthusiasm when saying "no" to the idea of a collection of pieces by a deceased author would have been a very easy thing to do. Andy Crank at the University of Alabama—a scholar of Kenan's writing who interviewed him, became his friend, and once discussed the idea of a "Portable Kenan" with him—gave invaluable comments, ideas, and encouragement, and also recovered "That Eternal Burning" from *A Time Not Here*. Miriam Berkeley photographed Kenan over three decades, beginning with the publication of *A Visitation of Spirits* when Kenan was in his twenties, and it is her gorgeous portrait on the book cover. Its painted treatment and graphic design comes from W. W. Norton's gifted art director, Steve Attardo. Managing editor Rebecca Homiski, project editors Amy Medeiros and Rebecca Munro, and copyeditor Katharine Ings helped make decisions that would have defeated the editor. Publicist Erin Lovett, marketer Michelle Waters, assistant Mo Crist, director Cedering Fox of WordTheatre, the Center for Fiction's Melanie McNair, actors Marinda Anderson, Michael Boatman, CG, and Ryan Jamaal Swain, writers Alexander Chee, A.M. Homes, E. Patrick Johnson, and Elias Rodriques, the folks at Epilogue Books, Flyleaf Books, and everyone who loved Kenan at the University of North Carolina–Chapel Hill, especially Susan Irons and Bland Simpson, all put generous time and heart into making a successful publication of this book—not easy in the absence of an author in the promotional driver's seat.

Tayari Jones, your commitment beginning with the very conception of this project, your contribution of both time and talent, and your support every step of the way made all the difference.

Randall, your busy ghost is a delight to us all, even as your being in the flesh is sorely and irredeemably missed.

In admiration and gratitude,
Alane Salierno Mason, editor
New York, March 2023

EDITOR'S NOTES

THE ROOSTER, THE RATTLESNAKE, AND
THE HYDRANGEA BUSH

Originally published as Kenan's introduction to the anthology of essays on North Carolina foodways that he edited, *The Carolina Table: North Carolina Writers on Food* (Hillsboro, NC: Eno Press, 2016), this essay included several references to other essays in the anthology that have been cut, given the different context here.

SWINE DREAMS

The version published in the *State by State* anthology (still available) addresses at some length the history and environmental consequences of the pork industry in North Carolina, drawing upon "Boss Hog," a story from the Pulitzer Prize–winning series by Melanie Sill, Pat Stith, and Joby Warrick in the *Raleigh News and Observer* (February 19–28, 1995). According to one of his bio notes, Kenan was at one point interested in writing a book on that subject. Here, however, it seemed too much of a digression. Meanwhile the previously cut material about hog gelding, too riveting to ignore, is now restored to an essay that takes a more personal form and includes Kenan's original subtitle.

GHOST DOG

A few lines that were cut in the published essay have been restored.

THE GOOD SHIP *JESUS*

Kenan revised his views on Baldwin's "bitterness" in his introduction to *The Cross of Redemption: Uncollected Writings* by James Baldwin, a volume he compiled and edited (New York: Pantheon, 2010). Academic citations within the article have been removed for readability but remain accessible in the online version on JSTOR.

THERE'S A HELLHOUND ON YOUR TRAIL

This graduation address was given to students in the documentary studies program of Duke University, May 10, 2015, and later published as a chapbook in 2016. A version directed to writing students, absent Gordon Parks, appears as "The Character of Our Character: Reality, Actuality, and Technique in Fiction and Nonfiction," pp. 45–55 in *As We Were Saying: Sewanee Writers on Writing* (Baton Rouge: Louisiana State University Press, 2021).

THAT ETERNAL BURNING

Kenan wrote this poetic response to Norman Mauskopf's photographs for a book of those photos titled *A Time Not Here: The Mississippi Delta* (Santa Fe, NM: Twin Palms Publishers, 1996).

CREDITS

"Ode to Billie Joe" was first published in the journal *Southern Cultures*, vol. 17 no. 3, 2011, pp. 33–34.

"Ghost Dog: Or, How I Wrote My First Novel" first appeared in *eJournal USA*, US Department of State, vol. 14 no 2, 2009, pp. 10–13.

"Prologue: Come Out the Wilderness," "Cyberspace, North Carolina: Where Am I Black?," and "New York, New York: Blackness on My Mind" from *Walking on Water: Black American Lives at the Turn of the Twenty-First Century* by Randall Kenan, copyright © 1999 by Randall Kenan. Used by permission of Alfred A. Knopf, an imprint of the Knopf Doubleday Publishing Group, a division of Penguin Random House LLC. All rights reserved.

"Notes Toward an Essay on Imagining Thomas Jefferson Watching a Performance of the Musical *Hamilton*" was first published in the journal *Southern Cultures*, vol. 25 no. 2, Summer 2019, pp. 12–18.

"The Good Ship *Jesus*: Baldwin, Bergman, and the Protestant Imagination" first appeared in the journal *African American Review*, Johns Hopkins University Press, vo. 46 no. 4, Winter 2013, pp. 701–714.

"There's a Hellhound on Your Trail: How to See Like Gordon Parks" was given as the 2015 commencement address to the Duke University Master in Fine Arts in Experimental and Documentary Arts graduating class of 2015 on March 10, 2015. and printed as a chapbook by the Center for Documentary Studies at Duke University.

"Finding the Forgotten" first appeared in *Garden & Gun* magazine, August/September 2016.

"Letter from North Carolina: Learning from Ghosts of the Civil War" was published by Literary Hub, August 18, 2020.

"That Eternal Burning" is excerpted from *A Time Not Here: The Mississippi Delta* by Randall Kenan, copyright 1997, and is reprinted courtesy of the publisher Twin Palms Publishers.

"Love and Labor" first appeared in the journal *Yalobusha Review*, University of Mississippi, vol. 4 article 2, 1998, pp. 5–11.

BLACK FOLK
COULD FLY

Randall Kenan

BLACK FOLK COULD FLY
Randall Kenan

DISCUSSION QUESTIONS

1. In *Black Folk Could Fly*, the world Randall Kenan describes growing up in—Chinquapin, North Carolina—is vividly specific, yet are there elements that are universal or relatable? What are some examples? Did you see yourself, your family, or your hometown in his?

2. Kenan recalls that when he was growing up, he had an "intense desire to be elsewhere" (p. 38). Yet he came to cherish his childhood despite its hardships. Have you had a similar evolution in how you feel about your past?

3. "The many feelings engendered by life in a small town are much more complex and tangled than most people who've never lived in one . . . could ever imagine" (p. 87), Kenan writes. If you've lived in a small town, do you agree?

4. Fred Rogers said, "All of us have special ones who have loved us into being." Who were they for Randall Kenan and why? How did they do it?

5. Kenan's writing is full of wonderful evocations of food. What were your favorites? In what ways did he make you think about barbecue and soul food differently?

6. Kenan loves to interrogate and unpack words and ideas, surfacing and questioning the assumptions people make when using them. The prime example is "race." He points out that race is an invalid idea scientifically, yet still so often used in America. How did this make you think differently?

7. Kenan sets out to write about Blackness as "an emotional condition" (p. xiii). What did the book teach you about being Black? Which assumptions did it make you reexamine?

8. Kenan laments Richard Pryor's late rejection of the N-word: "he lost sight of the true genius of Black people" (p. 149) to appropriate and use the word in their own ways. Do you agree?

9. Kenan was an intellectual who equally loved pop culture. From his riffs on James Baldwin and Ingmar Bergman to Eartha Kitt and *Star Trek*, what did you relate to most?

10. How does Kenan's voice resemble those of others you've read? How is it distinct?

11. Did the book make you smile or laugh? When and how?

12. Did the book move you? Which moments or relationships or themes?

13. "It is sentimental to think that the bits and pieces will always align; to think there is some hidden master plan. Destiny requires much more of us than simple trust. Faith is action" (p. 133). How did Kenan live this idea?

14. Kenan writes that he was born "rich in identity—Black, Southern, Queer" (p. 264). How does that idea make you feel about your own identities, both native and acquired?

15. At the end of the book is a letter Kenan wrote to his younger self, full of poignant wisdom and humor. Which pieces of advice rang most true to you?